T0203588

Technology transfer between the US, China and Taiwan

Examining the flow of technical knowledge between the US, Taiwan and Mainland China over the last sixty-five years, this book shows that the technical knowledge that has moved between these states is vast and varied. It includes the invention and production of industrial goods, as well as knowledge of the patterns of corporate organization and management. Indeed, this diversity is reflected in the process itself, which is driven both by returning expatriates with knowledge acquired overseas and by successful government intervention in acquiring technology from multinational firms.

Technology Transfer Between the US, China and Taiwan engages with the evolving debates on the merits, importance and feasibility of technology transfer in the process of economic development globally, and uses the example of Taiwan to show that multinational corporations can indeed play a positive role in economic development. Further, it reveals the underlying tension between international cooperation and nationalism which inevitably accompanies international exchanges, as well as the delicate balancing act required between knowledge acquisition and dangerous levels of dependency, and the beneficial role of the US in East Asia's technological development.

With contributors from disciplines ranging from history, geography, urban planning, sociology, political science and electrical engineering, this multi-disciplinary book will be of great interest to students and scholars working across a broad range of subjects including Taiwan studies, Chinese studies, economics, business studies and development studies.

Douglas B. Fuller is Senior Lecturer at King's College, UK.

Murray A. Rubinstein is Senior Research Fellow at the Weatherhead East Asian Institute, USA.

Routledge Research on Taiwan
Series Editor: Dafydd Fell, SOAS, UK

The *Routledge Research on Taiwan Series* seeks to publish quality research on all aspects of Taiwan studies. Taking an interdisciplinary approach, the books will cover topics such as politics, economic development, culture, society, anthropology and history.

This new book series will include the best possible scholarship from the social sciences and the humanities and welcomes submissions from established authors in the field as well as from younger authors. In addition to research monographs and edited volumes general works or textbooks with a broader appeal will be considered.

The series is advised by an international Editorial Board and edited by Dafydd Fell of the Centre of Taiwan Studies at the School of Oriental and African Studies.

Technology transfer between the US, China and Taiwan

Examining the flow of technical knowledge between the US, Taiwan and Mainland China over the last sixty-five years, this book shows that the technical knowledge that has moved between these states is vast and varied. It includes the invention and production of industrial goods, as well as knowledge of the patterns of corporate organization and management. Indeed, this diversity is reflected in the process itself, which is driven both by returning expatriates with knowledge acquired overseas and by successful government intervention in acquiring technology from multinational firms.

Technology Transfer Between the US, China and Taiwan engages with the evolving debates on the merits, importance and feasibility of technology transfer in the process of economic development globally, and uses the example of Taiwan to show that multinational corporations can indeed play a positive role in economic development. Further, it reveals the underlying tension between international cooperation and nationalism which inevitably accompanies international exchanges, as well as the delicate balancing act required between knowledge acquisition and dangerous levels of dependency, and the beneficial role of the US in East Asia's technological development.

With contributors from disciplines ranging from history, geography, urban planning, sociology, political science and electrical engineering, this multi-disciplinary book will be of great interest to students and scholars working across a broad range of subjects including Taiwan studies, Chinese studies, economics, business studies and development studies.

Douglas B. Fuller is Senior Lecturer at King's College, UK.

Murray A. Rubinstein is Senior Research Fellow at the Weatherhead East Asian Institute, USA.

Routledge Research on Taiwan
Series Editor: Dafydd Fell, SOAS, UK

The *Routledge Research on Taiwan Series* seeks to publish quality research on all aspects of Taiwan studies. Taking an interdisciplinary approach, the books will cover topics such as politics, economic development, culture, society, anthropology and history.

This new book series will include the best possible scholarship from the social sciences and the humanities and welcomes submissions from established authors in the field as well as from younger authors. In addition to research monographs and edited volumes general works or textbooks with a broader appeal will be considered.

The series is advised by an international Editorial Board and edited by Dafydd Fell of the Centre of Taiwan Studies at the School of Oriental and African Studies.

Technology Transfer between the US, China and Taiwan

Moving knowledge

Edited by
**Douglas B. Fuller and
Murray A. Rubinstein**

Routledge
Taylor & Francis Group

LONDON AND NEW YORK

First published 2013
by Routledge
2 Park Square, Milton Park, Abingdon, Oxon OX14 4RN

Simultaneously published in the USA and Canada
by Routledge
711 Third Avenue, New York, NY 10017

*Routledge is an imprint of the Taylor & Francis Group,
an informa business*

British Library Cataloguing in Publication Data
A catalogue record for this book is available from the British Library

Library of Congress Cataloging in Publication Data
Technology transfer between the US, China, and Taiwan: moving
   knowledge/edited by Douglas B. Fuller, Murray A. Rubinstein.
   p. cm. – (Routledge research on Taiwan series)
   Includes bibliographical references and index.
   1. Technology transfer – China. 2. Technology transfer – Taiwan.
   3. Technology transfer – United States. I. Fuller, Douglas B.
   II. Rubinstein, Murray A., 1942 –
   HC430.T4T43 2013
   338.951'06 – dc23   2012040400

ISBN: 978-0-415-64220-0 (hbk)
ISBN: 978-0-203-08065-8 (ebk)

Typeset in Times New Roman
by Florence Production Ltd, Stoodleigh, Devon, UK

Contents

Figures

Tables

Contributors

Douglas B. Fuller is Senior Lecturer in Comparative Management and International Business in the Department of Management at King's College, University of London. He has previously taught at Chinese University of Hong Kong and the School of International Service at American University, USA. His research focuses on technology policy in developing Asia, particularly Greater China, and he has published articles in the *Asia Pacific Journal of Management, Industry and Innovation*, the *Journal of Development Studies* and other journals.

Murray A. Rubinstein is Senior Research Fellow at the Weatherhead East Asian Institute, USA. He is also Professor Emeritus at Baruch College, USA. He has written two monographs and edited or co-edited five books related to Taiwan and Christianity in China.

J. Megan Greene is Associate Professor of Modern Chinese History and Director of the Center for East Asian Studies at the University of Kansas, USA. Her research focuses on the role of science and technology policy in state-led development efforts in the Republic of China both on the mainland and in Taiwan.

Akintunde I. Akinwande is Professor in the Electrical Engineering and Computer Science Department of the Massachusetts Institute of Technology, USA.

Charles G. Sodini received a BSEE degree from Purdue University in 1974, and MSEE and Ph.D. degrees from the University of California, USA, in 1981 and 1982, respectively. He was a member of the technical staff at Hewlett-Packard Laboratories from 1974 to 1982, where he worked on the design of MOS memory. He joined the faculty of the Massachusetts Institute of Technology in 1983, where he is currently the LeBel Professor of Electrical Engineering. His research interests are focused on mixed signal integrated circuit and system design. Along with Professor Roger T. Howe, he is a co-author of an undergraduate text on integrated circuits and devices entitled 'Microelectronics: an integrated approach'. He also studied the Hong Kong electronics industry and co-authored a chapter with Professor

Rafael Reif in a book entitled *Made by Hong Kong*. He continued to study the globalization of the electronics industry and contributed to the book *How We Compete* authored by Professor Suzanne Berger. Dr. Sodini was a co-founder of SMaL Camera Technologies, a leader in imaging technology for consumer digital still cameras and machine vision cameras for automotive applications.

Jinn-yuh Hsu is Distinguished Professor in the Department of Geography at National Taiwan University. He has published papers on the social and technological connection between Silicon Valley and Hsinchu region in Taiwan. He is currently working on a book project of the development of special zones, including the export processing zones and technology parks, in Taiwan.

Yu Zhou is Professor of Geography at Vassar College, USA. She is also Zijiang Professor, in the Institute of China Innovation (ICI) at East China Normal University. Her research has been in the areas of globalization and high-tech industry in China, and transnational linkages, and she is the author of the book *The Inside Story of China's High-Tech Industry: Making Silicon Valley in Beijing* (2008).

You-Ren Yang is in the Graduate School for Transformation Studies, Shih Hsin University, Taiwan.

Chu-Joe Hsia is Professor and Director at the Graduate Institute of Building and Planning, National Taiwan University.

Introduction

Douglas B. Fuller and
Murray A. Rubinstein

The essays in this volume focus on the flow of technical knowledge from the United States and Taiwan and from Taiwan and the US to Mainland China over the last six and a half decades.[1] This technical knowledge encompasses the invention and production of industrial goods as well as knowledge of the patterns of corporate organization and management that allows for the efficient production of such goods and knowledge of the ways to integrate such production to the world market and to the demands for such products. Most of this volume will focus on the IT industry, but this book also addresses scientific and technical transfer outside of the IT industry.

The larger backdrop to the international dimensions of technological development in Greater China is the evolving debates on the merits, importance and feasibility of technology transfer in the process of economic development globally. In the immediate post-World War II period when faith in economic planning, albeit Keynesian rather than central planning, was at its height in Western market economies, developmental economists, such as Lewis, Prebisch, Rosenstein-Rodan and Hirschman, to varying degrees regarded state involvement in technology development to be important, perhaps essential, and were concerned about terms of trade working to the disadvantage of developing countries (Rodrik 2011). Among these economists, there was a general emphasis on state involvement to overcome market failures rife in emerging economies. The neo-liberal revolution of the 1980s affected development economics as well and gave rise to the Washington Consensus that assigned blame for the lack of development to government failure rather than market failure. According to this prescription, markets malfunction in the developing world due to government interference. Remove state interference and markets, and terms of trade would work to the advantage of developing countries.

In parallel with this general debate on development was the specific discussion of the role of technology transfer and multinational corporations (MNCs) in technological development. Dissatisfaction with the development outcomes, particularly in Latin America, gave rise to critiques of the systemic forces keeping developing countries on the periphery of the global economy in dependency and world systems theories. More subtle varieties of this critique appeared in the late 1960s in the work of Cardoso and Faletto's dependent development, which recognized the structural constraints on peripheral economies while also recognizing new possibilities (Cardoso 2009). Even in these more subtle attempts, MNCs were viewed more as the problem than the solution, both to development generally and technological development in particular.

Empirical work on the specific issue of technology transfer tends to downplay or dismiss the positive role that foreign firms can play in technological upgrading. Foreign firms only contribute to development when they are forced to do so by effective state intervention (Fosfuri and Motta 1999; Jomo and Felker 1999; Mani 2004). Singapore is the sole case where foreign direct investment (FDI) played a central role in technological development and Singapore's policies were geared toward leveraging technology from these MNCs (Mani 2004). Nevertheless, Taiwan's example also suggests that MNCs can play a positive role in economic development with proper state policy and China's deep engagement with transnational technology communities points to informal conduits of knowledge beyond MNCs that can help facilitate technological development today.

This transfer of knowledge, at least in its early stages prior to and immediately following World War II, is an often neglected aspect of economic development in Greater China and the linkages between the US and the two Chinas, the Republic of China (ROC) and the People's Republic of China (PRC). When economists examine the East Asian economic miracle of the second half of the twentieth century and interplay of the US with Taiwan and now, more recently, with Mainland China, they usually look at large-scale processes, patterns and trends and also at the nature of multi-sectoral or aggregate development. They also tend to look at patterns and levels of trade and see this as the core pattern of nation-to-nation interaction.

Beyond economics, the scholars who have examined technology transfer to Greater China have tended to fall into one of two perspectives. On the one hand, there are those, such as Annalee Saxenian (2006), emphasizing the positive impact of returning expatriates who are seen as bringing back all the critical tacit technological and organizational knowledge and thereby contribute tremendously to technological development. On the other hand, the state-centered explanations, such as Wade (1990), tend to view Greater China through the prism of successful government intervention in acquiring technology from multinational firms. In this volume, we embrace both these views while contextualizing them in history, politics, global industrial change, industry networks and even the idiosyncrasies of some of the key individuals involved in the process.

Indeed, the main merit of this volume is the multi-disciplinary approach used to address the multi-faceted phenomenon of flows of knowledge from the US to Greater China. The contributors to this book hail from the disciplines of history, geography, urban planning, sociology, political science and electrical engineering. The varied disciplinary background is obvious in the different approaches taken across the chapters. The electrical engineers offer technical insight into the technological changes that helped shape the organizational changes and opportunities for development in the IT industry over the last two decades. The political scientists and sociologists pay attention to the capabilities and constraints of the institutions supporting technology policy and high-technology industry and the political and social bases of these institutions. The historians provide insights into the long-term evolution of some of the same institutions and further illumination of the micro-level processes of technology transfer through biographical accounts of the major participants. The geographers and planners utilize their disciplinary knowledge to examine how networks of production and established communities of technological practice are transferred across the Pacific and the Taiwan Strait.

In providing this account of the complex interactions between the US and Greater China, we also offer a corrective to those accounts that tend to interpret American actions as simply a self-aggrandizing exercise of imperial and hegemonic power (see for example Cumings 2009). It is not that imperialism and hegemony were not present in these interactions, but what is missing in accounts like Cumings' account are any acknowledgement of the major beneficial role of the US in East Asia's technological development. Furthermore, this contribution to East Asian technological development has clearly reduced American hegemonic and imperial power so it cannot be construed solely and simply as expansion or perpetuation of American hegemony.

Despite the diverse approaches, there are a number of themes and debates running through the book. First, there is the tension between international cooperation (for the latter part of the era covered, such activities are often lumped together under the wider phenomenon-cum-moniker of globalization) and nationalism, While the book documents extensive cooperation, between individuals, organizations and national governments, this cooperation itself often contained contesting nationalisms. Moreover, these nationalisms or national objectives have often been the very motivation for such cooperation and cross-border exchanges now celebrated by proponents of globalization as the very epitome of that phenomenon. Whether the patriotism of returnees desiring to help Taiwan or China's technological development motivating them to return home or the long-held national strengthening objective of the Kuomintang (KMT) (the Republic of China's Nationalist Party) causing the KMT to seek technology partners abroad or the Cold War objectives of the US government causing it to embrace, if only temporarily, the same nation-building goals of the KMT, nationalism lurks just below the surface of the international exchanges covered in this volume.

In the wake of the Cold War, the growing rhetoric of globalization has served to justify and explain these cross-national flows and transactions while further obscuring the nationalist counter-currents running within them. Paying attention to these counter-currents is crucial to understanding the real social and political processes of globalization. These counter-currents are especially crucial if Karl Polanyi's insights into how radical economic liberalization unleash counteracting social and political forces (what he dubbed the "double movement") during the first era of globalization in the nineteenth and early twentieth century are still valid and relevant today. The editors and authors of this volume suspect they are still valid and the following chapters provide ample evidence of counteracting nationalist impulses that may loom very large if the current global financial crisis proves to be the curtain call for the second era of globalization.

There is a bundle of closely connected themes about organization and knowledge flow that also runs through the chapters. The first is the idea that tacit knowledge is embedded in individuals, practices and organizations. Only by engaging intensively with these loci of tacit knowledge can this tacit knowledge diffuse to others. The nature of tacit knowledge thus also points to individuals as key for knowledge transfer. However, they may serve as keys to knowledge transfer not only because of the tacit knowledge they have, but also due to their serving a bridging function in networks (see Chapters 5 and 6) and decisive leadership in making policy breakthroughs and organizational innovations (see Chapters 2 and 3). Finally, the organization of production and tacitness of the knowledge involved are intimately interrelated (see Chapters 4 and 5). Ways that make knowledge explicit can cause radical changes in the organization of production. In turn, these changes in the organization of production can dramatically alter the opportunities for firms from the developing world.

Another theme is the delicate balancing act between knowledge acquisition and dangerous levels of dependency. Developing countries want advanced technologies, but they are all too aware that acquiring such technologies through cooperation with foreigners may come at the cost of their technological and economic independence. When engaging in technology transfer, the issue is how can such transactions foster interdependence between the two sides rather than dependence.

Turning to the contents of the individual chapters, the first two chapters take a historical and biographical approach to trace the practices of technology transfer over time and in historical context. J. Megan Greene's chapter takes the long view of the KMT party-state's technology policy by tracing the continuities as well as changes in the formal state organizations involved in science and technology policymaking and the nature and sources of foreign assistance from the Nanjing decade through 1980. Murray Rubinstein in Chapter 2 examines the evolution of economic policy over the course of Taiwan's economic miracle from three perspectives: the international and domestic political situation of the Cold War and divided China; the American and Taiwanese institutions involved in economic and technology policymaking; and some of the individual participants in industry and policymaking, such as James Klein and K.T. Li.

In Chapter 3, Fuller examines the policymaking of the last two decades and argues that to the extent that Taiwanese policymaking has been successful it has still been shaped by the constraints of a very different industrial structure than that found in the other two "developmental states" with which it is commonly associated, Korea and Japan. Indeed, the very ability to use returnees to bootstrap Taiwan's IT sector was dependent upon Taiwan's politically shaped industrial structures and policies. The developmental mission the Taiwanese state had in common with technonationalist Korea and Japan thus led to different strategies and outcomes when faced with Taiwan's different constraints in terms of industrial structure and domestic political considerations. Taiwan ended up with a successful techno-hybrid model embracing greater integration with and even dependence on foreign, particularly American, technology firms (a techno-globalist approach) in order to foster technological development, one of the goals of technonationalism.

Turning away from politics and toward global industrial trends, Akinwande, Sodini and Fuller in Chapter 4 argue that Greater China's rapid rise in prominence in the IT industry is related to a revolution in industrial organization in the sector that opened up new possibilities for firms from what had formerly been the periphery to the technology core of the Triad i.e. North America, Japan and Europe. This re-organization not only lowered the barriers for entry for small-and-medium-sized enterprises (SMEs) from the developing world, but also dramatically altered the power dynamics within the industry undermining the previous dominance of vertically integrated, large-scale firms from the Triad.

And less one think that all flows of technology are alike, Zhou and Hsu in Chapter 5 provide a much needed reminder that the returnees coming back to Taiwan and Mainland China in fact often engage in quite dissimilar activities even as the general outcome, spurring technological development, is the same. Hsu and Zhou relate these differences to the different starting points and concomitant structural differences between the Taiwanese and Chinese returnee communities.

The final two chapters consider a new flow of technology from Taiwan to Mainland China. Using a rich empirical case study of Taiwanese network IT production in Suzhou, one of the major centers of IT production in China, Yang and Hsia in Chapter 6 delineate how Taiwan's particular set of networked production determines the extent to which local Chinese manufacturers can move up the value chain within these Taiwanese networks even as the Taiwanese relocate their manufacturing to China. Fuller's Chapter 7 examines how cross-Taiwan Strait economic integration generally, and within the critically important IT sector in particular, has benefited each side even as this integration has imposed some costs of adjustment. This concluding chapter explores how these benefits and costs are likely to evolve over time in order to examine the issue of the political palatability of continued intense economic and technological engagement across the Taiwan Strait.

Notes

1 One of the chapters actually looks at these interactions all the way back to 1927, but the bulk of the book examines these flows since the end of World War II.

References

Cardoso, F. (2009). "New Paths: Globalization in Historical Perspective," *Studies in Comparative International Development*, 44: 296–317.

Cumings, B. (2009). *Dominion from Sea to Sea*. New Haven, CT: Yale University Press.

Fosfuri, A. and M. Motta (1999). "Multinationals without Advantages." *Scandinavian Journal of Economics*, 101(4): 617–630.

Jomo, K.S. and G. Felker (Eds.) (1999). *Technology, Competitiveness, and the State: Malaysia's Industrial Technology Policies*. New York: Routledge.

Mani, S. (2004). "Government, Innovation and Technology Policy," *International Journal of Technology and Globalization*, 1(1).

Rodrik, D. (2011). *The Globalization Paradox*. New York: W.W. Norton.

Saxenian, A. (2006). *The New Argonauts*. Cambridge, MA: Harvard University Press.

Wade, R. (1990). *Governing the Market*. Princeton, NJ: Princeton University Press.

1   The KMT and science and technology, 1927–1980

J. Megan Greene

Technology transfer from the US to China has been going on to one degree or another at least since the Opium Wars and the subsequent opening of the treaty ports. Although much of the Western technology acquired by China in the nineteenth century had military applications, by the late nineteenth century the emergent industrial sector had also become a locus of technology transfer. As the KMT came to power in 1927, it rapidly became apparent that this modern Chinese state would need to develop strategies to foster and manage technology transfer that could assist with national development. To this end, both in China, between 1927 and 1949, and in Taiwan, after 1945, the KMT constructed a series of institutions that were designed, at least in part, to develop and manage relationships with foreign states and firms that might lead to the transfer of technologies that China needed. As this chapter shows, there was considerable continuity in the approach to technology transfer taken by the KMT over the long period between 1927 and 1980. However, throughout this period the KMT also demonstrated a high degree of flexibility, and in particular an ability to adapt to changing international and domestic circumstances by adjusting their approach to interacting with foreign states and businesses and creating new institutions when needed. This chapter examines the efforts of the KMT to foster technology transfer both in China, from 1927–1949, and in Taiwan, from 1949–1980. It describes the institutions the KMT constructed as well as the ways these institutions served to build and manage relationships with foreign states and businesses that had technologies the KMT needed.

Building institutions and networks: the KMT and technology transfer, 1927–1945

As the KMT looked to shape itself as a potential ruling party governing a modernizing China in the 1920s, the merits of accepting technical assistance from abroad were quite evident to its leaders. By the time the KMT established its government in Nanjing in 1927, for example, it had taken a considerable amount of technical assistance from the Comintern in the form of military and political advisers as well as the weaponry that it had used in its bid to gain control of the country. Although the faction of the KMT that ultimately led the new Nanjing government did not regard the Comintern as a reasonable source of further assistance, it did not take long for the new government to begin developing other networks through which China might acquire modern technology and knowledge. It would be inaccurate to suggest that the leaders of the Nanjing government were systematic in these efforts, but they none-theless developed several patterns of interaction with foreign-trained Chinese and foreign states and institutions that would continue to serve them well over the long run.

Over the course of the Nanjing Decade and during the Sino-Japanese War the KMT established patterns that it continued to employ even after it relocated to Taiwan. It constructed institutions to promote the modernization of China's scientific and technical sphere, including agriculture and industry; it recruited talented and skilled technicians, many of whom were trained overseas, into leading positions in these institutions; it established cooperative relationships with foreign governments and foundations through which knowledge and technology could be transferred; and it developed structures that would facilitate overseas training.

Academia Sinica

Even as it constructed its new government, the KMT created a new academic research institution, Academia Sinica, that party leaders imagined would have the potential to attract highly trained Chinese students back to China from the US, Europe and Japan to serve national needs. An early dimension of the KMT's approach to technology transfer, therefore, was an emphasis on recruiting highly skilled and foreign-trained Chinese talent into state-sponsored institutions. These researchers and scholars would bring to the service of the state the fruits of the training they had received abroad. In so doing, the state tapped into a desire on the part of many of the intellectuals who had studied abroad in the early decades of the twentieth century to use their knowledge to strengthen and modernize China. One such group of intellectuals was the Science Society of China, which was organized by a group of Chinese students studying at Cornell University in 1914. When these young scholars established the new journal *Science* later that same year, they did so with the hope that it would "promote science, encourage industry, authorize terminologies, and spread knowledge."[1] The Nanjing Government hoped to capitalize upon the desire of foreign-trained Chinese intellectuals to spread the knowledge with which they had returned home. Although the technology transfer that took place in Academia Sinica and other state-sponsored academic research institutions did not necessarily yield direct or immediate results for China's industrial or agricultural development, it nonetheless helped to transform the broader scientific and social scientific research and instructional environment in which technicians who went on to work in more applied fields were trained.

The NEC and the NRC

The Nanjing Government also constructed two economic development commissions in which research and development activities were undertaken by technicians in the employ of the state. The National Economic Commission (NEC) was established in 1931 by a group of reform-minded KMT leaders at odds with Chiang Kai-shek. It planned and implemented projects to develop China's economy, particularly in coastal regions. The NEC's primary goal was to end Chinese dependency on foreign manufactures and to encourage the development of domestic manufactures. To help accomplish this goal, it undertook projects ranging from highway construction and water management to agricultural development, particularly in cotton cultivation and sericulture.

The National Resources Commission (NRC) was initially a secret group, created in 1932 to help Chiang Kai-shek make plans to develop China's economy in preparation for war with Japan. Its primary role was to manage state-owned enterprises such as industries and mines, and in so doing it oversaw a considerable amount of technology transfer and diffusion of technical expertise. By 1933 the NRC was not only employing "chemists, geologists, and engineers; it also trained them, granting domestic scholarships for future service and sending individuals abroad (for example to foreign mining institutes) to study."[2] NRC director Weng Wen-hao, himself a foreign-trained geologist, believed that the best way to pay for the technical assistance that China needed was to expand Chinese exports, and so he began to plan the "exploitation and export of mineral deposits" that would pay for the upgrading of state-owned enterprises.[3] The NRC's plan was to simultaneously "recruit foreign assistance and establish an independent industrial base."[4]

In 1936 the NRC devised and began to implement a three-year plan that it administered in cooperation with Germany's state-operated industrial development agency, Hapro. The plan was drafted with German assistance and all of its projects fit into a broad framework of Sino-German economic exchange. German firms would provide machinery and technical expertise for a particular set of Chinese industries including a steel mill, a coal liquification plant, a nitrogen plant and machine and electrical manufacturing works. Germany would also provide technical assistance for a set of mining and oil drilling projects. The Chinese would pay for these services with their tungsten and antimony mines, and with the manufacture of ferrotungsten.[5] Owing to the outbreak of the Sino-Japanese war, the plan never reached completion, but parts of it were well underway by that point, and it serves as a good example of Sino-foreign economic cooperation that involved the transfer of a range of technologies.

Although cooperation with Germany broke down during the wartime period as Germany looked increasingly to Japan as its East Asian partner, the KMT continued to look abroad for scientific and technical assistance for military and industrial development. It sought foreign aid and training and it also examined foreign institutional models as it considered how best to develop its scientific and technical infrastructure. As Qian Changzhao, vice secretary of the NRC, observed in a 1942 speech, China would have to depend upon foreign cooperation to effectively build its industrial base in the post-war era. In the same speech, however, Qian also expressed his concern that it might not be easy to get the sort of cooperation that China most needed, since it was in the interest of the foreign powers to keep Chinese industry operating at a basic level rather than developing in more technologically advanced directions.[6]

The NRC and foreign assistance during World War II

The NRC, the Ministry of the Economy, and the Ministry of Education all actively sought to capitalize on foreign alliances to enhance their Science and Technology (S&T) capacity. Private, non-governmental organization and foreign government aid were all important sources of scientific and technical information and exchange during the wartime period. The China Foundation provided more than US $2 million for science teaching and research professorships during the war.[7] The United Nations Relief and Rehabilitation Administration (UNRRA) financed S&T education and research in China between 1944 and 1947. Both the UN and the US sent foreign advisors in fields such as medicine, engineering and agriculture, many of whom offered courses and seminars at Chinese universities. The US provided fellowships for Chinese students and educators to study in the US,[8] and UNRRA sent educational equipment and books on medicine, agriculture and engineering to universities and technical colleges.[9] Of the US government, the NRC requested publications and films on a variety of topics. Among the publications supplied by the US government were numerous scientific and technical journals, and educational films on topics such as animal fertilizer, the art of auto repair and railroad construction.[10] Just how detailed the information in these films was is unclear, but both the films and the journals would have given researchers and perhaps even the general public access to foreign knowledge that might otherwise have been hard to come by. The NRC also requested France to assist with the construction of a coking plant, and at least one hydro-electric plant, and to provide instruction on methods for prospecting underground materials.[11]

In addition, the NRC's National Bureau of Industrial Research (NBIR) sent groups of engineers to the US from 1943–1945 to learn new techniques, get training, engage in technology transfer and establish relationships with American firms. This training program resulted from an offer by S.D. Ren, a Chinese-American Vice President of the Universal Trading Corporation in New York who wrote to the head of the NBIR to offer help. Ren was quickly enlisted to find places in American firms for "twelve technical experts along twelve different lines . . . [who would be] . . . sent to United States to visit factories and research institutions to study specific technical problems."[12] Clearly, the intent of the program was to spread its impact as widely as possible by sending only one engineer in each of twelve fields. The participants were placed in factories and research institutes in fields as diverse as automotives, ceramics, vegetable canning and paper manufacturing. Y.T. Ku, Director of the NBIR, hoped that they would "acquire some technical experience on specific problems which have not yet been solved satisfactorily in our Bureau."[13] The range of problems and, indeed, the range of industries in which these problems existed, was quite broad. Letters from the engineers reveal that they were at least as heavily influenced by the working environment in the American industrial sector (and in particular the pattern of long-term employment) as by any specific technologies they came across. "We can see," they wrote, "that China's greatest difficulty will not be in the initial training of men, but in creating for them a sense of political and economic security, which will allow them to continue along one line, in one plant for decades on end."[14] This first group was followed by others, so that by 1945 at least 363 people had been sent to factories and government bureaus in the US to do short-term internships or study courses.[15]

The NBIR also undertook to identify Chinese talent studying and working abroad and attempt to recruit them to return to China. Y.T. Ku appears to have written numerous letters to such people in the early 1940s inviting them "to take part in the reconstruction and industrialization of our great country."[16] Such people would return to China with valuable skills and knowledge that they had acquired abroad and would be able to put that knowledge to work for the nation as it reconstructed itself following World War II.

In addition to the quest to acquire specific technologies and knowledge that was undertaken by the NBIR, other Chinese state institutions were looking at foreign models as they tried to develop themselves. So, for example, China's Science and Technology Planning Committee looked at foreign models for how it should be constructed. Among these models was the US Office of Scientific Research and Development, established in 1941 by Franklin Roosevelt to coordinate, initiate and support research related to national defense.[17] Similarly, in 1943 the Ministry of Education hosted a visit to South-west China by Britain's Professor A.V. Hill and Sir Shant Bhatnagar from India who spoke with representatives of the NRC, NBIR, Academia Sinica, Ministry of the Economy and Ministry of Education about British and Indian models for similar institutions.[18]

Post-war institutions and dependence on the US

As World War II drew to a close, the foreign aid that the ROC government had depended on as it fended off Japan began to dry up as the US government, in particular, became increasingly uncertain about whether it made good sense to continue to support Chiang Kai-shek's government, a government generally regarded by the Truman administration as corrupt and ineffective. A strong China lobby in the US pressured congress to support the KMT, and so in April 1948, the China Aid Act was passed that gave the ROC government

$125 million.[19] The nature of the relationship had changed, and new institutions were required to facilitate the new relationship. In response to the China Aid Act, the KMT set up an institution to administer US economic aid.

CUSA

The Council for United States Aid did not live long in China, but rapidly retreated with the KMT government to Taiwan. There, it played an important role in facilitating all sorts of cooperation between the US and the ROC, including technology transfer. CUSA was chaired by the premier (president of Executive Yuan), and populated by other ministers of government, but was financially separate from government and ministries, making it semi-autonomous.

> Its basic purposes were to select aid projects, to procure and allocate aid commodity imports, to utilize the sales proceeds of such imports in the Local Currency Program, to supervise the execution of aid projects, and to maintain liason with the US AID Mission.[20]

It did not have to get legislative approval for its expenditures, and was also independent of the ROC civil service, so it could pay decent wages. Because it did not have to be preoccupied with the question of returning to the mainland (after the ROC moved to Taiwan) it "could concentrate upon the development of Taiwan."[21] As the circumstances of the KMT government changed in the late 1940s and early 1950s, CUSA and another institution, the Joint Commission on Rural Reconstruction (JCRR) played increasingly significant roles in managing technology transfer between the ROC and the US. Many of the KMT's early economic planning institutions, such as the NEC, NRC, and NBIR, on the other hand, did not get reconstructed in Taiwan, and were gradually replaced by new economic planning agencies.

JCRR

Like CUSA, the JCRR was also created in 1948 "as an organ to implement the China Aid Act."[22] It differed from CUSA, however, in that it was jointly run by Chinese and American commissioners, all of whom were appointed by either the president of the ROC or the president of the US. Most of the JCRR staff were educated in the US, and it served as an excellent vehicle of technology transfer.[23] From 1951 on, the JCRR sent Chinese technicians who had been working in various agricultural agencies abroad for training. Between 1951 and 1979, JCRR sent 1,372 people abroad for advanced training through programs such as the JCRR Technical Assistance Training Program and the Sino-Japanese Technical Cooperation Program as well as a number of smaller programs.[24] The Technical Assistance Training Program was paid for by US aid and administered by CUSA, JCRR and the US AID mission. "Before 1966, all trainees in the TA Program received non-degree practical training, usually for only a few months. Beginning in 1966, academic training leading to advanced degrees was also included in the program."[25] Under the Sino-Japanese Technical Cooperation Program, which was started in 1960, JCRR selected agricultural technicians to be trained in Japan, the costs of which were paid for by the Japanese.[26] The training that technicians received through these programs was in areas such as crop production, farmer's organizations, irrigation, forestry and land use, livestock production and animal husbandry, fisheries, agricultural economics, rural health, dairy farming and agricultural economics.[27]

In addition to sending Chinese and Taiwanese abroad, JCRR also used American technicians effectively. As Richard Hough wrote in 1968:

> The contribution of US technicians was not limited to advice alone; their involvement in decision-making was deep and meaningful. JCRR's closely knit staff of US and Chinese technicians provided a fertile climate for the transfer and adaptation of American technology and the devising of innovations valid for the Chinese situation.[28]

American advisors played a significant role in guiding Taiwan's agricultural development, and in determining precisely which agricultural methods and techniques could be best adapted to Taiwan's situation.

The Atomic Energy Commission

The ROC government constructed a different sort of institution with a much more specific technology transfer mission when it established the Atomic Energy Commission (AEC) in 1955 following the signing of the atomic energy agreement between the US and the ROC. Its first director was Zhang Xiaofeng who subsequently established Tsinghua University's Nuclear Science graduate program.[29] Taiwan's AEC was tasked with negotiating international agreements with institutions like the International Atomic Energy Agency and the US Atomic Energy Commission, as well as soliciting financial and technical assistance for Taiwan's nuclear science research programs. These new programs were made possible by the 1955 atomic energy agreement, which established procedures under which the ROC could lease uranium and other necessary materials from the US.[30] In 1957 Taiwan's AEC arranged for the purchase of a swimming pool reactor from the US which was then set up at Tsinghua to be used for research purposes.[31]

The Tsinghua University Institute of Nuclear Science (INS) was established in 1957, and even though its swimming pool reactor was not functional until 1961, the program began accepting and training graduate students as early as 1957.[32] By 1957, in an effort to collect as much knowledge on the subject as possible, the ROC was already sending scientists to international nuclear conferences. According to the *China Yearbook 1958–1959*, "representatives were sent from China to the International Conference on the Application of Radioisotopes in Scientific Research held in France in September 1957, and to the Chicago Atomic Energy Exhibition and Nuclear Conference in March 1958."[33] Funding for this appears to have come from the US government by way of CUSA. By 1959, the US Agency for International Development (AID) was supporting the research of a number of Tsinghua scientists.[34] There were limitations, however, on how much and what types of technical assistance the US would grant Taiwan in the field of nuclear physics. Although the Tsinghua program clearly had connections to the ROC's military nuclear weapons program at the Zhongshan Institute of Science and Technology, it nonetheless claimed to be interested only in researching and developing nuclear energy, and this was the sort of nuclear physics that the US was willing to support. When in 1958 the ROC government requested actual nuclear warheads and training in nuclear weapons operation from the US, however, the US government would not help.[35]

National Council on Scientific Development

Yet another institution that the ROC government constructed to help facilitate scientific and technical development in Taiwan was the National Council on Scientific Development (NCSD), which was jointly administered by Academia Sinica and the Ministry of Education, and the membership of which was constituted almost entirely of academic researchers in the sciences, humanities, and social sciences. Established in 1959, it took a number of years for the leadership of this institution to begin to conceive of it as having any relevance to Taiwan's broader strategies for economic development. Although its stated purpose was to oversee the scientific and technical development of the ROC, at least until 1965, the NCSD's primary goal was the improvement of research and teaching facilities and conditions for academics in Taiwan. To achieve these ends, the NCSD made numerous successful overtures to the US AID Mission as well as to other American institutions such as the Fulbright Foundation and the Asia Foundation to solicit funding. The NCSD also developed connections to American academicians and held various joint activities such as the Sino-American Conference on Intellectual Cooperation in 1960.

When, in 1964, Academia Sinica and the US National Academy of Sciences collaborated to establish a new Sino-American Committee on Science Cooperation, however, the NCSD came under pressure to take on a broader set of goals, perhaps the most important of which was to implement, beginning in 1965, a Scientific Manpower Development Program. The program was a direct response to a growing awareness within Taiwan's scientific community that Taiwan's economic, academic and perhaps even social progress was being hampered by an excessive outflow of talent. To counteract this problem, the program aimed to:

build up highly qualified scientific and technological manpower by establishing efficient and well-equipped research centers; [. . .] reduce the exodus of talented youth and scientists from the country; [. . . and] provide the country with a steady supply of competent scientists and highly trained technological manpower.[36]

Although its early efforts were almost entirely limited to a relatively ineffective quest to establish five new research centers that NCSD members believed would both train new manpower and attract some departed talent back to Taiwan, the NCSD nonetheless continued to be successful in attracting assistance for these ventures from the US, largely through the assistance of the Sino-American Committee on Science Cooperation.[37]

The role of US aid

As these institutional examples make clear, the US, though not the sole source of technical assistance for the ROC after its move to Taiwan, was the main source. Between 1951 and 1965, when US aid came to an end, the US gave the ROC an average of US $100 million a year, most of which was military assistance. Of that sum, funds for technical assistance averaged around US $2.4 million a year.[38] As Neil Jacoby observed, however,

> this instrument produced more development per dollar than did any other. The transfers of knowledge, skills, and technology to the Republic of China resulting from the presence of US technicians in Taiwan, and the sending of Chinese participants abroad for training, had enormous multiplier effects.[39]

Although these effects could best be seen in fields such as agriculture, education, public administration and public health,[40] US aid also helped promote a transfer of knowledge, technology and business practice to local industry. As Denis Simon has noted, the AID mission organized

> a constant flow of US businessmen to the island. These persons were often asked to visit Chinese factories and production sites, and to provide their own suggestions about how to improve managements, organization, and production facilities. [. . .] Visiting technical personnel worked through AID-sponsored organizations such as the China Productivity Center, which was designed to assist local producers improve the efficiency and productivity of their firms.[41]

These person-to-person interactions were the most common method through which technology transfer was accomplished during the US aid period and beyond.[42]

Working with industry

It was not until 1958, however, that many foreign enterprises began to take an interest in working in Taiwan. According to Tucker, prior to 1958, ROC economic planners were too focused on import substitution for American taste, which meant that foreign investors had no incentives to invest because they were discouraged from taking profits from the island. The market wasn't open enough for Americans. This changed when Chen Cheng became premier, and between 1958 and 1960 Taiwan's economic planners started opening things up. In the early 1960s US companies started moving to Taiwan, although their presence was not immediately welcomed by Taiwanese industries, which were accustomed to having a fair amount of protection. So, for example, when Singer (sewing machines) moved into Taiwan in 1963, it "met vehement protest from local manufacturers." However, government officials, who were clearly thinking more broadly about the economic benefits of inviting foreign firms into Taiwan, "countered that technology transfer and local procurement would compensate for initial sales losses." To make Taiwan alluring to foreign enterprise, the ROC government "willingly offered the American company tax concessions, a ban on competing imports, and unrestricted repatriation of profits as inducements. The US government enhanced the offer with promises of cheap credit and insurance against loss due to war or expropriation."[43]

Between 1958 and 1970 (inclusive), the ROC government approved 28 technology cooperation agreements between local industries and firms in Europe, 65 with US firms, and 398 with Japanese firms (from 1952 to 1958 there had been no such agreements with European firms, 8 with US firms, and 21 with Japanese firms).[44] By and large, the agreements with Japan tended to be shorter term and involved less sophisticated technologies than those with the US.[45] In other words, technology transfer from US companies generally yielded greater overall benefits to industry in Taiwan.

The Hornig Mission and a new model for US assistance

With the termination of US aid in 1965, Taiwan's economic planners were especially eager to explore new models of scientific and technical cooperation that might yield technical assistance along the lines of what they had received through the US aid program. One approach was to encourage more business-to-business interaction of the sort described above. A second approach was to set up new channels through which the US could continue to advise Taiwan in much the same way it had done prior to 1965. To this end, Premier C.K. Yen, on a visit to the US in 1967, asked President Lyndon Johnson if he would send a group of scientific and technical advisors to Taiwan. The result was the Hornig Mission of the fall of 1967.

The Hornig Mission was led by Donald F. Hornig, Special Assistant to the President for S&T, who was joined by the president of Bell Telephone Laboratories, a representative of Arthur D. Little, and a group of five US government science advisors. The visit was arranged and organized by K.T. Li, then Minister of Economic Affairs, who worked closely with a new government institution, the Committee for Science Development, as he set up activities for mission participants. In his welcoming remarks, Li described the mission as an opportunity for frank discussion of Taiwan's situation with regard to science and technology.[46] It is clear from records of these discussions, however, that both Chinese/Taiwanese and American participants were also thinking a great deal about what sort of continuing technical assistance the US might be able to provide Taiwan.

Documents provided to the Hornig Mission participants by the Committee for Science Development[47] made quite clear the degree to which that committee, at any rate, perceived a need for continuing technical assistance from the US. In the document "Prospects of Industrial Development and Research Needs in the Republic of China," for example, the Committee for Science Development laid out a series of plans for development of specific economic sectors followed by an assessment of needs. In a number of cases the document observes that technology to facilitate development will need to be acquired from abroad. For example, in a discussion of the need to increase energy output to facilitate industrialization by expanding its nuclear power capability, the document notes that "Taipower will obtain necessary technical information from the EEI, AEC, foreign utilities and engineering firms on commercial basis."[48] Similar sorts of statements regarding the need for technology transfer pepper the descriptions of other areas targeted for development, both in infrastructure, and in industry and agriculture.

The prepared documents in conjunction with site visits and other activities clearly helped to shape the discussions between the American delegates and their Chinese/Taiwanese counterparts. In a September 23, 1967 meeting of Hornig Mission participants and representatives of numerous ROC government institutions, for example, there was a great deal of discussion about the sorts of assistance the US might be able to provide. Hornig started off by observing that

> the new US industries investing here have a large stake in continuing development and can play an important role by participating in seminars and colloquia, retaining university professors as consultants, providing scholarships, and other mutual assistance between industries and the educational institutions.[49]

In other words, industry could and should play a role in spreading knowledge and facilitating the development of Taiwan's S&T educational infrastructure. Still, some of the Chinese/Taiwanese participants in the meeting remained concerned about whether this sort of interaction would be adequate. Dr. K.C. Chen of Tsinghua University pointed out, for example, that for the five research centers that the ROC was trying to establish to succeed, they "must have an exchange of scientists with the US." Hornig agreed, but argued that the facilities would have to be excellent in order to attract good scientists.[50] In response, James Fisk, president of Bell Telephone Laboratories, noted that Bell labs typically brought visiting scientists for a year or two at a time. He also volunteered "to accept several of your scientists,"[51] at which point Hornig said that he expected "other US industrial research facilities could be made available for similar visits."[52] Y.S. Tsiang of the JCRR followed up with a request for "suggestions on what specific methods, in addition to institutional relationships and exchange programs, are recommended to make US science experience available to us here." Hornig answered that he and his colleagues needed to consider this question further, but he proposed "a stronger bridge between JCRR and USDA," "a bridge to the US Bureau of Standards" and "bridges for transfer of expertise in other US government departments." He also observed that links between industries were desirable, but that he could not "commit US industry to such a relationship."[53] He went on to "propose that we keep in close touch on scientific matters and suggest that each side designate representatives through whom continuing dialogue can take place."[54]

Clearly, the message that Hornig and his companions took back to Washington was that there was still a role for the US to play in assisting Taiwan to achieve its technological and industrial aims. A White House press release on the Hornig Mission noted that mission participants

> pointed out the need for continued US cooperation in developing the capacity in Taiwan to carry out industrial research, and to provide advanced education. They noted the important role played by American industry in introducing new technology, business methods and modern industrial plants.[55]

The Hornig Mission yielded at least two concrete results. First, at the suggestion of Hornig, President Johnson appointed Bruce Billings (who had formerly worked for the JCRR) to be stationed at the US Embassy in Taipei as a science advisor.[56] Second, in 1969 a new Sino-American science coopera-tion program was set up between the US National Science Foundation and Taiwan's newly formed National Science Council. As K.T. Li later wrote, this program was not insignificant.

> Since 1970 the Sino-American joint venture has sponsored 61 long-term visits (up to two years) by outstanding scientists, two-thirds of whom were Chinese American, and 363 short-term visits of up to three months. The two agencies have also promoted co-operative research, binational seminar, and the free flow of scientific information and ideas.[57]

In other words, as Donald Hornig had suggested it should, the Hornig Mission led to the establishment of mechanisms for continued technology transfer under the auspices of state institutions.

Just as the NBIR had in the 1940s, from at least 1964, when the Sino-American Committee on Science Cooperation undertook a survey of Chinese-American scientific manpower in the US, ROC officials, and K.T. Li in particular, paid considerable attention to the Chinese-American community. As Li wrote, the 1970 US census

> recorded 48,000 Chinese-Americans in the professional, technical and related fields, including about 5,000 college and university teachers and professors, 9,000 engineers, 4,000 physicians, dentists, and related practitioners, 4,000 technicians, and 3,000 research workers. These people, some of whom were a part of the brain drain from Taiwan, have made significant contributions to science, technology, and education in the USA. Several large US companies, including Boeing, IBM, and Bell Laboratories, have large "Chinese communities" in their engineering and research departments. Some US companies offer Chinese food in their cafeterias, mahjong for the wives, and Chinese lessons for the children in order to provide an attractive employment package. Despite these, many of these Chinese Americans have . . . already returned temporarily or permanently to Taiwan. Their past performance in the US professional environment gives us confidence that we can establish a strong technological base in the Republic of China.[58]

Li himself made a point of keeping close contacts with the sizeable community of Chinese American scientists and engineers and meeting with them on his trips to the US, and as one of his biographers observed, "these channels greatly facilitated the upgrading of Taiwan's industry in the 1980s."[59]

Technology and diplomacy: the ROC as a source of technology

Just as technology flowed into Taiwan through these various channels, it also flowed out of Taiwan as part of the ROC's extensive diplomatic efforts to retain its seat in the UN and to continue to be internationally recognized in the 1950s and 1960s. From 1954 on, the ROC invited technicians from developing countries to come to Taipei for training, and over the course of the next 20 years, more than 7,500 technicians came from 50 countries. Much of this training was undertaken by the JCRR, which offered courses on agriculture, land administration, technology and skills, animal husbandry, and fishing and aquaculture.[60] Most of this training was funded by the US through US AID, and, according to Nancy Tucker, "the CIA facilitated many of the initial contacts needed to convince governments to utilize Nationalist expertise."[61]

Beginning in 1961, the ROC sent technicians, most of them working in agricultural fields and sent through JCRR, to developing countries in Africa, Latin America and elsewhere in Asia. The first such team was a group of 15 technicians sent to Liberia in 1961. By 1970 there were 702 technicians working in 23 African countries, and 111 others working in Asia and Latin

America.[62] Although most of this technical assistance was in agriculture, ROC technicians also offered training and assistance in fisheries, aquaculture, animal husbandry, sugar refining, road construction and handicrafts.[63]

Clearly, the level and type of technology being transferred from Taiwan to other places was considerably different than that being transferred from the US to Taiwan, but this trickle down system was politically useful to both Taiwan and the US, and it was more effective than direct technical assistance from the US to the countries receiving ROC aid might have been, in part because of the greater developmental parity between Taiwan and the countries it assisted.[64] Ultimately, although these efforts may have yielded a great deal in terms of economic development in the countries in which they were made, they did not yield the diplomatic results that the ROC had hoped for. The tidal wave of support for UN recognition of the PRC was simply too strong.

By the time Taiwan was derecognized by the US in 1978, such technological missions were very much on the wane, in particular because the number of states with which Taiwan had formal relations had significantly diminished. Taiwan's foreign relations crisis also made it all the more imperative for the state to try to come up with creative strategies to facilitate continued transfer of technology into Taiwan. Many of the efforts along these lines made by the ROC government in the 1970s and 1980s were rooted in the patterns of inter-action that had been established in the 1950s and 1960s, and others stemmed from ideas that had been generated through these early interactions.

The creation of STAG

In the 1970s ROC institutions continued to negotiate opportunities for Taiwan's scientists and technicians to study abroad in fields that were of particular interest to economic planners. One such institution was the Industrial Technology Research Institute (ITRI), an institution designed to conduct research and development activities that would serve Taiwan's small and medium-sized enterprises, which in the mid 1970s sent a group of 38 scientists to the US for short-term semi-conductor training.[65] In addition, the ROC continued to look for ways to lure foreign companies to import technology to Taiwan, so for example, in 1978, the Ministry of Economic Affairs invited the board of Texas Instruments (TI) to Taiwan with the intention of luring TI to set up R&D units in a planned science park in Hsinchu. Although this plan did not yield the expected results, advice given by Patrick Haggerty and others from TI did lead to the creation of a new institution, the Science and Technology Advisory Group (STAG) in 1979. This new institution was composed of a set of semi-permanent foreign advisors who met periodically with ROC technocrats, scientists and captains of industry to guide science policy as it pertained to industrial development. Like the 1978 TI visit, STAG meetings were in many respects modeled on the Hornig Mission. Also in 1979, the Science-based Industrial Park in Hsinchu, which had been in the planning stages for at least a decade, finally got up and running. The Hsinchu science park was envisioned as a place in which both foreign and Taiwan owned industries would set up research and development units in close proximity to each other and also to ITRI and several universities. The hope was that the park would develop into a community of researchers who would share knowledge and technology. A second expectation for the park was that it would help to lure skilled Chinese/Taiwanese technicians back to Taiwan, and that they would bring with them the skills, knowledge and technology that they had acquired abroad. Although it took some time, by the 1990s the park seemed to be achieving these ends, and was having at least enough success that the Taiwan government decided to try to emulate the model in several other locations around the island.

Conclusion

The KMT state played an active role in facilitating technology transfer both during its early years in China and after its move to Taiwan. It did so by maintaining open lines of communication with foreign states, recruiting foreign public and private entities to develop industrial interests in China and then in Taiwan, keeping in contact with overseas Chinese and constructing institutions that might facilitate all of these things. Although the role played by these institutions remained fairly constant, the institutions themselves shifted over time. Many of the institutions constructed by the KMT during the Nanjing Decade ceased to exist after 1949, and were replaced by new institutions designed to get the most out of the relationship with the US. When US aid ceased in the mid 1960s, still other institutions came into being that could facilitate technology transfer. And as these institutions failed to behave as flexibly as they needed to in the late 1970s, they were supplemented by yet another set. At no point was the ROC without a set of institutions that could help to implement its strategies for encouraging technology transfer. Moreover, even if the KMT political leadership wasn't always convincingly competent, state economic planners from the early 1930s on always appear to have had a clear sense of the sorts of technologies that the nation needed to acquire, and a set of plans for how to get them. And they were assisted in these endeavors by having a set of foreign partners who were willing to help, although again, those partners shifted over time. While there is no question but that a great deal of technology has been transferred to the ROC through person-to-person and business-to-business methods, it is nonetheless important to acknowledge and understand the role that the ROC state played at least up until the 1990s in trying to facilitate this process.

Notes

1 Peter Buck, *American Science and Modern China, 1876–1936*, Cambridge, MA: Cambridge University Press, 1980.
2 William C. Kirby, *Germany and Republican China*, Stanford, CA: Stanford University Press, 1984, p. 97.

3 Ibid. 98.
4 Ibid. 99.
5 Ibid. 207.
6 Qian Changzhao, "Qian fuzhuren weiyuan xunci" [Vice head Qian's Lecture] (1–21–1942) in *Ziyuan weiyuanhui Weng Wenhao, Qian Changzhao yanlun* [Speeches by the NRC's Weng Wenhao and Qian Changzhao]. Nanjing Second Historical Archive, NRC, 28(2) 314, p. 13.
7 *The China Handbook, 1937–1945*, New York: The Macmillan Company, 1947, p. 343.
8 Ibid. 83–85.
9 Wilma Fairbank, "A Study of Chinese Educational Needs and Programs of US-Located Agencies to Meet Them," Report to UNESCO, 1948, pp. 79–82.
10 Nanjing Second Historical Archive, NRC, 28–1533, and NBIR, 448–543
11 Communications between Weng Wenhao and the French Ambassador to China, Henri Maux, Nanjing Second Historical Archive, NRC, 28(2)-695
12 Weng Wenhao to Ambassador Clarence Gauss, 7-25-1944, Nanjing Second Historical Archive, NBIR, 448–544.
13 Nanjing Second Historical Archive, NBIR, 448–544.
14 Letter to Dr. Ku and Co-workers from Wm. Han-chu Lee, *et al.,* January 1945, Nanjing Second Historical Archive, NBIR, 448–540.
15 Ibid.
16 See, for example, "Letter from Tsai Hong-Ji to Y.T. Ku," Nanjing Second Historical Archive, NBIR, 448–543.
17 "Letter from V. Bush to Ku Yu-hsiu," Academia Sinica, AS-Jingjibu, 18-22–104. The charter of the US Office of Scientific Research and Development and other information sent by Bush was all translated in its entirety into Chinese, which does not appear to have been a very common practice at the time. This suggests to me that the Committee was quite serious about adapting the US model to the Chinese case. Translations of the documents can be found in Nanjing Second Historical Archive, NRC, 28–1641.
18 Nanjing Second Historical Archive, Academia Sinica, 393–699.
19 Michael Schaller, *The US Crusade in China, 1938–1945*, New York: Columbia University Press, 1979, p. 301.
20 Neil H. Jacoby, *US Aid to Taiwan: A Study of Foreign Aid, Self-Help, and Development.* New York: Praeger, 1966, p. 61.
21 Ibid. 62.
22 Ibid.
23 Nancy Bernkopf Tucker, *Taiwan, Hong Kong, and the United States, 1945–1992*, New York: Twayne Publishers, 1994, p. 55.
24 Joseph A. Yager, *Transforming Agriculture in Taiwan: The Experience of the Joint Commission on Rural Reconstruction*, Ithaca, NY: Cornell University Press, 1988, pp. 211–212
25 Ibid. 212.
26 Ibid.
27 Ibid. 213.
28 Richard Lee Hough, "Models of Rural Development Administration: The JCRR Experience in Taiwan," Southeast Asia Development Advisory Group, No. 37, New York: The Asia Society, 1968, pp. 6–7.
29 Yen Chen-hsing, "Dui fazhan woguo yuanzi neng de zhanwang" [My Views and Hopes in Relation to Our Development of Atomic Energy] in *Yuanzineng weiyuanhui lubao* [*Chinese AEC Bulletin*] 2: 3 (June 1966), p. 1.
30 "Agreement for Cooperation Between the Government of the United States of America and the Government of the Republic of China Concerning Civil Uses

of Atomic Energy," 18 July, 1955, reprinted in Stephen P. Gibert and William M. Carpenter, Eds., *America and Island China: a documentary history* (Lanham, MD: University Press of America, 1984) pp. 168–72.

31 Bruce Billings, "The Republic of China and America: Seven Decades of Science and Technology Relations," in Sun Tung-hsun and Morris Wei-hsin Tien, Eds., *ROC and USA 1911–1981* (Taipei: American Studies Association of the Republic of China, 1982), p. 27; *China Yearbook 1958–59*, p. 416.

32 *China Yearbook 1958–59*, 416.

33 Ibid. 417.

34 Paul R. Byerly, Jr., "End of Tour Report, to AID/W from USAID/Taipei," 6 August 1963, Academia Sinica, AS-Qian, Box 77, p. 15.

35 "Memorandum Prepared in the Department of State," 30 December 1958, FRUS, 1958–1960, Vol. 19, China, pp. 509–10.

36 Ibid.

37 For more on the NCSD see J. Megan Greene, *The Origins of the Developmental State in Taiwan: Science Policy and the Quest for Modernization*, Cambridge: Harvard University Press, 2008.

38 Jacoby, pp. 38, 210.

39 Ibid. 210.

40 Ibid. 165.

41 Denis Fred Simon, "Taiwan, Technology Transfer, and Transnationalism: The Political Management of Dependency," Berkeley, CA: University of California Ph.D. dissertation, 1980, p. 418.

42 Simon, p. 421.

43 Tucker, p. 57.

44 Simon, p. 420.

45 Ibid. 422–24.

46 K. T. Li, "Welcome Address to Hornig Mission," Academia Sinica, AS-Li, B490–19, p. 2.

47 The Committee for Science Development, which was created in 1967 and placed under the National Security Council, took over the planning and coordinating functions that the NCSD had been intended to perform. At the same time, the NCSD was reorganized into the National Science Council, which took primary responsibility for doling out government grants.

48 Committee for Science Development, "Prospects of Industrial Development and Research Needs in the Republic of China," Academia Sinica, AS-Li, B490–44, p. 4.

49 "Minutes of Meeting with Dr. Hornig and his colleagues on Science Development in the Republic of China," Academia Sinica, AS-Li, B490, p. 3.

50 Ibid. 7.

51 Ibid. 8.

52 Ibid.

53 Ibid.

54 Ibid. 9.

55 "White House Issued Following Release Today: October 6, 1967," Academia Sinica, AS-Li, B490, p. 1.

56 Lutao Sophia Kang Wang, *K. T. Li and the Taiwan Experience*, Hsin-chu: National Tsing Hua University Press, 2006, p. 172.

57 K. T. Li, *Economic Transformation of Taiwan*, London: Shepheard-Walwyn Publishers, 1988, p. 172.

58 Li, 1988, p. 175.

59 Wang, p. 173.

60 Yager, p. 211.
61 Tucker, p. 61.
62 Ralph N. Clough, *Island China*, Cambridge: Harvard University Press, 1978, p. 151.
63 Clough, pp. 151–152.
64 Ibid.
65 Sun Chen, "Toward a Knowledge-Based Economy: Taiwan's Experience in Developing Science and Technology-Based Industries," *Industry of Free China* (March, 1999), p. 95.

2 The evolution of Taiwan's economic miracle 1945–2000

Personal accounts and political narratives

Murray A. Rubinstein

In this chapter, we examine the contours of Taiwan's economic history as a ROC (Republic of China) province and as the seat of the ROC's émigré regime and the economic miracle that was launched with the help of the ROC's strongest ally, the United States. We meet the technocrat actors from both the ROC and the US who helped to the promote and finance the miracle and then create a consumer electronics sector that in turn helped produced a strong IT sector. Only then can we understand the investment of the ROC's private sector in the "open for business and investment" Peoples Republic of China of the mid 1990s and early 2000s.

We begin this overview with the coming of the ROC regime to Taiwan and end as new IT firms and other industrial firms are beginning to relocate their factories in southeast and mid-eastern coastal China

Post-war Taiwan and the birth of an "economic miracle"

The ROC military and civilian forces took over the island from the colonial Japanese government that had ruled what had been a province of the Qing Empire from 1895 in late August of 1945. The three years that followed, the Retrocession (to use the proper KMT terminology) were marked by all too many recorded examples of how the ROC civilian officials – carpetbaggers, to some – and military forces involved themselves in widespread corruption and acts of physical brutality – including rape – upon the civilian population. This was the situation that existed in 1947 when the Taiwanese revolted. That revolt, successful at first, was brutally put down after ROC negotiators had bought time by talking to Taiwanese elite leaders. The suppression resulted in at least 10,000 deaths and result in a population that would remain largely cowed and quiescent until the end of the 1960s.[1]

Only after the revolt of 1947 – the 2-28 Incident and its brutal suppression and their increasing failures to deal with the CCP military forces on the mainland – did the ROC officials realize that they had to make reforms in Taiwan if they were going to be able to hold that province. With the removal of Chen Yi and other reforms, things began to get better as the island's economy recovered some of its former capacity and a measure of anxious calm returned.

It was during this time that groups of ROC technocrats high within the circles of the bureaucracy began to come to Taiwan to aid in the reconstruction process. A number of these men would become the core of well-trained and experienced planners and doers that the ROC's second in command, Chen Cheng, would rely upon to restructure the economy in the decades following the ROC's 1949 loss of the mainland and its government's retreat to the island.

The year following the retreat saw the new island home of the ROC regime saved from invasion by a historical event taking place a few thousand miles away. History was now favoring the defeated, demoralized and virtually defenseless regime, now led once again by Chiang Kai-shek. The American government's involvement in the defense of South Korea and its subsequent bloody and prolonged military engagement with the new People's Republic of China led the Truman administration to order a carrier group in the Taiwan Strait and then led the US to become the protector of the ROC.

Let us flesh out this scenario out in a bit more detail. In late 1950, the UN's war in Korea, with American troops doing most of the fighting, moved into its critical stage. The American and British forces, under the command of General Douglas Macarthur, the commander of American troops in the war against Japan, and then the leader of the American occupation that followed, had been able to destroy the North Korean armies and advance well north in communist North Korea's heartland. It was only then that the general and his troops found that the People's Liberation Army (PLA) had moved across the Yalu River to defend a sister socialist regime. That massive and well-trained army, the victor in the Chinese Civil War, drove the surprised American and British forces down deep into the south. It was then, with the US engaged in full blown combat on the Korean Peninsula with the PRC, that the Truman administration sent naval forces into the Taiwan Strait to protect the government of the ROC. The US would continue to recognize and support the ROC for almost thirty more years.

Early in 1951, a high profile and multifaceted American foreign aid initiative began in this now smaller and weakened ROC in Taiwan. That US "nation building" initiative would turn out to be the most successful effort of its kind in American post-war history. It was that initiative and the high-level cooperation of US and ROC technocrats that was at the core of the socio-economic change that produced the Taiwanese miracle – and the high-tech miracle that was an essential and dramatic element in that process of economic transformation.

Before we examine the stages of that economic transformation it is important to meet three sets of actors. The first set consists of American civilians who were members of the Agency for International Development Mission, the arm of the State Department. These men were sent to the island to plan and then implement the Truman-led government's foreign aid programs. The second set of actors were American military officers who were to help rebuild the ROC's armed forces and who also set up listening stations and sites for the analysis of data gathered by ROC agents and their networks still on the mainland. CIA agents worked with these men who were able turn Taiwan into America's forward base for the gathering of intelligence about the now hostile PRC. The third set of actors was those Chinese technocrats, newly arrived on the island, who worked with the ROC leadership to reinvent Taiwan as the "Other China." In the pages ahead we will focus on the civilians, American and Chinese, who helped create the "economic miracle."

The Taiwan "Miracle" can be broken down in four overlapping periods or stages. These are as follows:

1   the stage of import substitution;
2   the stage of export-driven industrial development;
3   the stage of the development of computer-centered high-tech industries;
4   the stage of economic relations with, and transfer of, technology to Mainland China.

In the sections of this chapter that that follow, I will discuss, somewhat briefly, each of the first two of these stages. I will then examine the American presence in Taiwan, a presence that is an important aspect of the export-driven stage and is also related to the decisions that helped bring about the third stage.

The import substitution stage

Import Substitution Industrialization (IS) is the starting point for the Taiwan Miracle, and, as much research on development has shown us, it is also a first formal stage of development that many high-growth developing economies go through. It can be thought of as a necessary "rite of passage." This stage begins in the early 1950s and ends in 1960, as the second stage, the export-driven stage begins to take shape.

A first step the government's leaders and planners felt they had to take was to rebuild what had been there, under the Japanese colonialists, as a foundation for future economic expansion. They needed economic support to do so and thus the presence of American foreign aid officials and advisors, with vast sums of direct foreign aid at their disposal, became almost essential for both the survival of the regime and for the redevelopment of its economy. American officials in the halls of the grand buildings at Foggy Bottom, at the embassy in downtown Taipei (near the preserved West Gate of the old Qing government's headquarters) and from the heights of the western neighborhoods of Tianmu and Yangminshan looked at Taiwan as a potential model – an Asian test case – for its attempts to administer foreign aid funds and practical advice.[2]

Their American allies provided the capital they needed to tide them over these difficult first years but this gift came with strings attached: Americans. They would have to be brought into the newly rationalized system of economic planning. There was another problem with the Americans: they disliked the kind of direct ownership of industries and commercial enterprises and control that key ideologues within the KMT and the government espoused and put into practice. As we have noted, it was government officials and party officials that took over many of the Japanese enterprises once the Japanese had surrendered the island.

As the 1950s went on, the first three of the basic challenges were met. Fiscal policies, while notably draconian, were introduced that did stabilize the currency. Funds were found for the large military and the American sea and air umbrella provided the degree of security the regime felt it needed. And, with American help and with an American presence on a number of joint committees, a successful land reform program was launched.

Infrastructure, in terms of hard-on-the-ground assets – roads, rail lines, port facilities, and the basic industries that allowed the transportation systems to be re-constructed, expanded and maintained – had still to be fully developed for economic expansion and the creation of a powerful industrialized Taiwan to become possible. That process would take place in the 1970s.

The human infrastructure had to be re-developed as well. Thus the school system that had begun under the Japanese had to be expanded and improved upon. Primary schools, middle schools, high schools, colleges and universities had to be rebuilt and expanded to meet the growing needs of the now multi-regional Han (and Aborigine) populations and these schools to be equipped and staffed with well-trained teachers. A modern curriculum had to be developed. The planners such as K.T. Li, a graduate of Nanjing University who had done graduate work in physics at Cambridge, realized all too well that an educated workforce was required for development.[3] Medical care had to be improved, as did the general level of public health and safety.

Certain aspects of the development of science and technology had been a priority of the Nationalist government during the Nanjing Decades and the war years, and this interest continued once the government had re-established itself in Taiwan (see Chapter 1). Americans became important here for the advice and deep expertise they could provide. We see this in the development of the nuclear energy program the government began and in the realm of high-level technical education and in the education in the pure sciences.[4]

With the help of missionary doctors and teachers, secular teachers and experts working with US government agencies, training programs were developed that were designed to meet the needs of a better class of industrial workers.[5] Thus this development of the human infrastructure was stressed almost as much as the industrial/transportation infrastructure.

However, the physical infrastructure presented a more challenging problem. The Japanese system had been an extensive one and was being rebuilt, but the bureaucrats and planners and their American counterparts realized that more had to be done to improve the system of roads and rail lines. The Japanese infrastructure that was in place provided but a starting point, even after it had been repaired and returned to full operation. As the Import Substitution Program took hold, the planners realized that there was already, and would continue to exist, a need for new roads and inter-county highways, for new rail systems, for the improvement of the older harbors and port facilities and for the development of new ones.

Plans were drawn up and then expanded upon. However, even contemplating such development forced the planners to realize that specific industries had to be put in place to produce basic materials – the steel, concrete and macadam – that were vital to make possible the large-scale construction projects and infrastructure development that were needed. As each of the stages of Taiwan's developmental miracle took place, both human and physical infrastructure was expanded to meet the changing needs of the expanding economy. This was not accomplished piecemeal but within a coherent system that was built on a series of large-scale, multi-year plans. Such plans and initiatives helped defined the nature of each of these progressive developmental stages.

During the 1950s, the Import Substitution Strategy was implemented by determined economic planners of the economy who were running a strong and demanding state apparatus. A draconian, regulatory solution was put in place. To end the demand for goods, high tariffs were put in place and the people were forced to save money and limit their levels of consumption. The people of the island felt the pain of the scarcity that this policy produced.

There were some novel and effective on-the-ground solutions that were put in place. Many of the basic needs of the populace such as education, health care, food and clothing were provided by members of the Protestant and Catholic missions that moved to the island in the late 1940s and early 1950s, and the churches and denominations in the US that supported this Christian missionary enterprise. Taiwan had become the center of what had been a large humanitarian and education effort that the missionaries had begun on the Chinese mainland. With the coming of the anti-foreign and anti-religious CCP, however, such mission bodies found themselves driven from their old homes along the coast and in the Chinese interior. Taiwan became both refuge for Chinese Christians and the new base for the missionaries themselves and it was to this area of relief that such missionaries made the largest contribution. But even such efforts were limited.

However, as the general economic conditions and the quality of life on the island slowly began to improve, there were increased demands on the part of the Taiwanese populace for basic consumer goods and more. The pent-up demand for consumer goods was making itself felt. The easiest solution to this problem was to import such goods. However, to import such goods was to create a trade deficit and, in doing so, further worsen a problem of a large-scale budget imbalance that the expenditures on the military system had brought about. But the demand was still there and here the strategy of Import Substitution, now in effect and now increasingly visible, came into its own. Industries that produced products for the domestic market had to be put in place or expanded and the joint committees and ministries involved in this process began to move forward.

But more industries producing a wider range of products for domestic consumption and possibly export had to be started. The Chinese planners on the Joint Committees attempted to find firms capable of entering these industries. As they did so, they felt the pressure to meet American demands for higher levels of privatization. Thus the board in charge of such matters began moving at what seems to have been a feverish pitch, finding individuals and groups willing to take over given state industries and running them.[6]

They also pushed for start-up companies as well. Willing investors were found, especially after the land reforms had provided former landlords with newly available capital for such projects. The Land Reform Policy implemented in the 1950s helped strengthen the hand of the Taiwanese private sector by providing the large landowners with considerable sums of money for the land they surrendered. However, these Taiwanese individuals who benefitted by the land reform were seen as a challenge by those ROC officials who wanted to strengthen the Waishenren (Mainlander) capitalists who had come to Taiwan from the major centers of business and industry in China.

The stage of export-driven industrial development

The second of these stages, the stage of export-driven industrial development, is a vital one in the minds of many observers of comparative economic development. By 1958, the Import Substitution Policy had made considerable progress and the privatization that the US was pressing, and that K.Y. Yin and K.T. Li had agreed to, was now underway, though on a scale still unacceptable to the AID advisors. However the budget deficit caused by military spending remained: The ROC's President and his inner circle of ideologues and departmental heads refused to let go their dream of the re-conquest of the PRC or so they said in public statements. They also felt that a large defense establishment was needed to protect the regime against the threat of a PRC invasion. The US officials now felt that new strategies had to be devised to deal with the budget issue and to also wean the ROC off the milk of fiscal survival that was American foreign aid dollars. New initiatives and strategies were called for to make the end of foreign aid possible. The multiple plans and initiatives designed to meet that goal of the end to foreign aid were summed up in the grand strategy that was the term "the Export–driven (or Oriented) Strategy."

The impetus for this change of direction came from the Americans. The US had leverage over Taiwan and had the power over what the ROC could or could not accomplish economically and militarily. The great problem of the ROC government's deficit and the reasons for that deficit – its dream to reconquer the Chinese mainland – forced the US to act in the late 1950s, four years after the US and the ROC signed a mutual defense treaty. By 1959, the US was against such a large scale and quixotic military operation and wanted its ally to reduce its level of spending on the military sector. It can be said that, in ways both good and bad, the treaty of 1955 defined the course of ROC history.

One heavy psychological and ideological cost of that treaty was the understanding that Chiang's regime would not continue to pursue its futile and provocative policy of attempting to recover the Chinese mainland. But the US wanted more – it wanted Taiwan to reduce military expense or find a way to obtain the revenues needed to balance the budget. It also wanted the ROC to open its system up to private enterprise and reduce its strong –one might say strangle – hold on the Taiwanese economy. To push these agendas, the American officials then announced the formal end of foreign aid grants to the ROC. This step was taken to force the government to commit itself to strategy that would promote fiscal self-reliance, if not total economic separation.[7]

The director of AID in Taiwan, Wesley C. Haraldson, met with high-level Taiwanese officials at the end of 1959 and strongly suggested an export-driven strategy as a general policy of dealing with the various economic issues. He then went still further. He and some Taiwanese planners saw the need for a wide-ranging set of changes that were designed to develop a strong foundation for the export driven economy that was to be developed. He suggested a number of proposals and these were used as the basis for what became known as the Nineteen Point Program. Generalissimo Chiang recognized that he had to give up his dream of a triumphant return to the mainland and his hope of an ever flowing source of American financial aid and went along with the export driven strategy and the Nineteen Point Plan, thus setting in motion those steps that would result in, within a decade, that period of expansive economic growth that would be term "the Taiwan Miracle."[8]

From 1958 to 1963 the pieces of the bold grand strategy were mapped out and by 1964 the initial steps to achieve the success of the strategy had been taken. Each year thereafter elements of the grand plan were implemented and sets of new, related initiatives were also put in place.

Before we move on to see how these strategies work it is useful to ask some questions about motivations and objectives. The first is this: Why did the planners feel the need to adopt this new direction in the economy? One reason was that the US felt that the foreign aid they were providing had to end. Taiwan had shown that it had not been able to deal with the problem of ROC budget deficits as the US advisors had strongly urged them to do. They pressured the ROC to cut its military budget – the major source of those deficits, – but it was something the party ideologues and Chiang Kai-shek himself was reluctant to do. To do so – to cut military spending – would be to admit that the ROC leaders no longer had the will to attempt to take back the Chinese mainland.

The US did not want to pull out its aid or other types of support quickly. They could not abandon an old ally, one that had a considerable lobby in Washington, that worked to ensure powerful US support for the continued existence of the ROC, but they wanted to show that they could do something. They also wanted Taiwan to be able to wean itself off the aid and stand on its own as an economic force in East Asia.

What were the reasons the ROC went along with these suggestions? If the ROC leaders and planners adopted a strategy that would allow their vulnerable nation to become a more important economic and strategic entity for inter-national production of the US and other advanced economies in addition to its role in the American security alliance in East Asia, this role would benefit the ROC politically, at home and abroad.

Finally, where there other agendas at play here? The answer is yes. For example, Taiwan would now also serve as an assembly area for many products produced by American manufacturers, thus fitting into the expanding world economy before one thought of the terms "globalization" or "technology transfer." By setting up such plants on Taiwanese soil, American corporations such as the Long Island, New York-based electronics manufacturer, General Instrument, would be able to cut labor costs and at the same time produce higher pre-tax profits, more of which the company could retain due to Taiwan's lower taxation. Taiwan would also gain because it would be the home of a new, vigorous and cutting-edge group of companies. These US-based com-panies would gain higher revenues and the US government would be sure that an American company that might have failed on native soil could still produce respectable levels of tax revenues. Furthermore, the US government would also be cutting its expanding foreign aid budget during these years of Cold War competition with the Soviet Bloc.

There was to be a considerable lead time provided for this introduction of new industrial strategies and the ending of foreign aid. The US advisors made sure that the ROC planners worked closely with them in a variety of ways to make the new system work and make the transition to partial self-sufficiency easier. One must add that not all aid was cut nor did many American govern-ment personnel leave Taiwan. There would remain the formal diplomatic presence, at least until the formal end of diplomatic relations in early 1979, and there would remain both the sizable Military Assistance Group (MAG) with its own specialized personnel, personnel who worked directly with the Taiwanese military and those other members of the American military estab-lishment who ran the US military facilities, such as air bases and less visible quasi-military and intelligence sites on the island.

But did the complex strategy, with its tax rebates, its investment incentives and its set of new EPZs (Economic Production Zones) work as planned? The record of the next twenty years shows that it far exceeded its planners' expectations, particularly those of K.T. Li, but only after considerable hard work by both Chinese officials and their American counterparts.

When the formal program ended in 1964, only K.T. Li was left standing. His close friend and mentor K.Y. Yin had died in 1963 of what many observers believed was overwork. Li now became not only a key member of a number boards and committees, but was also a member of the cabinet. He and those around him tried to sell the idea to companies in the US. General Instrument, a company we shall focus upon later, became the first American firm to buy in. Other electronics firms came in the years that followed and by the early 1970s the American consumer electronics industry was firmly transplanted on Taiwanese soil.

Other industries also came to Taiwan in the late 1960s and over the course of the 1970s, such as the clothing industry and the shoe industry. Major American shirt companies, such as Hathaway, moved facilities to the island, for example. Outerwear manufacturers could also be found and thus, at the outlet stores in Taipei, one could purchase seconds of the shirts and also goose-down vests and goose-down jackets at prices well below those in the US. The recreational shoe industry was represented as these companies produced the running shoes and the high-end sneakers that became so popular in the 1970s. The name brands would be exported but brands with local names were readily available to the consumer at greatly reduced cost.[9]

This somewhat anecdotal evidence is reinforced by the aggregate data that is available. C.Y. Lin tracked this process in detail in his important book written in the early 1970s and shows us that from 1960 to 1970 the exports from the industrial sector grew from US $200 million to US $1.1 billion. He then notes that this, in turn, produced greater growth in overall industrial growth and the efficiency of the industrial sector as well as higher levels of worker productivity.[10] The most telling effect of all of this dynamic expansion was the fact that the net deficit on balance of payments ended and became a growing surplus by the mid 1970s and grew even greater in the decades that followed, in spite of the first oil embargo begun by the Yom Kippur War of the fall of 1973 and other similar large-scale diplomatic and military incidents and problems.

By the early 1970s, the ongoing and ever increasing pace of economic expansion began to strain the nation's existing infrastructure and demonstrated the need to create new island-based heavy industries that could produce the materials needed for large-scale industrial expansion and infrastructural improvements. The Ten Great Projects were designed to deal with the weakness in the basic transportation system and the power grid and also deal with the question of the growing demand for semi-finished products and for oil and its by-products. In his remaining decade and a half of life – the most productive time in his rather amazing and fruitful career – Chiang Ching-kuo, now the key figure in government and after 1978, the President of the ROC, approved the launching of this large-scale and expansive program.[11]

The Ten Major Projects focused on the transportation sector of the infrastructure. The projects included the development of new port facilities, new super-highways linking north to south, and the construction of a large-scale and modern airport that was to be located in Taoyuan County an hour to the south and west of Taipei. The growing demand for electric power for industrial, commercial and consumer use was also addressed. Atomic-powered plants were planned and then constructed north of Taipei and in the south on the large, scenic area near Olanbi.

The government involved itself in projects that demonstrated that the 1950s policy of import substitution had not yet died. A large-scale steel factory was planned and then built, with the help of a major German concern near Kaohsiung.[12] A shipyard was also built in the same area, the area that had long been the home of the local shipyards that had serviced East Asian fleets since the Japanese years. Nor was the demand for fossil fuel neglected. Large scale oil refineries were built, both as a source of automotive and rail system fuel, but also as the basis for a textile and clothing industry based to a large extent on petroleum-based threads and fabrics.[13] Each of these facilities were built and then put into operation with different degrees of success.

By the mid 1970s, it was clear that the shift to the export-driven strategy had been a solid success that produced record levels of growth in the Taiwanese industrial economy. The decision to focus on producing exports had been the correct one. The entire nation felt the impact of these large-scale economic changes. Taiwanese were enjoying their individual and collective success but were beginning to demand change in many of the ways their government and their nation was run. And though Taiwan was regarded as a Little Dragon, it was one that, after the Shanghai Communiqué and the de-recognition by the US, was increasingly isolated by the larger world.

What I have presented thus far is the large-scale context of the evolution of the high-tech center that we are going to focus upon in this essay. Now let us shift to that smaller sphere of US technical cooperation and of the joint US/ROC effort to construct a new industrial economy with a consumer electronics segment at its cutting edge.

The American consumer electronics industry in the Taiwanese developmental miracle: the case of General Instrument Taiwan, Ltd. and its long-term, Taiwan-based president James Klein

In what direction would the newly planned export-driven economy move? What industries and types of Western firms would be involved in working with the Taiwanese authorities and potential Taiwanese suppliers (SMEs)? The answers to these fundamental questions would begin to appear in the early 1960s. It was during this period that a confluence of forces in America and in Japan produced the decision, made by corporate leaders in each of these economic powers, to shift elements of their developed – or, in the case of Japan, still evolving – consumer electronics industries to a newly industrializing Taiwan, open to these companies and to the assembly of their various product lines. This section focuses upon the American facet of this decision. Let us begin with the development of General Instrument.

General Instrument (GI) was a company that produced electronic parts that evolved on the east coast of the US and that represented what some of its employees and others have called the Jewish coast of the electronics industry. Firms located on the west coast had their own distinct cultures, cultures my informants described as decidedly WASP in nature. GI evolved in this close-knit, often interconnected yet very competitive industry and produced those specific components and parts, diode, rectifiers, transformers, switches and embryonic chips, that the major consumer electronics companies needed to assemble the radios, televisions and high end and specialized electronic equipment that the American military required to fight the Cold War.

Now let us again meet K.T. Li, one of the architects of the hi-tech section. Li and his mentor, K.Y. Yin, had developed the idea to bring American companies into Taiwan to act as exemplars and models for the development of the industrial sector and the consumer electronics industry. By 1963–1964 he began to talk to such companies and one he talked to was GI. In 1964 he invited the leading executives of GI to Taiwan to try to convince them to set up manufacturing plants in Taiwan. As things turned out, GI was the first company he talked to and the first company that accepted his offer. With GI's commitment in hand he knew he had taken the first of many steps to implement the export-oriented strategy that he and his American counterparts had laid out in the early 1960s. Taiwan would now also serve as an assembly area for many products produced by American manufacturers, thus fitting into the expanding world economy before one thought of the terms "globalization" or "technology transfer."

What we see is that GI built a path that other American firms would take. How was GI able to establish itself and create the foundation for Taiwan to become the new home of the American consumer electronics industry? One answer can be found by profiling the careers of the people that GI sent to Taiwan and then examining just what they did. One of the first of these was Richard Adler. A later and ultimately more important arrival was James R. Klein.

Richard Adler was an extraordinary and fascinating man and a throwback to an earlier age of American business, as was the company he worked for. He was a person possessed of many different talents, with a decidedly unique style that he projects to this day. He fit the GI executive profile as a bit of a brilliant, smart-ass rogue. Thus he was the perfect man to be able to succeed in fulfilling the challenges and problems that an American engineer/administrator faced in Taiwan. Within a few years after his arrival he was able to set up and operate an electronics component factory that produced high-quality, made-to-spec products in an area that had, a short time before, been a rice paddy suburb of Taipei – an area that today houses the original GI factories and high-rise, very exclusive apartment complexes in what was then still a largely undeveloped, mostly non-industrial, agricultural island nation.

GI went into production by the late 1960s but it took an incredible amount of effort, know-how and sheer imagination to get the plants to that point. In interviews conducted in July of 2004, Richard Adler talked about this early period and provided details about just what had to be done and just how things were done. Suffice to say, according to Adler, the problems of construction of facilities and the problems of obtaining and installing the equipment needed to produce various components, antennas, cable converters and the many other products that these factories did eventually produce were many and had to be solved one at a time.

By the mid 1970s, according to Adler, many of these problems had been dealt with but other problems of a different nature remained. These were problems of personnel and management and the man who was brought in to deal with these problems was James Klein.

Klein arrived in Taiwan in 1974 and took over, after some tense weeks as General Instrument's Vice-President for Personnel. He would succeed in this position and as the President of General Instrument Taiwan, Ltd. (GIT) beyond his and his superior's greatest expectations. GIT's development under James Klein must be seen within the context of the larger linked processes of what is termed the second stage of the Taiwan economic miracle, the expansion and evolving sophistication of Taiwan's hi-tech industries development and the ongoing development of the US-ROC-tech-transfer nexus. However it can also be seen for what it is – the case of the right man taking the right job for himself, his company and his adopted new home, Taiwan. Now we must look at the man and his work.

His first years on the island spanned the four years from 1974 to 1977. These were crucial ones for James Klein, for his company and its four divisions and for the community of transplanted American consumer electronics firms.

Over these first two or three years in-country, Klein had to face many problems and many challenges. He first found that he was forced to defend himself from the man whose position he was taking. The man refused to recognize him or accept the decision of the high company executives and went on with his normal routine, never trying to recognize the change or help Klein learn about what he had to do. This forced Klein to operate on his own and learn about the company and its culture in an informal way. He did gain the confidence of a number of the people of the same line rank and above and then found a way to ease the personnel man out. It was all-in-all a set of lessons well learned. Had he not had experience in a number of different corporations as an officer or as a freelance consultant, he would not have been able to survive this difficult situation. It was an unwanted test, but he came through it looking good and all the better for the ordeal.

As Klein got to know the company in Taiwan, he became aware of the most difficult problem it faced – very high worker turnover. The line workers were young women and they were housed a about a half mile away at facilities run by a Catholic priest. The walk from the housing facilities to the factories was through paddy fields. Xindian is now a thoroughly urbanized suburb that lies southeast of Taipei.

But what of the employee turnover problem GIT faced? Given the conditions these women lived in and worked in and the rigorous and disciplined lifestyle that they were forced to lead, it seems little wonder that the turnover rate was around 12 percent per month and an astounding 144 percent per year. The time it took to train workers for what were very delicate tasks in potentially dangerous environments was high, as were the overall stress levels. When one added the ugly factor of sexual harassment on the part of the male managers of these young female country girls, one can imagine the scale of the problem GIT and similar companies faced.

Klein had two decades of experience figuring out the solution to similar problems and he did some onsite research and conducted interviews with mangers and with the heads of each division. He developed detailed proposals and argued for the acceptance of his new approaches to the problem. He won over the man who was then president of GI Taiwan and other officers and the plan was implemented. It succeeded in a fashion that was far beyond anyone's expectations and James Klein became a "local hero."[14]

This was but a first step. Klein then began to reorganize the whole salary system and the incentive system for managers. It was the type of reorganization that did create enemies on a local level but support from those above. He had also created a powerful network of friends and allies and by 1975 had become de-facto president of GIT. That title was formalized by his actual promotion to President in 1977. However, having the title "president" did not really mean having substantive power. The president, according to Klein, "operated as legal representative and when hired assumed that they had full power and responsibility."[15] However, the reality at GIT was that the division managers thought otherwise. Even before he took over formally, Klein had begun to chip away at the managers' belief that real power lay with them and the GI Taiwan Division president wielded little real power. He had worked on a number of problems in such areas of concern as personnel, training, labor relations and the increasing level of government involvement and at each stage, did what he could to strengthen the hand of the president. He also had a direct line to the GI Corporate president in New York City. However, before he held the title and the "theoretical power of the position," power that he wanted make real in the everyday world of GIT, he couldn't do much. He still needed the status and the formal approval of command from corporate headquarters in NYC. Once authority was given to him he was able to make changes in the organizational structure of GIT that, in turn, shifted power from onsite managers of GIT to himself, president of GIT.

What Klein did, once he was formally president, was seemingly simple. He made each of the division managers into "production managers." Their task was to make things – products – based upon the production schedules for their respective US heads of divisions. Everything else was reported to the president. This included "personnel/training, finance/accounting purchasing, security, administration, union relations, government relations, import/export, receiving and customs."[16] This was an extensive amount of power and, with the acquisition of a state-of-the-art IBM 360/40 computer, even more power was put into Klein's hand for he had management information system tools to help him.

The control on the divisions was tightened even more as time went on, with the president's office providing basic services and also help with basic problem solving in the divisions. Control of hiring and retaining personnel was one key item and here new structures were set up to bring many more Han-Taiwanese into the mix. Implementing this policy meant that many more local people were able to reach the ranks of middle management. Such middle managers were the core group in the reform and the democratization process that was taking shape in Taiwan.[17]

What these changes meant was that the president now held real power. He also possessed an additional power – to monitor the effectiveness of operations in each plant. The president could see what was going on and this meant fixes could be applied and problems could be solved without recourse to communicating directly to US management in NYC.

These changes were implemented rapidly and they made GIT a much better company so that by the 1980s it was in Klein's words, "the Big Dog on the island, largest employer, top exporter, and a clear reputation."[18]

Klein would build off this success and he would, over the years that followed, expand his own role in GIT and strengthen GIT's presence in Taiwan and in other parts of East and South East Asia.[19] I simply mention this here but it is a tale told in greater detail elsewhere.[20] By the time the end of his tenure as GIT's President came, in the early 1990s, Klein would have been able to use all his hard won skills to break up GIT into individual pieces. Each of these pieces, the GIT divisions, would then be offered up for sale by the mother company's new owners, Foresman Inc. and its very powerful and charismatic CIO, a man named Donald Rumsfeld. With his work accomplished, he moved to the US and to the home that he and his wife Helen had purchased at Sea Pines Plantation on the South Carolina golf mecca of Hilton Head Island.

What K.T. Li and Chiang Ching-kuo came to realize was that they had allowed a tiger to enter the gates. They might have thought that with the end of foreign aid from the US would come the end of a forceful American presence in Taiwan. That presence could be seen on each street in the new sections of Taipei and the major cities and industrial and high-tech zones to the south. By the early 1990s that icon of American fast food culture, McDonalds, could be found on the major thoroughfares of the city. Many Taiwanese preferred American fast food to the classic street food or small local restaurant food that could be found a few streets or alleys distant. By the late 1990s Starbucks had invaded the central city as well and were a major competitor to the smaller, more intimate and more infamous and raunchy coffee shops that had dominated the city in previous decades. Thus American food and beverage culture and American movie culture began to win the cultural war. American presence in general and the American corporate private sector were now truly forces to be reckoned with.

Once in Taiwan, the Americans had their own agenda and had been able to carry it out with the help of such ROC friends as K.T. Li himself. The newly invited, and now invested, American FDI firms had their own ways of working and had their own networks and pressure groups in place by the end of the 1970s and thus had a major stake in the Taiwanese economy. But the ROC leadership also realized that they held the keys to a major new direction in the industrial economy – the development of computers and computer peripherals and the production of computer chips.

Let us see just how they did this.

The computer-centered high-tech industry stage of the Taiwan miracle

The fifteen years from 1977 to 1992 saw Taiwan enter a new and more complex period in its economic, societal and political history. The new sets of problems the technocrats and planners who had defined and implement the governmental policies that made the "miracle" possible now faced were different in scale and in nature from what they had dealt with in the export driven stage. They were, in a sense, trying to cope with their very success, even as that success forced government officials to move in directions they did not want to go, but had to in the new socio-economic environment of a Taiwan that they, as members of the public sector, had been able to create with the cooperation of the new and more aggressive and more dynamic private sector. Those who were statist and basically anti-capitalist in their thinking found that they themselves had played the role of Dr. Frankenstein and had unleashed the monster of a more open private sector economy. Thus they discovered that they faced quite different problems and had to develop strategies and on-the-ground tactics that allowed them to operate easily in this new and, in their eyes, chaotic environment of economic change.

The tone for the changes to come was set by the new leader, Chiang Ching-kuo. Ching-kuo was the son of the Generalissimo who had become Prime Minister in 1968 and president upon the death of his father in 1975. He had been the man who had been convinced that the infrastructure needed to be dramatically improved and had the power to push forward the Ten Major Projects to their successful conclusion. This was an important step, but he felt he needed to be more conversant in economic issues before he and his government could move ahead with the next stages of development. But there was something more here as well. Chiang had long deferred to his father's judgment and to his father's willingness to go along with K.Y. Yin and his successor, K.T. Li. Now that he had served as Prime Minister and was heir apparent to his father as President he wanted to have his own group of economic thinkers with him. The ideological and interpersonal dimensions to this struggle will be spelled out in the next section. Here I simply want to make mention of it as part of the background to the changes in large-scale economic developments that would take place in the years from the late 1970s to the early 1990s.

Chiang Ching-kuo was not alone in this thinking about what had to come next: By 1974 he had received a policy paper that had shown him that some of the best Taiwanese economists were thinking ahead as well. Some of these men were members of the prestigious Institute of Economics at Academia Sinica. Others were based in the US and were on the faculties of major universities. These men, citizens of the ROC who were in major positions in the west, were still willing to contribute to the development of their home country. Liu Ta-chung (T.C, Liu) of Cornell, Fei Ching-han (John Fei) of Yale, Chiang shi-chieh (S.C. Tsiang) who held joint appointments at Rochester and Cornell, Ku Ying-chang (Anthony Koo) of Michigan State, Tsou Chih-huang (Gregory Chow of Princeton) and Hsing Mo-han of the Chinese University of Hong Kong.

These men were all allied with the Milton Friedman-connected, free market (or "classical liberal") Chicago School, rather than the more statist liberal (or New Dealer) Keynesian school. In the report that they put together, "A discussion of Future Economic and Financial Policy in Taiwan," they first commented on and praised the effort of Chiang Ching-Kuo and then made the case for their common economic thinking and the need to privatize Taiwan's economy, while continuing to make use of government intervention only in careful and more modest ways. This paper dealt with other issues as well and stirred a debate, but some of the changes that they did advocate were adopted in this period. What they had done was bring to Chiang Ching-Kuo's attention a viable and authoritative case for the large-scale privatization of the Taiwanese economy.

What one can also say is that this report was one that could and did serve as the foundation of the changes to be put in place a decade later, during a dramatic period of rapid political, diplomatic and social change.[21] When more formal plans were developed in the mid 1980s, a number of these same experts were consulted once again and a number of these men were brought together again as the government formulated new sets of initiatives to define the nature of the now even more sophisticated and complex economy.

Over the course of late the 1970s and the 1980s, the consumer electronics industry and the information technology industry became the very center of the economic miracle. A bit earlier in the decade, ITRI and the Electronic Research Service Organization, under the ITRI umbrella, were established in 1973. It was during this time that discussion about the manufacture of wafers (electronic chips) had been discussed and a tentative step was taken. RCA, one of the American consumer electronics firms brought into Taiwan in the late 1960s signed a technology transfer agreement with ITRI and a private firm (but with the government holding 40 percent of the stock), United Microelectronics, was set up. This firm became one of the pioneers in the area of chip manufacture and would produce a wide range of chips for consumer products over the course of the 1980s. The second major firm in the field, a firm with a more ambitious agenda, Taiwan Semi-conductor, was set up in 1986. Morris Chang, the former president of the American firm General Instrument (and parent of the General Instrument Taiwan Ltd), took command of this new and, soon thereafter, major actor in the rapidly evolving technology sector.

But let us go back a bit. In the late 1970s, both Li and Premier Sun and key figures in industry did not think the time was yet right for moving aggressively.

Organizational groundwork had to be done. K.T. Li, the grand master of the export promotion strategy and more, had lost his struggle with the president but a new and important place in government was found for him. Chiang Ching-kuo was a better judge of people than his father and a far more successful strongman turned governmental leader and he recognized the contributions Li had made and the depth of his knowledge in the field of science and technology. Thus Li was given command of a fair amount of governmental policy planning in this increasingly important private sub-sector. He was a smart man who read the situation correctly and took the opportunity granted to him by the man he had served but often disagreed with to set down the path for Taiwan's technological future.[22]

First was the issue of formally organizing the new effort. This began with the convening of a major conference, the First National Conference for Science and Technology Development, which began in 1978. It was promoted by K.T. Li and here he had the support of both Premier Sun, and the now officially elected ROC President, Chiang Ching-kuo. The attendees, pushed by the conveners, produced a basic document that Li then used as the basis of the program for development of pure science and technology. It had a broad set of three large-scale objectives, each with its own subset of goals. Furthermore, an administrative organ within the government was created and it was the task of members of the newly formed National Science Council to put these plans into effect. Within three years, the called-for large-scale research plan had been drawn up.[23]

The next step was to concretize the new IT initiative by creating a home for research and development and new modes of production. Here Premier Sun took command. He too had a science/technology background and saw the value of bringing together technical education resources with centers of corporate R&D and with onsite production facilities. The result was the Hsinchu Science and Education Park. It was formally launched in 1979 and became a model facility of its kind and a display area for the industry that would evolve with great speed over the course of the 1980s and 1990s.[24]

Sun and Li had another purpose in mind in establishing the Hsinchu facility: They saw it as a way of convincing Western trained Taiwanese scientists that great opportunities awaited them in Taiwan and not in the US. By the 1970s, with the growth of the consumer electronics industry many of these "overseas Taiwanese" began to come home but this new park made the new direction of Taiwan's industrial sector as clear as could be. It was a beacon seen by Taiwanese engineers and scientists as far away as Poughkeepsie, the IBM stronghold in New York's not so bucolic Duchess County.[25]

The strategy to make Taiwan a place for the professionals to return to did work out by the late 1980s. Salaries had risen, opportunities were abundant and native Chinese language ability was an advantage, not a hindrance. Ownership and high-level management positions were a good possibility for those ambitious and talented enough and there were many who were in that category. After 1988, there was one other strong reason for the engineer or physicist or chemist to return home: The Chinese mainland's economy was taking off and one direction that new economy was taking was in technology. From the late nineteenth century, if not the late Ming and High Qing that the Jesuits came to know and to contribute to, the Chinese had been fascinated by Western science and strove to master it as best they could. Even the *laobaixing* ("the old hundred names," i.e. common people) were fascinated, as the new scholarship on the quasi-cult surrounding the introduction of electricity shows us. It was also easy for those who wanted to learn more about public figures like Yin, K.T. Li, Premier Chen and Premier Sun, to discover just what types of backgrounds and skills these able and famous policy makers and leaders had had. The list of new and successful firms in IT such as Acer with its president Stan Shih make this point quite clear to all.

Development of the hi-tech sector was a key element in economic development but there was more high-level planning going on and it was on a scale that would affect the entire ROC economy. In the mid 1970s major figures in economic theory who were loyal to the ROC, though based in American universities, had been brought in to assess the Taiwanese economy. Those reports were now returned to by the men around Chiang Ching-kuo. He was in poor health now and his vice-president and his premier were now taking over many of his responsibilities.

Premier Sun had been involved at this level and now felt that the grand initiative begun in the 1970s had now to be continued. What amounted to a master plan on the macro-economic level was now being called a means of charting the course of a maturing economy that was on the verge of becoming what the US had become, a service oriented economy that was able to invest in other areas and to place its manufacturing sector in places where costs of production were lower, but still of good quality (see Chapters 3 and 7 of this volume).

By the mid 1990s, the new economy that had been re-imagined in the 1980s had begun to take shape. But there was more. There was the new domestic and international political openness of Taiwan. This new aspect – this totally new direction – was a result of those political, fiscal and foreign policy initiatives that the dying Chiang Ching-kuo had launched in 1987. He had ended martial law, thus opening the political system and moving Taiwan from soft totalitarianism to quasi-democracy. At the same time he had opened the way for Taiwan and the mainland to come together economically. He had ordered that those people who had relatives in China could now visit them. This seemed like a small step but many grasped its real significance – China was a place where one could visit and then quietly assess the possibilities of trade and investment. Furthermore the limits on the amount of currency one could take out were changed and this allowed for greater levels of cash flow. In the next few years quasi-public agencies for mainland relations were set up in Taipei and similar bodies were set up in Fuzhou, the capital of Fujian, the Chinese province that most Taiwanese had come from.[26] In my three research trips to Fujian, from 1990 to 1995, I saw evidence of the various levels of the evolving ROC/PRC relationship.[27] I saw the surge of what I termed pilgrimage tourism. I saw trade in religious items and I saw the reconnection of Taiwanese religious institutions with those in the mother province. Christians, Buddhists and members of major folk religious communities developed these new networks. I also learned that Taiwanese investment in the evolving Chinese economy had become possible and that the trade and industrial officials on the national, the provincial, and the county/city levels in China were now trying to woo Taiwanese investors to their home areas in the same way that K.T. Li had wooed Americans to Taiwan in the 1960s. Taiwan's new renewed involvement with the mainland had begun.

We can see this renewed contact with the PRC as outgrowth of the stage of hi-tech development or as yet another stage in the Taiwan miracle. I prefer to think of it as a continuation or extension of this third crucial stage, the stage in which the high-tech industries came to the forefront of the Taiwanese economy and made Taiwan a world leader in an important global phenomenon, the expansion and transformation of the IT sector. What was new about this stage is the way Taiwanese manufacturers in this and other industries took full advantage of Chiang Ching-kuo opening to the PRC. In the first years of the 1990s, these companies attempted to get a feel for the mainland and attempted to assess its potential as both trading partner and as a site of investment for funds, equipment and personnel. Both of these activities increased dramatically after 1990. Movement of capital and expertise increased exponentially in the years that followed.[28]

Let us trace this development in a more systematic way. Formal regulations governing investment and trade were introduced in 1989. These sanctioned indirect trade, investment and technological cooperation. However as early as 1990, it was clear that events were moving faster than they realized, and thus a system of reporting investments and the amount of business being done was put in place.

In this first phase of Cross-Strait trade and investment, the shifting of facilities that were labor intensive and low tech was made possible. This shift was made because the economic leaders in Taiwan realized that the PRC had a competitive edge here and the best way of regaining that advantage was to produce such goods themselves in the cities of China's southeastern provinces. New laws and regulations were thus promulgated as a way of getting a handle on what was going on. The PRC provincial and central authorities responded by developing new industrial zones that were designed for foreign – here read Taiwanese and Huaqiao (Overseas Chinese) – investors, who would put their money near such cities as Fuzhou, Xiamen and coastal areas such as Meizhou Bay. They also put into effect programs that would provide tax breaks and site preparation for these investors and ran a yearly trade and investment fair to entice further investment.

President Li responded to this ever larger investment in the PRC's economy by promoting a Go-South investment policy that would, had it succeeded on a larger scale, have had Taiwanese investors investing in plants, equipment and personnel training in the nations of Southeast Asia, including Vietnam. Direct air links from Taipei and Kaohsiung to such cities as Hanoi, Saigon and Kuala Lumpur cemented this process even further.

The Taiwanese hi-tech sector that had been bankrolled by the Chiang Ching-kuo administration had become became part of the larger China-bound FDI mix during the 1990s and major firms began to invest in the PRC with ever larger sums of money. By 1999 only about 50 percent of the personal computers (PCs), peripherals and integrated circuits (ICs) produced by Taiwanese companies were actually manufactured on Taiwanese soil.[29]

The ROC economy suffered the effects of the dot-com crash of 2000 and growth slowed by almost half from almost 7 percent to about 4 percent and this had a direct effect on the investment in the PRC. A new administration also came to power. What was needed was a more direct set of linkages to the mainland so the development of the three mini links became a matter of high priority. We have now followed the process of Taiwan's economic development and of the ROC/PRC post-1989 economic relationship as it evolved until 2001.

Conclusion

This chapter has taken us far and suggested the nature of the development of the Taiwanese economy since the retrocession of the 1940s. We have seen the role of major political actors such as Chiang Kai-shek and his son Chiang Ching-kuo and of key high-level technocrats, most notably K.T.Li. We have also seen the role of key American governmental agencies such as AID. What we have also seen, through the eyes of one American corporate expatriate executive in a pioneering US electronics firm, is the role that this industry played in the first, larger-scale stage of technology transfer from the US to Taiwan. This same industry played a role in the development of the Taiwan-based high-tech industry that evolved over the course of the 1970s and 1990s and continues to evolve over the course of the first decade of the new millennium. We are now ready to examine the next stage of the tech-transfer process and its role in the evolution of cross strait economic development. The chapters that follow focus on that complex process.

Notes

1 On the Japanese period in Taiwan see Harry Lamley in Murray A. Rubinstein, (Ed.) *Taiwan, A New History*, Armonk, NY: M.E. Sharpe, 1999.
2 There is a wealth of literature one can tap into to study this first stage and the later stages of the Economic Miracle. I have suggested two of these in my introduction, the collaborative Li-min Hseuh, Chen-kuo Hsu, Dwight K. Perkins study and the more recent Yongping Wu study.

  I will also make frequent reference to Sophia Wang's recently published English translation of her biography of K.T. Li. The Chinese version of this manuscript had already been published as a book in Taiwan. Dr. Wang has produced a translation and expansion of the Chinese language version. See Lutao Sophia Kang

Wang, *K.T. Li and the Taiwan Experience*, Taiwan: National Tsinghua University Press, 2006.

A number of other books on Taiwan's economic evolution were published during the decades under discussion. Such books are very close to the source and give the flavor of the periods that their authors examine. These works include K.S. Yum, *Successful Economic Development of the Republic of China in Taiwan*, New York: Vantage Press, 1968, and Yuan-li Wu, *Becoming an Industrialized Nation*, New York: Praeger, 1985.

K.T. Li, one the major architects of the process contributed to the literature as well. See his K.T. Li, *The Experience of Dynamic Growth on Taiwan*, Taipei: Meiya Press, 1976. A later volume, also by K.T. Li, but with introductory essays by Gustav Ranis and John C. Fei has proven very useful. See K.T. Li, *The Evolution of Policy Behind Taiwan's Development Success*, New Haven, CT: Yale University Press, 1988.

The basic book on the American foreign aid program in Taiwan is Neil H. Jacoby, *US Aid to Taiwan: A Study of Foreign Aid, Self-Help and* Development, New York: Frederick A. Praeger, 1966.

Conference papers such as Peter Chow's "From Dependency to Interdependency: Taiwan's Development Path toward a Newly Industrializing Country," and Chu-yuan Cheng, Taiwan's Economy Under Chiang Ching-Kuo. My own take on this subject of economic development can be found in Chapter 13 in Murray A. Rubinstein, (Ed.), *Taiwan, A New History*, Armonk, NY: M.E. Sharpe, 1999.

3   K.T. Li has written about this facet of Taiwan's infrastructural development in his various books. See his K.T. Li, *The Experience of Dynamic Growth on Taiwan*, *Taipei*: Meiya Press, 1976. See also Sophia Wang's new book, Lutao Sophia Kang Wang, *K. T. Li and the Taiwan Experience*, Hsin-chu: National Tsing Hua University Press, 2006. The citations in this essay are taken from the manuscript version of Sophia Wang's important book.

4   See J. Megan Greene, *The Origins of the Developmental State in Taiwan: Science Policy and the Quest for Modernization*, Cambridge, MA: Harvard University Press, 2008.

5   On the missionary presence see Murray A. Rubinstein, *The Protestant Community on Modern Taiwan: Mission, Seminary and Church*, Armonk, NY: M.E. Sharpe, 1991.

6   Sophia Wang traces this process in her book, *K. T. Li and the Taiwan Experience*.

7   See Li-min Hseuh, Chen-kuo Hsu and Dwight H. Perkins, *Industrialization and the State: The Changing Role of the Taiwan Government in the Economy, 1945–1998*. Cambridge, MA: Harvard University Press, 2001. See also C.Y. Lin, *Industrialization in Taiwan, 1946–1972*, New York: Praeger, 1973, 83–84.

8   The specific proposals that made up the Nineteen Point Plan may be broken down into a number of sections that covered related issues. The first such section dealt with overall economic development. The specific proposals dealt with plans to promote savings and develop capital markets as a means of raising the overall rate of investment.

The second group of the points was designed to make the government have a better control over budgetary problems. Issues of tax regulations and of the program of subsidies were covered here. A third set of points dealt with the banking system and here again issues of state control versus private control were focused upon, but with the decision made to have the state continue to have sway with its system of publicly held (i.e. governmentally held) banks holding the dominant position in the financial system.

The final set of points involved the sticky one of exchange rates and here progress was made toward moving to a single such exchange rate. What observers on the scene and what later groups of scholars have suggested is that the plan was not carved in stone and it contained points not yet fully fleshed out, but it did give the

US a feeling that their concerns were now being addressed. Furthermore, it provided the basis for the more open economy that key figures within the ROC planning community could build upon and make use of in their own attempt to create a more viable and powerful private sector.

9   These comments are based on observations made while your author and his family were living in Taipei – and playing the consumer – in the late 1970s and when he was visiting each year over the course of the 1980s, 1990s and the first half of the first decade of the twenty-first century. See also Ying-yi Tu, "The Textile and Apparel Industries, Appendix A. in Hsueh, *et. al.*, *Industrialization and the State*, 186–224.

10 Ching-Yuan Lin, *Industrialization in Taiwan, 1946–1972: Trade and Import Substitution Policies for Developing Countries*, New York: Praeger, 1973.

11 Chiang Ching-kuo's long, eventful and productive life are spelled out in Jay Taylor, *The Generalissimo's Son: Chian Ching-kuo and the Revolutions in China and Taiwan*, Cambridge, MA: Harvard University Press, 2000. On Ching-kuo's role in economic development see the masterful essay by Chu-yuan Cheng of Ball State University, "Taiwan's Economy Under Chiang Ching-ku" (unpublished ms.).

12 See Hsueh, Hsu and Perkins, *Industrialization and the State*. See also Chu Yuan Cheng, "Taiwan's Economy under Chiang Ching-kuo," (conference paper).

13 Ying-yi Yu, "The Petrochemical Industry," Appendix B, in Hsueh, Hsu and Perkins, *Industrialization and the State*, 224–265.

14 I have interviewed James Klein in depth and at length over the past three years. The data I made use of in this section comes from interviews conducted and taped at the Klein residence at Belfair Plantation in Bluffton, South Carolina in January, 2004.

15 Klein, "Memoirs," (handwritten ms. (December 29, 2004,), 1.

16 Ibid. 2.

17 Ibid. 3.

18 Ibid. 4.

19 Klein, "Summary of the1980s" in "Memoirs," (handwritten ms. (December 29, 2004), 21.

20 I will have a chapter on Klein as GIT president in a biography of James Klein that is also a study of the American governmental and corporate presence in Taiwan from the 1950s through the 1990s.

21 See the discussion of this in Hseuh, Hsu, and Perkins, *Industrialization and the State*, 67–69.

22 Hsueh, Hsu, and Perkins, *Industrialization and the State*, 60.

23 Ibid. 59.

24 Ibid. 60–61.

25 This comment is based on conversations with Taiwanese Chinese engineers and IT specialists made at Vassar College (actually on the Vassar Golf Course) in the summer of 2007.

26 On this political development see Murray A. Rubinstein, Chapter 16, "Political Taiwanization and Pragmatic Diplomacy," in Murray A. Rubinstein, Ed. *Taiwan: A New History*, Armonk, NY: M.E. Sharpe, 1999, 2007, 436–480.

27 Over the course of these years I was studying the phenomenon of pilgrimage tourism, but also trying capture a sense of the roots of the larger Taiwanese experience by examining those key areas along the Fujian coast where the Fujian immigrants to Taiwan (who would become over time, Han-Taiwanese) had come from.

28 See Michael Chase, Kevin Pollpeter and James C. Mulenon, *Shanghaied?: The Economic Implications of the Flow of Information Technology and Investment Across the Taiwan Strait*, Santa Monica, CA: Rand Corporation, 2005.

29 *Shanghaied?* pp. 7–8.

3 Taiwan's techno-hybrid development model

Taiwan's industrial policies for high-technology sectors 1975–2012*

Douglas B. Fuller

Introduction: technoglobalist means for technonationalist ends

Taiwan's technology policy[1] toward the high-technology sectors embodies seemingly contradictory principles. The Taiwanese state has actively cultivated a rich set of international interactions with firms from advanced industrial countries. The state has not tried to terminate these links despite the fact that these interactions arguably create more dependence on the outside world than independence from it. This globalist orientation appears to clash with another fundamental principle of Taiwan's technology policy – innovation as a nationalist project to build up the domestic technology and industrial infra-structure in order to develop the national economy as a whole. How has Taiwan resolved this apparent contradiction in its technology policy?

In the spectrum of East Asian technology policies from the explicitly technonationalist strategies of Korea and Japan[2] to the MNC-embracing policies of Singapore, Taiwanese policy occupies an intermediate position. The goal of establishing domestic technological capabilities that do not depend completely on serving as a base for foreign MNCs is one shared with Korea and Japan and rejected by Singapore, the regional headquarters of Japanese and American multinationals. Taiwan parts company with its technonationalist Northeast Asian cousins in its willingness to accept a level of international participation in its strategic technology sectors, and the mutual dependence entailed by its technology strategy of fostering international linkages. Instead of pushing out or isolating foreign firms once the transfer of technology to local champions is complete, Taiwan has maintained these linkages between local firms and foreign ones in the home market and abroad. In short, Taiwan has used technoglobalist means to leverage ongoing international linkages in order to realize the technonationalist ends of enhancing the ability of domestic firms to compete in global markets. These technohybrid[3] tactics have engendered a dependence on (or at least an interdependence with) the outside world that would be anathema to the technonationalism of South Korea and Japan. Thus, the contradiction between the nation-building project and the technoglobal one is only resolved through sacrificing the technonationalist ambition of more complete control over the forefront of technology.

Taiwan's hybrid mix of technoglobalist means and technonationalist ends has four key features: (1) low-cost competency building to create strategic suppliers; (2) the use of multiple technology channels; (3) tolerance of foreign multinational firms in the domestic economy; and (4) the problem of full-setism. The first three features explain how Taiwan has leveraged international industrial linkages to build up its national economy. The fourth feature demonstrates that the tension between technoglobalist tactics and technonationalist ends has not been completely resolved, even in a country where international economic interdependence has not been rejected on nationalist grounds.

The first feature is low-cost competence building to create strategic suppliers. The Taiwanese have built up strategic suppliers of international firms rather than promoting expensive, vertically integrated national champions like the Korean *chaebol*. These suppliers have gained new competencies through their interactions with international customers. The Taiwanese state worked to build up the capabilities of firms and the general industrial infrastructure through its R&D apparatus: licensing foreign technologies, negotiating the licensing on behalf of Taiwanese firms and granting subsidies to encourage local firms to enter high-technology markets. Despite the active state role, tight budget constraints circumscribed this interference by the state. The political interference did not extend to rigging the financial market in favor of very large firms in order to have the scale economies for independent innovation, an intervention that typically involves massive state subsidization of the favored firms. Smaller state efforts had to be focused on building up a limited scope of competencies to have any punch.

In general, the state focused on the narrower set of capabilities that the large branded MNCs demanded from their suppliers, rather than attempting to build national champions with a broad range of competencies. This low-cost approach accounts for the great divergence in size of the high-technology firms between Taiwan and its Northeast Asian neighbors. Korean and Japanese high-technology firms tend to be large conglomerates whereas their Taiwanese rivals, even today, are typically more middling in scale and more narrowly focused in scope. This strategy also accounts for the continued dependence, which is often reciprocal, between Taiwanese strategic suppliers and their foreign partners and customers. By focusing on building a narrow range of process technologies suitable for suppliers, Taiwanese firms did not acquire the broader scope of competencies needed to innovate independent of a set of cooperative arrangements with firms possessing complementary innovation assets.

The second feature in building Taiwan's innovation system and high-technology sector is the cultivation of multiple technology channels. The state's R&D efforts and licensing of technologies from abroad has been one critical channel. The state often used its research equipment and employees to form new, privately managed companies. The Taiwanese firms also capitalized on an increasingly intensive set of interactions with key customers to gain new technologies. While the state's efforts helped this MNC-supplier channel of technology, the Taiwanese firms were also able to capitalize on the trend in the electronics industry of branded firms outsourcing manufacturing. This strategy of outsourcing created an incentive among foreign-branded firms to increase the competence of their main suppliers. The state did not stand idly by, but took the initiative to make this trend work to Taiwan's advantage.

Another major means of acquiring technology has been the wave of returning engineers and technicians from abroad, principally the US. The senior management of most Taiwanese high-technology firms was educated abroad and had subsequent foreign work experience, particularly in American IT companies. The technology embodied in returning human capital was critical because the returnees were trained at the best US research universities. They also brought back practical skills learned on the job in US centers of innovation that could not have been taught in the university system of Taiwan or even the US.

The third feature in Taiwan's efforts to build a high-technology future is the acceptance of multinationals' presence in strategic sectors, even after Taiwanese domestic firms have achieved capabilities equivalent to those of the foreign-based companies. There have been few adverse policy consequences for ventures with prominent foreign backing, such as TSMC and TI-Acer. In the case of TSMC, the state actively sought out foreign involvement. Philips has had major manufacturing operations in electronics in Taiwan and has received no pressure to move out once Taiwanese firms have similar prowess in electronics manufacturing. Indeed, Taiwanese policy tries to lure foreign firms that can round out the industrial infrastructure for high-technology industries, but forgoes the efforts to force the foreign firms into joint ventures with local firms to achieve that elusive goal of control. As of 1999, three foreign high-technology firms were among the top twenty manufacturing firms in Taiwan, and they were in sectors in which there is significant local competition.[4] Simply put, the Taiwanese have been concerned about bringing value-added activities to Taiwan, but have been relatively unconcerned about national ownership compared to their Northeast Asian neighbors, Korea and Japan. On the other hand, Taiwan has been reluctant to give foreign MNCs Singapore-style sweetheart deals in order to lure them to Taiwan although recent policy shifts in Taiwan (discussed later on in the chapter) appear to push Taiwanese policy closer to the Singapore-style wooing of MNCs.

The final feature is the problem of the Taiwanese state and industry falling prey to full-setism. Full-setism[5] is the idea that a nation should engage in every key activity in a given sector, the full set of the key activities in that sector. The problem with this approach is that it does not give due consideration to the fit between the capabilities of the local economy and the overall requirements for a given sectoral activity. Taiwanese authorities and private business have fallen prey to full-setism in both sectors examined in this chapter. Technology policymakers ignored the inherent conflict between Taiwan's industrial structure skewed to SMEs and the large economies of scale needed to compete in DRAM (dynamic random access memory) and HDD (hard disk drives). Full-setism is a recurring problem of Taiwanese technology policy. Its recurrence suggests that the Taiwanese authorities have been fundamentally motivated by technonationalist ideas to build up their domestic economy, just like their East Asian neighbors. Forging strong global linkages provided a different means to the same end of nation-building. Given the nationalist ideology, the occasional bids for a more complete national economy in defiance of economic constraints should not come as a surprise. There is a temporal aspect to Taiwan's technological policy that should not be ignored. The ability of the state to determine Taiwan's technological policy orientation has diminished over time. The twin trends of the growth in size of the new high-technology firms and the willingness of the older conglomerates to enter high-technology sectors once the industrial infrastructure for these new sectors matured caused the shift from public to private dominance over Taiwanese industrial policy. The decline of the state's power relative to private enterprise has not changed the overall direction of policy. In a case that parallels Japan's, the decline of state power has not heralded a distinctly different approach to industrial policy. Taiwanese policy embodies elements both of technona-tionalism and technoglobalism, and may yet produce an even a denser set of international linkages with private enterprise leading the way. In Japan, technonationalism arguably still informs the interactions among Japanese and foreign firms, even if the overt role of the state has declined.

This chapter examines two sectors, integrated circuits (ICs) and personal computers (PCs). These sectors have figured prominently in Taiwan's technology policy. Both have had their share of success and failure, but they have also had somewhat divergent outcomes. Taiwan's IC sector exemplifies the best that this technoglobalist strategy for nation-building has to offer a developing country. Taiwan's IC industry has created true interdependence between its leading strategic suppliers and their international customers. The Taiwanese foundries and their foreign chip-designing clients are equal partners. Each depends on critical technologies that the other possesses. In contrast, the same strategy applied to PCs has led to development of the industry and enhancement of Taiwan's PC technology, but the Taiwanese PC makers, important suppliers to the branded firms, have few critical technologies that the branded firms cannot easily acquire elsewhere. In PCs, dependency has generally been the price of development although a few powerful brands have emerged in Taiwan in the last decade.

Having it all: development and interdependency in the IC industry

The development of the industrial and R&D infrastructure

The fundamental conflict in the early years of IC industrial policy in Taiwan was between tight technology budgets and lack of private alternatives. Private firms were unwilling to invest in risky high-technology industries, and the government was not prepared to commit sufficient resources to create public firms or to lure private investors. Furthermore, the international leaders of the IC industry at the time were all large, integrated device manufacturers (IDMs). Technology policymakers tried to find a niche for Taiwan's small firms in an industry dominated by large firms from the leading industrial states. With a lack of large-scale funding from public and private sources, technology policymakers focused on building government research assets that would compensate for the lack of endeavors by private or even public firms. This research apparatus would later be deployed to develop other industries in the future.

The institutional infrastructure building began with the founding of ITRI in 1973. Subsequently, research institutes under the ITRI umbrella were formed. The most important of these was the Electronics Research Service Organization (ERSO), founded in 1974. Premier Sun also established the Science and Technology Advisory Group (STAG) in 1979 under the premier's office to advise and oversee technology policy. The Hsinchu Science-based Industrial Park (HSBIP) was founded in 1980. This park provided tax breaks and other incentives for the high-technology companies within its confines. It also ensured that adequate supplies of water and electricity were available to business located in the park. These supplies are critical to the operation of the IC industry. Around the HSBIP, the state built up the training capabilities of local universities, particularly Tsing Hua and Chiao Tung. Chiao Tung boasts the National Nano-Device Laboratory, a very large and advanced fabrication facility for training students.[6]

Leveraging MNCs to create a domestic industry

Combining government R&D facilities and technology from multinational corporations, the Taiwanese state was able to spin off firms from ERSO. Spinning off in the Taiwanese context meant ERSO trained personnel in the acquired foreign technology and then allowed these ERSO-trained engineers and ERSO equipment to leave ERSO's control to become privately managed companies.[7] However, given the political opposition to excessive expenses for high-technology promotion, these firms were not national champions flush with cheap capital provided by the state, but small firms built on the cheap.

The two main state initiatives in the IC industry led to UMC and TSMC being spun-off from ERSO. Each project not only faced political pressure that kept budgets tight, but was predicated on cooperation with a foreign MNC.

The first project to acquire IC technology involved RCA transferring the technology to set up a fab (fabrication facility) in ERSO in 1976–1977 and cost only US$ 15 million. In 1980, the fab was spun-off from ERSO to form UMC, a privately managed firm in which the state, through Chiaotung Bank, owned 49 percent. The firm did not represent a departure from the standard IDM model of keeping design and fabrication in-house.

The second project, the VLSI Project, aimed to bring Taiwan's IC technology up to the very large-scale integration (VLSI) level of one-micron geometry in process technology and design. This controversial new plan had a budget of only US$ 72.5 million to be spent over six years (1983–1988) (Mathews and Cho, 2000: 169). The technology policymakers felt that a foreign partner was needed, both to provide technology, and, more importantly, to serve as an investor to protect the new project from further criticism about wasteful government spending. In 1986, Philips agreed to sponsor a stake (originally set at 27.5 percent) and the China Development Corporation, a parastatal bank owned by the governing Nationalist Party, contributed 48.3 percent. Other private investors made up 24.2 percent (Mathews and Cho, 2000: 197–198, fn 20). It has also been suggested that TSMC might have needed Philips for some of the crucial IC fabrication patents that Philips owned.[8]

The rise of the pureplay foundry model

The formation of TSMC with cooperation from Philips marks the beginning of the foundry model, an industrial relationship in which a firm fabricates but does not design its own chips. The foundry model that has made the Taiwanese IC industry into one of the world's largest is based on interdependence between the strategic supplier of foundry services and the customers, many of whom are foreign firms. The foundry clients have to find fabrication capacity for their chips and the foundry firms have to be able to fill their fabs with client orders. The Taiwanese state and business came to embrace this technoglobalist tactic, the foundry model, to build national industry rather than reject it as insufficient in terms of the technonationalist goal of technological independence.

TSMC's foundry model represented an innovation in the industry where the IDM model combining design, fabrication and sometimes packaging functions in one company was still the dominant format for the IC industry. The feasibility of the foundry model was unclear because the knowledge about the designs necessary to fabricate the chips was still not completely codifiable. In the IC industry, codifiability means the ability of the chip designer to encapsulate in the design plans of the chip everything that the fabricator of the actual chip has to know to produce the chip. This ability to transmit all the required information within the design itself was very difficult and helped to explain why most firms were still IDMs that brought the chip designers and fabricators together in one firm to figure out how to produce the chips.

The foundry model suited small firms, such as TSMC, trying to advance technologically because these firms could learn through serving their customers.

Initially, customers, such as VLSI Technologies, passed on technologies to TSMC without which TSMC would have been unable to fabricate their chips (Mathews and Cho, 2000: 172). Later on, as TSMC's expertise grew with a wide range of products and processes, the main learning process from customers came in the form of feedback that could be leveraged to refine and expand TSMC's fabrication methods. It was also important that TSMC did not design and produce its own chips because this allayed the fears of potential customers that the foundry contractor would steal its designs.[9]

Although the codifiability issue made the foundry model a gamble, the pureplay foundry business eventually replaced the IDMs as the greater part of Taiwan's IC production even as Taiwan grew to become the world's fourth largest IC producer. In Taiwan, the technoglobalist strategic suppliers to the world beat out the more technonationalist IDM firms that tried to combine and control all the major IC activities within their own domestic companies. The state did not try to limit the success of the technoglobalist foundry model that it had created in order to favor the IDMs, including the many new private firms that began to enter the industry in the late 1980s. Indeed, the state did not interfere with the gradual conversion of IDMs into foundries.

By 1994, the technology necessary to transfer designs to foundries had been completely developed. Many of the current managers of TSMC's fabs returned to Taiwan from the US to work for TSMC at this time because it became clear that this model would work well (IPC Interviews). The feasibility of codifiability, and the return of experienced engineers and managers from the US, helped to account for the gradual increase of the foundry share from a plateau of roughly one third of Taiwan's total fabrication in 1992–1995 to roughly two-thirds from 2000 onward. Many IDMs, including Taiwan's pioneering UMC, converted to the foundry model or were bought out by foundries.

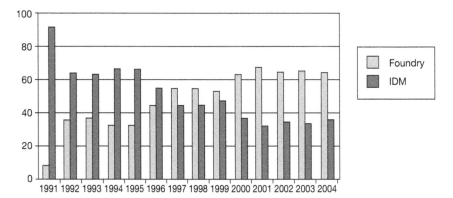

Figure 3.1 Percentage share of foundry and IDM in IC manufacturing
Source: IEK 2005.

Why did the foundry model succeed better than the other models in Taiwan? The mainstream IDM approach was very difficult because it required simultaneous development of the next generation of process and product design technologies. Given Taiwan's tight credit system, firms did not have the access to the large amounts of patient capital necessary to pursue this simultaneous development of process and product technology. Between 1993 and 1997, total R&D as a percentage of sales hovered just above 5 percent compared to 10 to 15 percent of sales in large US firms.[10] Priority was given to acquiring economies of scale and new equipment, which embodied an increasing share of the process technology. Capital investment averaged 69.5 percent of sales over the period 1993–1997. Even this high level of capital expenditure should be viewed in the context of a rapidly growing industry that showed a net profit growth of 34.1 percent from 1995–1997 (ITIS, 1998: VIII–15, VIII–19). Indeed, the only time Taiwanese fabrication R&D investment reached 10 percent or more was during the 2001–2002 downturn when overcapacity became a major issue so capital investment shrank dramatically in absolute and percentage terms and correspondingly more was spent on R&D. With the growth from 2003–2004, more capital investment was needed and R&D investment once again returned to 5 percent (IEK 2005: 9–19). The pure-play foundry model solved the ongoing Taiwanese dilemma of how to advance technology on small budgets by learning from customers and concentrating on advancing technology in only one area – IC fabrication.

The foundries' focus on and mastering of process technology did not make them independent drivers of the IC industry. Instead, Taiwanese foundry firms supplied process technology and state-of-the-art manufacturing capacity. Outsourcing IDMs and design houses sought fabrication capacity. The result was continual interdependence between the foundries and their customers. In industry upturns, the foundries have the upper hand as they have control of the scarce commodity, foundry capacity. In downturns, the IC designers and outsourcing IDMs have the upper hand as the scarce commodity is their chip orders and foundry capacity is abundant. Taiwanese foundries and American fabless design houses as well as some IDMs have tried to enter into long-term relationships to smooth out the cycle of dependency. Along with Philips' continued large stake in TSMC, the other major foundry in Taiwan, UMC, has sold equity to American design firms in return for dedicated fab capacity. Philips and TSMC have a fab in Singapore, and UMC has one fab in Japan[11] and another in Singapore in partnership with Infineon.

Extending the interdependence model: chip design firms

The other high-technology segment of the IC industry in which Taiwanese firms have been quite successful is the chip design segment.[12] From the start of significant design firms in the early 1990s to the first few years of the twenty-first century, the most significant products were chipsets.

Just as the Taiwanese foundries are competitors with each other and have their most valuable strategic partners abroad, the Taiwanese chipset designers have been fierce competitors and have allied with both domestic and foreign allies in their chipset wars. This model of competition is quite different from the Japanese case of technological upgrading through consortia. While the Japanese consortia may have been marked by as much inter-firm competition as inter-firm cooperation, the concept of upgrading was still to organize the national "us" against the foreign competition. The Taiwanese firms have a Taiwanese identity, but this does not dictate which firms will be their strategic allies or enemies.

Since the financial requirements of the design segment are modest and, given the significant human capital resources of Taiwan present in the large and growing pool of local college graduates as well as the returnees, one would expect the Taiwanese to excel in this area. Again, the state played an important role as the Computer and Communications Laboratory (CCL), a former division of ERSO, licensed foreign chipset designs to local firms.[13] The local industry also received much talent from the US firm, Chips & Technology.[14] The top managers of the three largest Taiwanese chipset firms, ALI, VIA and SIS, were all returnees from the US, and two of the three firms' managers were ex-employees of Taiwan's main chipset competitor, Intel.

Three Taiwanese chipset makers were able to enter into competition and/or alliance with Intel in this segment because Intel has relied on its cutting-edge processors to push sales of its chipsets. Intel chipsets did not necessarily give the best performance and thus the opportunity for other firms has opened up.[15] The Taiwanese chipset makers have competed in the world market and with each other by leveraging both domestic and international firms as allies.

VIA was able to compete in an Intel-dominated world for some time. VIA succeeded in selling a new chipset in defiance of the chipset standards that Intel has tried to set using technology from an American intellectual design firm, Rambus. VIA has not pushed the technological envelope too far as Intel appears to have done with Rambus technology.[16] VIA has had a strong relationship with the TSMC as a foundry partner and a strategic alliance with National Semiconductor through which it has access to a large IP portfolio. Acquiring the Cyrix processor division and R&D facility in Silicon Valley from National Semiconductor, VIA expanded into the design of low-end CPUs. ALI chose to be a partner with Intel though Intel's difficulties with Rambus technology impacted ALI as well. ALI also partnered with TSMC to work out the fabrication problems that the chipset designs can present. Both VIA and ALI were also connected to Taiwanese computer manufacturers, major chipset consumers. The odd man out, SIS, never succeeded in establishing a good relationship with either of the Taiwanese foundries and has no major international allies though SIS has licensed technology from abroad. SIS took the controversial and financially risky strategy of turning from a fabless design house into an IDM through a construction of a fab. The alliances played themselves out in the introduction of the new Pentium 4 chipsets in 2001 as

Intel refused to grant a license to VIA, its most potent competitor. VIA responded by producing Pentium 4 chipsets without a license, which has resulted in Intel lawsuits against VIA in a number of countries. In contrast, Intel had much better relations with ALI and SIS with licenses rather than lawsuits as the end result.[17]

In the end, however, none of these firms went on to displace Intel in PC chipsets. SIS's risky strategy, which did not conform with Taiwan's industrial and financial structural biases toward focused firms with lean capital investments, ended with UMC taking over the fab in 2004. VIA, once a global top-ten design firm, now is not even among the ten largest design firms in Taiwan. ALI was bought out by another Taiwanese design firm in 2004.

The story of Taiwan's design sector does not end with this relatively modest success of playing second fiddle to Intel. Mediatek, the very firm that bought ALI, was part of a wave of Taiwanese design firms that have displaced or competed neck-and-neck with foreign competitors in other chip segments. Mediatek (ranked sixth globally among fabless design firms) first displaced American firms, such as ESS, in multimedia chipsets for MP3 and DVDROM, and the firm has now made substantial headway in baseband chips for mobile phones. MStar (ranked eleventh globally) has also made substantial headway into the baseband chip market. Novatek (ranked twelfth globally) has become one of the largest producers of LCD driver chips, a crucial component in LCD displays. Realtek and Himax rank fifteenth and nineteenth globally, respectively.

Full-setism and the DRAM dilemma

Despite the successes of the Taiwanese state in building an industry infrastructure and spinning off the revolutionary TSMC, the Taiwanese state and cooperative private entrepreneurs have not been infallible. The technology policymakers and business entrepreneurs flirted with the idea that to build a nation requires a complete set of advanced industries. In this particular case, the idea was that to have a really vibrant national IC industry, one needed to have a DRAM industry. The Taiwanese efforts to build such an industry are a pointed reminder that behind their more internationalist strategy the Taiwanese still have a nationalist project.

After the failure of the first short-lived DRAM venture, Quasel, in 1986, Taiwanese firms made a second attempt to enter the DRAM product segment. The joint venture, TI-Acer, began production in 1991. Mosel Vitelic built a fab in 1994 with process technology transferred from Oki (Mathews, 1995: 95). With their joint venture with Infineon (Siemens), Promos Technology, Mosel Vitelic got 64M DRAM technology from Infineon and a partner in wafer fabrication in 1996. Nanya Plastic entered into an agreement with Oki and began production in 1996. Powerchip, a subsidiary of Umax, received technology from Mitsubishi and began operations in 1996. Taiwanese government officials and private businesses encouraged these ventures because theybelieved that DRAMs would remain a critical driver of IC process technology and that as a large consumer of DRAMs, Taiwan should acquire access to a stable supply of this critical component. The last large ERSO-led research project, the Sub-micron Project of 1990–1994, helped Taiwanese firms develop process technologies below the 1 micron-width and also created a new DRAM spin-off, Vanguard, with technology transfer from Oki.

The problem with these ventures is that the Taiwanese DRAM producers have become captive suppliers of their foreign partners, and have had to assume most of the investment risk as well. Because Taiwanese firms pay fees to the suppliers of the DRAM technology, the slim margins that DRAM fabrication generates are even smaller. None of the Taiwanese firms has been able to develop the latest DRAM designs on its own. Given the need for large shares of the world DRAM market to be able to fund such research, around 15 percent (Fuller *et al.* 2003), none of the Taiwanese has been able to reach R&D economies of scale. In essence, the Taiwanese DRAM firms are dependent on their foreign customers for technology and orders. In contrast to the foundries, they have no hold over their clients because they own little propriety process technology, and DRAM design and manufacturing are so tightly linked that it is unrealistic that they would be vendors for a wide range of clients.

There has, accordingly, been a gradual exit from this market. When TI left the DRAM business, TI-Acer was stranded without a source for the next generation of technology and Acer sold the TI-Acer fab to TSMC to increase TSMC's foundry capacity. TSMC has converted Vanguard to foundry production. Nanya almost closed down when they could not receive the next generation of DRAM technology from Oki, and were only saved when they received the technology from IBM in return for setting aside part of its capacity for IBM. As shown in Figure 3.2 below, after frenzied investment in the mid 1990s, DRAM has declined in market share vis-à-vis foundry to roughly half of foundry's market share.[18]

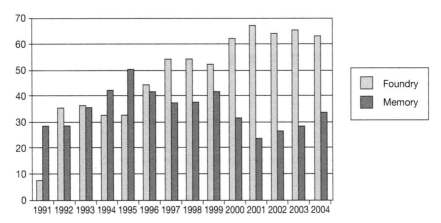

Figure 3.2 Percentage share of foundry and memory in IC manufacturing
Source: IEK 2005.

The dependence on foreign technology among Taiwan's memory producers has continued to the present. The Taiwanese government proposed combining memory chip assets in a government-backed venture during the 2009 downturn, but Taiwan's memory ventures were reluctant to merge with each other and the Legislative Yuan was reluctant to commit money to the venture, another bit of evidence of the shift away from the state-directed in this sector (see section 2.6). With the state attempt at reorganization of the industry a failure, the DRAM makers are in great difficulties. Promos is on the verge of bankruptcy. Nanya now partners with Micron of the US, and Powerchip has been partner to Japan's Elpida. However, Elpida is now itself bankrupt and in the process of being bought by Micron. Such an acquisition would leave most of what's left of Taiwan's DRAM makers dependent on a single foreign firm, Micron's, technology.

The shift to private initiative

After the Sub-micron Project, the state's major efforts in IC fabrication were over because the private firms, many of which were spun-off from public ITRI, were large enough to pursue research on their own. In fact, as early as the start of the Sub-micron Project, state projects came under attack from large private firms that felt the state efforts were unnecessarily displacing their own efforts. In the wake of a heated dispute between UMC and TSMC over which firm would own Vanguard, the Legislative Yuan halved ITRI's budget in anger at the perceived waste of public funds on large private firms. The state stayed quiet for a number of years, but in the late 1990s ERSO tried to organize a new consortium called ASTRO to research future generations of fabrication technology. However, TSMC and UMC had major R&D activities of their own and secure cooperative relationship with foreign MNCs so they refused to join. This refusal doomed the project since it was predicated on joint government-business cooperation.

The rise of private initiative is not a defeat for Taiwan's technological development. In terms of US utility patents, in 2001 ITRI only had 219 whereas three major private firms had more: TSMC (691), UMC (589) and Hon Hai (309). These three private firms also were ranked among the top thirty of US high-technology utility patent holders for that year (Floyd and Meyer, 2002: 19, 25, 40). Moreover, Taiwan's IC fabrication industry has received over one thousand US utility patents annually since 2000 (IEK, 2005: 9–29).

The cup half full: development and dependency in the Taiwanese PC industry

The Taiwanese computer manufacturers have developed as suppliers for the large international computer firms. While the Taiwanese PC firms have a superficial similarity to the IC foundries, the PC suppliers are in a more inequitable relationship with their foreign partners than the IC foundries are.

The Taiwanese foundry model was itself an innovation. Among the Taiwanese PC suppliers, there has not even been much of this type of organizational innovation. However, the dependence on the international branded firms in the Taiwanese PC industry is not entirely disadvantageous. As Dedrick and Kraemer (1998) have argued, the Koreans and the Japanese tried to go it alone without extensive cooperation with the American firms under the Wintel standard and they failed in this endeavor. Because they never embraced the extreme form of technonationalism, the Taiwanese were able to succeed in being close followers of the lead firms and avoid the losses of costly bets on failed alternative standards. Thus, the cup half empty due to dependence on the branded PC firms may be the cup half full with technological upgrading and industrial expansion that the technonationalist Koreans can only look at with envy. As time has passed, Taiwan's strategy has looked better and better. For example, the rise of electronics brands without manufacturing includes top global brands in computers (Acer) and mobile phones (HTC).

Foreign firms, domestic suppliers and the state

In the PC industry, the state aided local firms to become suppliers to the foreign firms that had come to Taiwan to set up manufacturing facilities. Gradually, these local suppliers developed into full service original equipment manufacture (OEM)[19] firms and then into original design manufacture (ODM) firms producing complete PCs for the own brand manufacture (OBM) firms, principally American ones. The local supplier firms, sometimes with the help of the state, were able to leverage their supplier role to upgrade technologically.

Promotion of the PC industry started shortly after the promotion of the IC industry. However, initiative in this area was more equitably shared between the public and private sector. The PC industry narrowly conceived has been an assembly industry and thus did not have as high technological barriers as the IC industry. Thus, private firms were more willing to invest from the beginning to catch up to the technological frontier.

The dominant producers in this sector in the initial stage were American producers. The activities of these foreign producers in Taiwan were significant because they were pursuing the core manufacturing activities in the production of PCs whereas they only pursued the back-end tasks of assembly and testing in the IC sector. In the late 1970s, foreign manufactures made up the great bulk of computer-related production in Taiwan.[20] During the 1980s, the share of foreign computers manufactured in Taiwan gradually declined from 57 percent in 1984 to 30 percent in 1990 (Kawakami, 1996: 6). By 1995, the figure was down to 15 percent (Hwang, 1995: 45). Figures for the foreign manufacturing segment are no longer kept by Taiwan's Market Intelligence Center as this segment is insignificant. However, the state did not make any efforts to drive them out. The decline in production by these American MNCs is attributable to their strategy of increasing outsourcing of production.

The large foreign presence was critical in several ways. Kawakami (1996: 12–17) argues that the firms stimulated the components industry, offered technological assistance to their Taiwanese suppliers, nurtured human resources and served to demonstrate what new products were in demand in the international market. The very fact that these firms were already in Taiwan also made the transition from vertically integrated producers to OBM firms outsourcing to Taiwanese OEM firms that much easier.

The real beginning of Taiwanese PC production, as opposed to component production, began in the 1980s. The state had an important if unintentional role in this development. Many of the firms got their start producing knock-offs of the Apple II. With the ban on video game machine production due to concerns that they were wrecking the moral fiber of the younger generation of Taiwanese, many of these game-producing firms in desperation began to churn out Apple II clones often with not-so-original logos, such as pineapples and bananas. In 1982, Apple persuaded the US government to ban these machines. Soon, the state took a more active role in promoting the industry. In 1982, ERSO and eight private firms worked on a PC clone and finished work in early 1983 (Chang, 1992: 201). In total, ERSO undertook three major desktop computer projects with a variety of local firms.

While the ERSO projects were important for the PC industry, the two industry leaders, Acer and Mitac, were doing OEM for ITT since 1982 and Mitac was not part of two of the three big desktop computer projects run by ERSO. The logic behind the OEM relationship helps to explain how these firms were able to foster technological upgrading outside of ERSO while they were still very small companies. As Lee and Chen (2000) argue, OEM manufacturing firms can leverage their relationships with outsourcing partners to upgrade.[21] The experience of Mitac, Acer and other firms, such as the printed circuit board manufacturer, Compeq (called Compaq in English until lawyers from the original Compaq caught up with it), confirms this theory of upgrading. The intensive OEM relationships with foreign, particularly US firms, and the ability of relatively small firms to enter into PC production in the early years help to explain the fact that ERSO did not play as critical a role in the development and diffusion of technology as it did in the IC industry.

When not directly promoting industry, ERSO was also important in acting as an intermediary to acquire foreign intellectual property (IP) rights. For example, ERSO bought the rights from Seattle Computer Products for DOS and sub-licensed it to local firms until Microsoft bought back the rights from Seattle Computer Products in 1986.[22] ERSO also bargained with IBM to lower the royalty fees IBM wanted to charge Acer for using what it claimed were IBM technologies after Acer abandoned ERSO BIOS. This negotiation may have had something to do with ERSO's cross-licensing arrangement with IBM.[23]

Engineers and technologists, who were trained in the US, played a critical role similar to the IC industry. In the late 1980s, an estimated 180,000 engineers returned from work or university in the US (Hsu, 1997: 73). Acer's

Stan Shih stands out among Taiwan's IT entrepreneurs as he is one of the few who did not go abroad for work or education.

The state's promotion policies changed in the 1990s into more genuine joint public-private research efforts. CCL gained its independence from ERSO and concentrated at first on notebook initiatives. While the First Generation Notebook consortium set up by TEAMA and ERSO attracted forty-six firms because the cost of entering the consortium was only US $50,000, the number of firms shrunk in the second and third notebook consortiums to four and fifteen notebook manufacturers, respectively. The latter two probably more resembled truly collaborative public-private partnerships. Today, there are seven notebook firms producing over a million notebooks a year (Miller, 2006: 27). By now, all the major branded computer firms, including the Japanese, employ the Taiwanese to produce notebook computers (Miller, 2006: 26).

The glass ceiling of OEM/ODM

Serving as OEM producers to branded international firms helped to make Taiwanese firms competitive international PC makers, but the Taiwanese wanted to be more than firms dependent on orders from branded foreign firms. They have attempted to move up the chain into design. Taiwanese firms have definitely enhanced their design capabilities, but they have not yet captured enough of the design capability to be said to be in a truly interdependent relationship with the branded PC firms. These branded firms have a number of manufacturing firms to choose from, both Taiwanese and others.

Some (Schive, 2000: 2) celebrated the shift from OEM to ODM as a major breakthrough. The primary purpose of the outsourcing firm in an OEM relationship is to reduce production costs so OEM production tends to have low margins. Thus, the logic behind this move is to increase margins (Lee and Chen, 2000: 7). The addition of global logistics services has been a further bid to enhance or at least preserve value as global customers demand these services from OEM/ODM suppliers (Schive, 2000; Lee and Chen, 2000; IPC Interviews).

Interviews with Taiwan's leading desktop and notebook PC assemblers indicate that these firms regard the ODM strategy as an incomplete solution to enhancing value creation. Information from the interviews with Taiwanese firms suggests that the PC manufacturers moved their production to China because the pressure of low margins has dictated a continued search for cost-cutting measures. Thus, the increasing design capabilities of Taiwanese firms did not bolster margins enough to prevent the necessity of cutting costs by moving production to China.

The cost pressure on the OEM/ODM firms has been unceasing even as the absolute size of these firms and their shares of the world market have increased through consolidation. Notebook computers have been considered the most profitable and technologically sophisticated of Taiwan's IT products. Unfortunately, even here Taiwanese manufacturers have suffered progressive decline in their profit margins even as they have gone from 40 percent of the global market in 1998 to 72 percent of the global market in 2004 (Miller, 2006: 27). This capture of world markets has not led these firms to be strategic suppliers in a closely inter-dependent relationship with their customers, such as the foundry provider-design customer relationship. One reason is that aside from the large Taiwanese OEM/ODM firms, there are a number of large, versatile contract electronics manufacturer (CEM) firms from the US that operate plants around the world. The flipside of the existence of these competitors is the fact that the Taiwanese do not control much of the technology of design or manufacturing. Thus, they do not have any obvious advantage over any other firm capable of manufacturing a computer. In contrast, the Taiwanese foundries have developed substantial process technology as well as a performance lead over their would-be rivals.

One method the Taiwanese have pursued is to cut cost by moving production to low-wage parts of East Asia, principally China. During the 1990s, there was a progressive movement of Taiwanese IT hardware production out of Taiwan. The first items to leave were low-end peripherals, such as keyboards and mice. Then, scanners, monitors and motherboards followed in the latter half of the 1990s. In the late 1990s, desktop production began to move abroad and now notebook computer manufacturing is beginning to leave Taiwan. Production abroad of Taiwanese electronics production topped 50 percent in 2000. Starting in 2000, notebook production started to move to China. By 2003, nothing but pilot production of notebooks was left in Taiwan (IPC Interviews).

The movement of production overseas has only allowed the Taiwanese firms to continue to compete in a product market with razor thin margins. It has not enhanced the margins, enabling the Taiwanese firms to move away from products for which they are dependent on their branded customers. The

Table 3.1 Net profit margins (%) for Taiwan's major computer manufacturers

Company	1998	2000	2002	2004
Quanta	17.8	10.3	7.6	3.7
Compal	13.2	8	6.8	3.1
Wistron	2.6	5.4	2.2	-0.7
Asustek	32.9	22.1	12.1	19.3
Mitac	4.9	3.8	3.4	4.2
Inventec	7.4	4.1	4.9	1.8
Arima	8.6	6.3	0.8	−10.6
ECS	−13.8	7.2	4.5	−3.7
First Intl	0.4	0.3	−5.3	−12.3
Clevo	1.6	−4.6	1.9	3.7
Twinhead	5.6	−16.7	−11.9	−2.6
Uniwill	n/a	−5	−3	−0.8
Average	7.38	3.43	2	0.425

Source: Taiwan Stock Exchange Corporation, www.tse.com.tw.

Taiwanese PC firms have tried to resolve these problems of low margins and dependency by diversifying away from their dependency on the PC market. These firms are gradually moving toward a wider platform of products similar to the platform of the CEMs though the Taiwanese will probably be unable to diversify into as many areas. The CEM firms' computer production is only about 20 percent of their total product portfolio.

The logical move has been to develop communications products, principally mobile phone products. Eleven firms have received cell phone technology, but only six have received the technology principally from ITRI and five have received it from foreign sources, principally US ones.[24] Private firms have shown a greater measure of independence from ITRI, given their growing absolute size and growing capabilities over time. Nevertheless, the old pattern of making international alliances, while receiving aid from ITRI, remains.

What have clearly succeeded are those Taiwan brand-only electronics firms, most of which emerged out of ODM manufacturers. Acer is the most successful and spun off its manufacturing arm as Wistron relatively early. Asustek, a top-ten global PC brand, also emerged out of an ODM and spun off its manufacturing arm. The mobile phone maker HTC did not emerge from a manufacturer directly, but its founders all came from the OEM/ODM business. With these three high profile international brands, one should no longer view Taiwan as bereft of branded electronics firms or incapable of creating successful ones. Nevertheless, these brands fit into the Taiwanese tradition of narrowly focused firms as they are all brands within relatively narrow categories as opposed to wide-ranging brands such as Samsung, Panasonic and Philips.

Building up the infrastructure and flirting with the full-setism

The Taiwanese state has been active in promoting the building up of the industrial infrastructure for the PC industry in the 1990s. The state has targeted critical components of the PC for development in Taiwan, such as HDDs and active matrix liquid crystal displays (AMLCDs). The Taiwanese state continued to follow the leading international firms rather than setting up its own standards and also refrained from promoting outright national champions for these sectors. Some of the projects have failed simply because the fit with the local industrial structure was ignored in misguided bids to have a more complete set of critical components for the PC industry. HDD is an example of this. The promotion of AMLCD technology did not meet such a bad end because computer AMLCDs did not require large amounts of capital to fund both R&D and production capacity (Fuller *et al.*, 2003).

The pursuit of HDD is a classic example of Taiwanese susceptibility to full-setism fever. This industry is characterized by extremely high scale barriers to entry and short product generations in a manner eerily similar to DRAM. Despite their growing size, Taiwanese firms are still small compared to the Korean *chaebol* that have the capability to leverage their resources to enter product areas with high scale barrier and short product cycles. Furthermore, the HDD industry remains dominated by MNCs. Singapore was able to become the regional headquarters for these foreign HDD firms because it has pursued a technoglobalist policy of encouraging MNC investment with a host of incentives. The Taiwanese were much more reluctant to pursue such a MNC-focused strategy, particularly early in the move of HDD production from the US and Japan to developing Asia in the 1980s. The Taiwanese failed to build firms with scale economies to be efficient mass producers and also generators of the current generation of products even though they pursued their strategy of utilizing ITRI and serving as suppliers to foreign firms (Noble, 2000).

Toward technoglobalism?

Since 2003, Taiwan in a departure from past policy has actively begun to recruit MNCs to place R&D activities in Taiwan. This program appears to represent a move from the technohybrid to a pure form of technoglobalism. In fact, it mimics Singapore's technoglobalist policies of promoting foreign MNC R&D. Yet, this new policy is less of a move toward the technoglobalist than a move to bolster the current technohybrid model. First, the push to encourage R&D encompassed both local and foreign firms. Thus far, thirty-nine local firms and nine foreign firms have set up these R&D centers. Thus, in contrast to Singapore, Taiwan is still very interested in promoting its own local firms. Second, the MNCs are generally recruited to engage with local Taiwanese firms to diffuse their technologies to local firms. Indeed, MNCs interviewed explicitly said their main motivation in coming to Taiwan was precisely the cluster of Taiwanese IT firms because the engineering costs in Taiwan are higher than other emerging economies actively recruiting MNCs, such as India and China. Moreover, a number of these firms testified that the movement of Taiwan's manufacturing offshore has not deterred them from coming to Taiwan because the design activities of Taiwan's firms primarily remain at home (Fuller 2005).

Conclusion

The Taiwanese have pursued their nationalist aims of achieving technological and economic development through the globalist tactics of forging international ties, particularly by serving as strategic suppliers to leading firms from the advanced industrial economies. These ties have sometimes created true interdependence and sometimes only dependence on the advanced world, but they have arguably succeeded at least as well at building the IT industry as the policies of Taiwan's more technonationalist neighbors have. The state has developed a set of domestic institutions including ITRI, the science parks and the university system to facilitate the internal diffusion of technology acquired through these international links.

To describe Taiwan as using globalist tactics does not lessen the nation-building project behind this technohybrid strategy. This nationalist motivation explains why the Taiwanese state and even private firms have been and may continue to be susceptible to the fever of full-setism and its challenge of grander and greater nation-building projects.

Beyond demonstrating the potential of the technohybrid model, Taiwan's successes show us the opportunities for development when industry value chains can be segmented into discrete functions that are coordinated across corporate boundaries and geographic space. In the IT industry in the 1980s, the conditions began to ripen for segmenting the activities in the chain of production so that they could be geographically and organizationally dispersed. In other words, the activities could be coordinated across space and outside the hierarchy of a single firm or tightly controlled industrial network, such as Japanese vertical keiretsu. The Koreans and Japanese, pursuing their techno-nationalist dreams through large, vertically integrated national champions, ignored the possibilities for development through segmentation or decomposition of the value chain. Thus, they missed the advantages of focus that went along with segmenting the value chain into discrete and narrow activities, such as TSMC's focus solely on fabrication of chips. Without the happy confluence of Taiwan's technohybrid strategy of aiming to serve as suppliers to MNCs and the decomposition of the value chain in IT, Taiwan would never have been able to enjoy the success it did as the first-mover in re-organizing IT production and creator of whole new business models. The next chapter examines the decomposition of the IT value chain in detail.

Notes

* An earlier version of this chapter appeared in *Journal of Interdisciplinary Economics*, Vol. 18, No. 2 & 3. Copyright © Sage Publications. Reproduced with the permission of the copyright holders and the publishers, Sage Publications India Pvt. New Delhi.

1 In this chapter, technology policy will be used in the broadest sense to encompass the set of industrial and technology policies Taiwan pursued in order to promote the high-technology sector.
2 For discussion of technonationalism, see Richard J. Samuels, *Rich Nation, Strong Army: National Security and Technological Transformation in Japan*, Ithaca, NY: Cornell University Press, 1994.
3 The term technohybrid in the context of technonationalist and technoglobalist strategies first appeared in *Crisis and* Innovation, New York: Cambridge University Press, 2003.
4 See *Tianxia* [*Common Wealth Magazine*], August 2000's list of Taiwan's 1,000 largest firms.
5 Full-setism is defined somewhat differently in Japan.
6 There is a rumor that the NNDL will shut down, but the fact remains that this facility is much larger and more advanced than its equivalent at MIT.
7 The term control is consciously used here as equipment and even space within ERSO buildings were often lent to the new companies. Thus, there were often transfers of control, but not transfers of ownership. However, the personnel were no longer ERSO employees in any sense.

8 These patents concerned some basic complementary metal oxide semiconductor (CMOS) fabrication process technology. IPC Interview. Interviews were conducted under the auspices of MIT's Industrial Performance Center unless otherwise noted.

9 IPC Interviews confirmed the importance of learning through customer feedback and the foundry model as a safe bet for customers' IP.

10 For US data, see Hodges, D.A., J.T. Macher and D.C. Mowery, "Semiconductors" in *US Industry in* 2000, Washington, DC: National Academy Press, 1999, pp. 245–286. For Taiwanese data, see ITIS (Industrial Technology Information Service), *1998 Bandaoti Gongye Nianjian* [The 1998 Semiconductor Industry Yearbook], Taipei, Taiwan: Ministry of Economic Affairs, 1998, p. VIII–15.

11 UMC bought this fab from Nippon Steel, which is no longer a major shareholder in UMC Japan.

12 In addition to design and fabrication success stories, Taiwan has a very successful IC packaging segment, but this segment is not as technology-intensive as the other two segments.

13 Noble, 1998, p. 144.

14 Dedrick and Kraemer, 1998, p. 159.

15 Ibid.

16 Some have said that Intel's failure in attempting to set the Rambus standard is due to trying to push immature technology onto the marketplace. The result was a chipset with poor performance. This information is based on interviews with chipset manufacturers.

17 For VIA's large difficulties with Intel compared to its Taiwanese competitors, SBN (Semiconductor Business News), November 1, 2001 and TENS (Taiwan Economic News Service), September 26, 2001.

18 Figure 3.2 below refers to memory, but the vast majority of Taiwan's memory production was DRAM and its offshoots well into the first decade of the twenty-first century so in this case memory and DRAM can be considered basically synonymous.

19 In the Taiwanese context, OEM refers to the suppliers of manufacturing services rather than the branded firms hiring the manufacturing service firms. Outside of Taiwan, OEM usually refers to the branded firms.

20 Momoko Kawakami, *Development of Small-and-Medium-Sized Manufacturers in Taiwan's PC Industry*, Taipei, Taiwan: Chung-hua Institute for Economic Research, 1996, p. 3, argues based on the Ministry of Economic Affair's Industrial Development Bureau's *Annual Report 1982–1983* that in 1979 the only PC manufacturers in Taiwan were American, aside from possible procurement from the small component suppliers implied by Kawakami's data (pp. 16–17). However, at least one Taiwanese firm was involved in minicomputer Chinese language input device production since 1974, IPC Interview.

21 Ji-ren Lee and Jen-Shyang Chen, "Dynamic Synergy Creation with Multiple Business Activities: Toward a Competence-based Growth Model for Contract Manufacturers" in *Research in Competence-based Management Advances in Applied Business Strategy, Volume 6A*, JAI Press, 2000, argues that firms can upgrade from OEM to ODM, but, given Kawakami's evidence from the relation-ships between outsourcing firms and OEM firms in the early years of Taiwan's PC industry, this argument should also be extended backwards to the initial stage when the outsourcing firms had the incentive to upgrade the manufacturing abilities of local firms to at least a minimum acceptable level.

22 Gregory W. Noble, *Collective Action in East Asia*, Ithaca, NY: Cornell University Press, 1998, pp. 139–142 claims that the head of counterfeiting of the Taipei Computer Association bought the rights to DOS, but these rights were suspended when Microsoft bought the rights from Seattle Computer Products in December, 1986. However, as part of the IBM and ERSO cross-licensing agreement, ERSO

had acquired the rights to MS-DOS, but was unable or did not try to stop small firms from making copies beyond the bounds of its sub-licensing agreement so Microsoft suspended ERSO's sub-licensing rights. An e-mail correspondence follow-up to an IPC interview with someone well situated to know about the policies of the 1980s does not mention the TCA incident at all. This interviewee does state that acquiring MS-DOS did allow many small firms to enter the motherboard business.

23 Dedrick and Kraemer, p. 156 mention the cross-licensing arrangement, but do not provide the likely context of the general ERSO-IBM cross-licensing agreement.

24 Data received from a Japanese firm from its Taiwanese subsidiary's July, 2000 marketing report.

References

Amsden, Alice (1989) *Asia's Next Giant: South Korea and Late Industrialization*. New York: Oxford University Press.

Chang, Chung-chau (1992) "The Development of Taiwan's Personal Computer Industry," in N.T. Wang Ed. *Taiwan's Enterprises in Global Perspective*. Armonk, NY: M.E. Sharpe.

Chen, Dongsheng (1996) *Spatial Structures and Networks of Industrial Organizations* (in Chinese). Taipei: Executive Yuan National Science Council.

Dedrick, J. and K. Kraemer (1998) *Asia's Computer Challenge: Threat or Opportunity for the United States and the World*. New York: Oxford University Press.

Evans, Peter (1995) *Embedded Autonomy: States and Industrial Transformation*. Princeton, NJ: Princeton University Press.

Flamm, Kenneth (1996) *Mismanaged Trade? Strategic Trade Policy and the Semiconductor Industry*. Washington, DC: The Brookings Institute.

Floyd, D. and P. Meyer (2002) "2001 Global Patent Trends," *Global Equity Research Asia*. Lehman Brothers (June 17).

Fuller, D.B. (2001) "Globalization for Nation-Building: Industrial Policy for High-Technology Products in Taiwan." MIT Japan Program Working Paper Series.

Fuller, D.B. (2005) "The Changing Limits and the Limits of Change: The State, Private Firms, International Industry and China in the Evolution of Taiwan's Electronics industry," *Journal of Contemporary China*, 14(44), August, 483–506.

Fuller, D.B. (2007) "Globalization for Nation-Building: Taiwan's Industrial and Technology Policies for High-Technology Sectors," *Journal of Inter-disciplinary Economics*, 18: 203–224.

Fuller, D.B., A. I. Akinwande, and C. G. Sodini (2003) "Leading, Following or Cooked Goose: Innovation Successes and Failures in Taiwan's Electronics Industry," *Industry and Innovation*, 10 (2): 179–196.

Gereffi, Gary (1990) "Big Business and the State," in *Manufacturing Miracles*, Gary Gereffi and Donald L. Wyman, Eds. Princeton, NJ: Princeton University Press.

Gold, Thomas (1986) *State and Society in the Taiwan Miracle*. Armonk, NY: M.E. Sharpe.

Hodges, D.A., J.T. Macher, and D.C. Mowery (1999) "Semiconductors," in *US Industry in 2000: Studies in Competitive Performance*, Washington, DC: National Academy Press, pp. 245–286.

Hsu, Jinn-yuh (1997) *A Late-industrial District? Learning Network in the Hsinchu Science-based Industrial Park, Taiwan*. Ph.D. dissertation, UC Berkeley.

Hwang, Chin-Yeong (1995) *Taiwan – the Republic of Computers*. Taipei: Commonwealth Publishing.

Industrial Technology Information Services (ITIS) (1996) *Wo Guo IC Shichang Fenxi Zhuanti Yanjiu (Market Analysis of the Domestic IC Industry)*. Taipei: Ministry of Economic Affairs.

——— (1998) *1998 Bandaoti Gongye Nianjian (The 1998 Semiconductor Yearbook)*. Taipei: Ministry of Economic Affairs.

Industrial Economics and Knowledge Center (IEK) *2005 Bandaoti Gongye Nianjian [2005 Semiconductor Industry Yearbook]*. Hsinchu, Taiwan: Ministry of Economic Affairs, 2005.

Kawakami, Momoko (1996) "Development of the Small- and Medium-sized Manufacturers in Taiwan's PC Industry," Research Discussion Paper Series, No. 9606, November. Taipei: Chung-hwa Institution for Economic Research.

Lee, Ji-ren and Jen-shyang Chen. (2000) "Dynamic Synergy Creation with Multiple Business Activities: Toward a Competence-based Growth Model for Contract Manufacturers," in *Research in Competence-based Management Advances in Applied Business Strategy Series*, R. Sanchez and A. Heene, Eds. Greenwich, CT: JAI, Volume 6A.

Li, K.T. (1988) *Economic Transformation of Taiwan, ROC*. London: Shepheard-Walwyn.

——— (1995) *The Evolution of Policy Behind Taiwan's Development Success*. London: World Scientific Publishing.

Lin, Ching-yuan (1973) *Industrialization in Taiwan, 1946–1972*. New York: Praeger Publishers.

Mathews, John (1995) *High-technology Industrialization in East Asia: The Case of the Semiconductor Industry in Taiwan and Korea*. Taipei: Chung-hua Institute for Economic Research.

Matthews, John and Dong-sung Cho (2000) *Tiger Technology: The Creation of a Semiconudctor Industry in East Asia*. Cambridge, UK: Cambridge University Press.

Miller, Tom (2006) "Foreign Exporters: Computer Age," *China Economic Quarterly*, 10 (2): 26–30.

Noble, Gregory (1998) *Collective Action in East Asia*. Ithaca, NY: Cornell University Press.

——— (2000) "Conspicuous Failures and Hidden Strengths of the ITRI Model," Report 2000–2002 of The Information Storage Industry Center, Graduate School of International Relations and Pacific Studies, UC San Diego.

Park, Phillip Hoon (2000) "A Reflection on the East Asian Development Model: Comparison of the South Korean and Taiwanese Experiences," in *The East Asian Development Model: Economic Growth, Institutional Failure and the Aftermath of the Crisis*, Frank-Jurgen Richter, Ed. London: Macmillan Press.

Samuels, Richard (1994) *Rich Nation, Strong Army: National Security and Technological Transformation in Japan*. Ithaca, NY: Cornell University Press.

Samuels, Richard and William Keller, Eds. (2003) *Crisis and Innovation: Asian Technology after the Millenium*. New York: Cambridge University Press.

Schive, Chi. (2000) "A Study on Taiwan: High-tech Industries in the Spotlight," paper presented at the Workshop on Networked Production and Globalization, Academia Sinica, Taipei, Taiwan, July 8.

Science and Technology Advisory Group (STAG) (1996) *Xingzhengyuan Keji Guwen Zu: Jianjie (The Executive Yuan's Science and Technology Advisory Group: An Introduction)*.

Tianxia [Commonwealth], July 1987, August 2000 and May 1, 2003.

Wade, Robert (1990) *Governing the Market: Economic Theory and the Role of Government in East Asian Industrialization.* Princeton, NJ: Princeton University Press.

Wang, N.T., Ed. (1992) *Taiwan's Enterprises in Global Perspective.* Armonk, NY: M.E. Sharpe.

Wu, Se-Hwa (1992) "The Dynamic Cooperation between Government and Enterprise: The Development of Taiwan's Integrated Circuit Industry," in *Taiwan's Enterprises in Global Perspective*, N.T. Wang, Ed. Armonk, NY: M.E. Sharpe.

Yang, Ding-yuan and Hui-ling Chen (1996) *Yejing Tianze: Gaokeji Chanye Shengtai (The Law of Natural Selection in Business Competition: The Ecology of High-technology Industry).* Taipei: *Gongshang Shibao* [Industrial Business Times] Press.

4 Global reorganization of the IT industry and the rise of Greater China[1]

Douglas B. Fuller, Akintunde I. Akinwande and Charles G. Sodini

This chapter argues that the global IT industry has become increasingly modularized through the digitization of information and that this modularization manifests itself in the reorganization and relocation of the IT industry. This chapter has three main points. First, digitization combined with competitive pressure derived from utilizing this digitization to enhance the core competence of the firm have driven firms around the globe to re-organize along modular lines in order to survive. Reorganization along modular lines means that vertical specialization (also referred to as de-verticalization or the vertical disintegration or fragmentation of the production chain) is pervasive and that production is conducted through fluid often non-hierarchical networks of firms rather than governed by stable hierarchical networks dominated by single lead firms or global network flagships. Second, modularization also allows for new vertically specialized type of re-location of the IT industry, specifically re-location led by small firms moving functions to or arising in geographic regions formerly on the periphery of the global IT industry. Modularity in conjunction with better communications technology has allowed for spatially dispersed, vertically specialized activities whereas in the past spatially dispersed activities could only be managed by the vertically integrated firm. With the possibility of dispersed and vertically specialized activities, barriers to entry have come down dramatically. New entrants from parts of the world previously neglected by the global IT industry have pushed re-location of certain industry functions. Third, Greater China (defined here as Taiwan and the People's Republic of China including Hong Kong and Macao) has been the greatest beneficiary of this reorganization-cum-relocation. The innovative electronics firms that have arisen in Greater China have been vertically specialized and constitute a large portion of the technology-intensive electronics firms outside of the triad of North America, Japan and Western Europe.

Over the last two decades, the IT industry has undergone immense change through the twin processes of reorganization and relocation. While these processes started in the 1980s, they accelerated rapidly during the course of the 1990s. Academics during the 1990s began to recognize the massive changes in the IT industry. Langlois and Robertson (1995) recognized de-centralization, but confined such recognition of de-centralization to the limited finding that component suppliers that exist outside of the organizational hierarchy of the lead firms. Some studies concentrated on particular industry segments, such as PCs (Dedrick and Kraemer 1998) or HDDs (McKendrick *et al.* 2000). Many confined themselves simply to such processes as they occurred in the US (Best 2001; Sturgeon 2002), which is understandable as the US has been the driver of such networks. Others extended the influence of American modularity to their impact on Asia (Borrus 2000; Lester and Sturgeon 2003). Baldwin and Clark (2000) discuss the modularization of design in which firms acting independently of each other design parts of a system following the same set of design rules, but this modularization of design is fundamentally different and distinct from the modularization/fragmentation of the value chain.

While all of these studies have contributed immensely to scholarly under-standing of the changes taking place within the IT industry, more recent studies have expanded the explanatory scope about how the standardization and codification of knowledge have led to the disintegration and modular-ization of the electronics products chain. Sturgeon (2002) presents evidence of disintegration of production process as the manufacturing module was increasingly outsourced to contract manufacturers in the US. Sturgeon and Lee (2005) extend this analysis of the modularization of manufacturing to a comparison of the US contract manufacturers and the Taiwanese ODMs. Langlois (2003) sees this modularization of production becoming widespread in the post-Chandlerian new economy resulting in increasing marketization of production relations. Chandler in such works as *Scale and Scope* and *The Visible Hand* was concerned with integration as a way to buffer the firm from risk though the term buffering is Langlois' term rather than Chandler's, but Langlois argues that in the new post-Chandlerian economy buffering through markets as opposed to buffering through integration and management is the prevailing way to mitigate risk.

Debates over the impact of codification and vertical specialization in the production chain revolve around how production relations are managed. Langlois (2003) argues that marketization of production relations has occurred. His vision of modularity views the connections between modules in the chain mediated mainly by the market with the help of some limited social institutions, most prominently, standards (Langlois 2003: 374). Countering Langlois' vision of radical vertical specialization and marketization of production relations, a number of scholars (Brusoni 2003; Pavitt 2003; Ernst 2004; Sabel and Zeitlin 2004) have criticized Langlois for an under-appreciation of the non-market networks that actual coordinate production. They are not convinced that the links between activities, such as product design and pro-duction, are completely codifiable and therefore they believe these links cannot be modularized. Instead, they believe in the continued importance of tacit knowledge that can only be transferred by intensive personal interaction across the firms (Pavitt 2003).

Some of these network scholars[2] (Ernst and Kim 2002; Ernst 2004) argue that the disaggregation of the production chain is managed by global production networks (GPNs) with flagship firms that integrate and coordinate the networks diverse activities and exercise control over much of the network's resources. Even in areas where ICT has appeared to move the fastest to allow vertical specialization of the production chain, such as in the IC industry (Linden and Somaya 2001; Macher *et al.* 2002), Ernst (2004) argues that a variant of the global flagship network, the global design network, with its own flagship enterprises is necessary to coordinate the dispersion of IC design activity. It is precisely the existence of these global design networks that have allowed and facilitated the dispersion of design activities to developing Asia. Specifically, Ernst argues that the system-on-a-chip (SoC) revolution has actually increased the cognitive and organizational complexity of design necessitating vertical specialization mediated by the global design networks rather than the invisible hand of markets (Ernst 2004: 2).

Gereffi and his colleagues (Gereffi *et al.*2005) attempted to acknowledge the validity of both sides' claims by recognizing five different types of value chains with distinctive organizations of production and power relations. These types range from marketized value chains to hierarchical ones. Critically, they recognized that there are modular value chains where the degree of explicit coordination is quite low and the ability to codify and transmit complex information is quite high. The power relations of these modular networks are asymmetric with lead firms having some power over "turn-key" suppliers. Thus, their view of modular value chains falls somewhere in between the views of Langlois and the network production theorists.

Where this chapter departs from the previous work on managing vertical specialization within the value chain is not only to argue for the technical feasibility of modularity, the ability to codify knowledge between certain sets of activities, as Langlois has done, but also to argue that modularization has direct implications for control of the networks of production and for the relocation of industry. To present the debate in its starkest terms as Sabel and Zeitlin have done, production is either done through spot markets due to the feasibility of codifying knowledge between certain tasks in the chain or through power asymmetries within the organization of production. In addition to Gereffi and his colleagues' belief in these power asymmetries in modular networks, Sabel and Zeitlin's conception of iterated co-design still contains power asymmetries as they still view lead firms engaging suppliers in iterated co-design (Sabel and Zeitlin 2004: 10). This chapter's conception of modularized production is closest to Gereffi and his colleagues' conception of the modular value chains, but our view of modular value chains recognizes that these value chains often contain opportunities for equality in power relations. More accurately, for the most equitable of these modular value chain relationships, the asymmetries in power relations are so fleeting and often so tenuous that they essentially are non-existent in terms of being a basis by which to extract even medium-term advantage.

To make a clear differentiation from the GPN or iterated co-design models, our model of modularity predicts that most transactions within the value chain will neither be long-lasting nor require large amounts of direct human interaction that tacit technology transfer requires nor will they be hierarchical in the sense of one identifiable lead firm controlling or coordinating the value chain. Instead, the modular value chain in electronics will be characterized by short-term cooperation, low levels of direct human interaction across modules due to codification of the requisite technology and at best ephemeral hierarchy in the sense of having one lead firm controlling or coordinating the production chain. Addressing the claims of Ernst and Kim[3] and Gereffi (1996) concerning the one lead firm's capture of a disproportionate amount of value within the value chain, this chapter will argue that in most cases there is no one lead firm that occupies the high value-added modules relegating key and no key suppliers to lower rungs on the ladder of value-added. To the extent that lead firms can be identified in any given point in time, their dominance is very temporary, seldom lasting beyond one project, so Gereffi and his colleagues' idea of power asymmetries within these modular networks is also not an accurate depiction of power relations within IT's modular value chain.

How have these modular value chains arisen? Over the past decade, the digitization of information needed to produce electronic industry goods has driven a profound re-organization of the value chain of electronics. Digitization has enabled the modularization of the electronics value chain.[4] The basic idea of modularity of value chains is that value chains can be broken down into parts (modules) with clearly defined (a) functions and (b) interfaces between the different functions. These clearly defined interfaces simply hand over processes from one function to the next. The digitization, which one can conceive as simply the technical feasibility of modularization, has in turn led to segmentation of the value chain because digitization allows for clearly defined functions and the accompanying codification of the necessary information needed to establish an interface between functions in the value chain.

The re-organization of the industry has interacted with new influences, such as the rise of new sources of human capital, and old ones, such as the lure of low-cost locations and jumping trade barriers, to cause a re-location of many of the IT industry's activities. Scholars of GPN (Ernst and Kim 2002) have correctly pointed out that liberalization and deregulation of trade and investment have facilitated relocation of industrial activities and that these factors alone would not allow the possibilities of relocating specific activities without the reorganization of production. The difference in this chapter's relocation argument and that of the GPN school is the organizational framework of relocation. The GPN school views the relocation as occurring within hierarchical GPNs whereas the modular model sees it happening in much more diffuse, shifting and non-hierarchical networks of production.

The chapter will proceed in two parts. The first section will provide detailed explanation of the process of reorganization and examples of the operation of modularization in electronics and how it differs from other explanations of vertical specialization. The second section will explain how modularization has allowed relocation and give examples across the IT industry with particular reference to Greater China.

Reorganization

The section on reorganization is organized as follows. The first subsection presents a broad overview of modular organization and what drives reorganization along modular lines as well as presenting the unique features of modular organization. The second subsection presents the segmentation of modules along the electronics production chain. The third subsection provides evidence that modularization is now widespread across the IT industry value chain. The fourth subsection details the characteristics of modular production in juxtaposition to lead firm- or global flagship-led networked production. The fifth subsection rebuts other alternative explanations of reorganization.

The process and characteristics of reorganization

The causal chain from digitization of information to segmentation of the electronics value chain works as follows. Digitization has enabled the segmentation of the IT value chain through the codification of critical industry information that enabled well-defined interfaces or hand-offs between modules along the value chain to replace hierarchies internal or external to the firm to manage these hand-offs down the chain of production. Others (Sturgeon 2002) have argued that digitization and standardization were equally necessary to create the opportunities for modularity in the IT industry, but digitization accelerated and enabled much of the standardization. Simply put, without digitization, standardization would not have gone very far in segmenting the value chain. Thus, to the extent that standardization can be differentiated as something other than an outcome of digitization, standardization is a necessary but not sufficient factor.

Modularization of the value chain is feasible because of digitization, but technical innovation alone is rarely the determining factor for industrial reorganization. Firms adopted modularization because it enabled firms to hone their core competency. In areas where there is little value to be generated by modularization, modularization will not be pursued.[5]

Modularization has allowed for whole new models of organization, such as the rise of contract manufacturers (Sturgeon 2002), which have re-defined the scope of core competency in the electronics value chain. Firms re-defined their core competency in the context of the opportunities and competitive pressures offered by the evolving new organizations of the IT industry. For example, IDMs in the IC industry have dramatically re-defined their core competency toward design plus some manufacturing in light of the maturity and cost pressures of the leading pureplay foundries (Hurtarte *et al.* 2007). Similarly, branded PC firms have shed manufacturing while re-focusing on marketing, distribution and after-sales service. Firms or even whole societies that have resisted the new re-organization have suffered from a loss of competitive advantage as the new organization has taken away their core competence. The Japanese IT industry has been the most reluctant to embrace this model, but the costs of this reluctance have forced even Japanese firms to begin to adopt the new segmented approach to organization.

Modularization has allowed for new firm entry as firms occupy new niches created by modularization, such as the pureplay IC foundry entrants, or take advantage of the lower cost of entry in narrowly defined niches, such as IC design. Design firms arose well before digitization was mature, but they faced difficult barriers to coordinating production and technological barriers. Consequently, they were insignificant players in the industry at the time. IC design houses can now access an array of services that have arisen with reorganization. Reorganization may even have caused a virtuous cycle of new firm creation as firms think of new ways to focus on a segment or functions of the value chain, and look for partners to help them to facilitate this strategy. For example, the rise of the pureplay foundries helped to drive the rise of the ASIC vendors, firms that offer design services for the back end of chip design, as foundries looked to partner with ASIC vendors to enhance the services offered to their design house customers. Critically, the facilitation of entry of new firms goes hand in hand with re-location as many new firms filling new niches appeared in parts of the world with previous little experience in those activities, such as the rise of foundry fabrication in Taiwan and Singapore.

Intellectual property (IP) protection is critical for the process of reorganization to work. Moving to segmentation is not a seamless and riskless transition; focusing on a narrow segment is itself fraught with risks. Dependence on those outside the firm hierarchy increases dramatically. Obviously, the transaction costs in terms of information flows have decreased dramatically with digitization, but there are risks inherent in sharing this information. The vulnerability of one's IP increases even as the digitization makes the information flows less costly. Thus, IP protection is critical to the functioning of this new system because without adequate protection the costs of the new organization of the IT industry vastly outweigh the gains reaped from focusing on the firm's core competency. The ability to protect a customer's IP has become one way to create a competitive edge over one's competitors in the IT industry, as will be discussed below in the pureplay foundry example.

Despite the critical nature of managing the protection of IP and risk of dependence on outside suppliers, the tipping point has long since been reached that dramatically lowers the risk involved in vertical specialization. The number of suppliers available in most segments of the value chain has reached a point where a firm is not critically dependent on one supplier in the segment. In those areas where IP is most vulnerable to theft, firms build up competencies in IP protection that secure them more orders. An example of this phenomenon is the pureplay foundry. These firms must protect customer IP to be able to secure new orders. Even those firms operating in environments with poor IP protection laws, such as China, have had to conform to international best practice in order to be able to secure orders (Author Interviews). The fact that the Chinese foundry, SMIC, has been able to secure repeat orders from international customers, such as Broadcom, Toshiba and TI (Texas Instruments), shows that such firms have been able to protect customer IP even given the poor formal legal structure of China.

There are four central claims made for the modular model. First, to the extent that a single lead firm dominates control and value within the chain, global network flagship or Visible Brain (to use Pavitt's phrase), this control and value accrual are ephemeral. Second, to the extent that they are needed at all, very limited human resources need to be deployed to handle the codified interfaces between modules relative to the human resources required for managing vertical specialization in the past. Third, there are two distinct patterns of vertical specialization. New firms tend to specialize in a very narrow set of modules, often just one module. Established firms in the process of de-verticalizing their operations generally span more modules than new firms even as they hone their core competencies through vertical specialization. Finally, there is no modal combination of functions that predominates. However, there is one combination of functions that has empirically proven to be a failure: the combination of manufacturing services with own brand marketing. Firms that have attempted to offer manufacturing services and their own brand have had to split these conflicting modules into separate companies, such as UMC and Acer, or be content to be third tier suppliers in one of the two modules, such as Korea's MagnaChip.

The modules of reorganization

This section will present the modularization of the electronics production chain. For simplicity's sake, the electronics production chain will be further divided into the components value chain and the product value chain. In reality, these chains are both necessary parts of the larger electronics value chain. The modules within the chains will be described using actual firms and products.

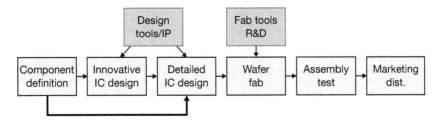

Figure 4.1 Electronic component value chain model

The electronic component value chain depicted in Figure 4.1 shows the specific functions that have emerged through its reorganization. We will explain the component value chain with the integrated circuit (IC) as the example since the IC is clearly the dominant key component in most electronic products. Before designing a component, firms often attempt to define the component to meet or create a new market demand. This component definition could be considered a form of proactive marketing. Some IC firms interact closely with product houses to determine what types of new ICs they need and then design to these specifications. For example, engineers at ST Micro spend significant amounts of time interacting with product engineers at Nokia to create the ICs that meet Nokia's specifications for new generations of cellular phones. The component definition function is the link between the electronic products and the key components it requires. Component definition is performed by both electronics products companies and by component companies.

The component definition is rarely done in isolation as the single function undertaken by a company. While both product companies and component companies do this function, this function differs from all the others in that the digitized interface does not flow in both directions. The component definition module has a clean, digitized interface with component design, but lacks such an interface with the product definition or design, the functions in the product value chain (see below), with which component definition interacts. Thus, product companies that outsource for non-standardized components must work with the component providers closely during the process of component definition as in the ST Micro and Nokia example above. In other words, overcoming this non-codifiable divide requires the type of intensive human interaction and perhaps co-location of resources predicted by at least some of the scholars who argue for the impossibility of a perfectly clean and codifiable interface between modules (Sabel and Zeitlin 2004:2).

Another way to overcome this digital divide between the product and component value chains is for the component definer to provide all necessary information to aid the product producer to design and manufacture to the component specifications. In this case, the component definer has already designed the component before the close interaction with the component customers occurs. Intel's large support staff that aids firms that design and manufacture PCs to design and manufacture for Intel's CPUs is a prominent example of this type of interaction. This type of relationship appears to be close to the role of the network flagship in the GPN framework though we shall return to the case of the PC later to show that even this case does not fully conform to the GPN framework. In any case, this large support staff is not co-located with Intel's design teams and is generally a one-way funnel of information from Intel to the product designers, a far cry from the iterated co-design of Sabel and Zeitlin.

The design function contains both innovative and detailed design. The innovative design function captures the higher value design skills where the design engineers must have a deep understanding and experience in silicon circuit and system design to translate the component definition into custom analog or digital circuits. Designers capable of performing this function require significant training and mentoring and usually have at least a Master's degree in electrical engineering. Therefore it has been difficult to find engineers with these skills in emerging economies though this situation is changing with the upgrading of engineering skills through modularized production networks. This function is highly valued and still can often provide a high barrier to entry. Detailed design consists of the relatively less complex tasks of translating the component definition or the innovative IC design into data that is ready to be sent to wafer fabrication. This data is called "mask data" referring to the detailed digitized drawings that will appear as layers in the silicon fabrication process. IP vendors, such as Artisan and ARM, and EDA tool providers, such as Cadence and Synopsys, provide much of the technology for both innovative and detailed IC design. Some fabless design houses, such as Broadcom and Silicon Labs, concentrate on the higher valued innovative design function, but generally perform detailed design as well. Others, such as Taiwan's VIA, are taking advantage of this design segmentation by performing the detailed designs in lower skilled/lower cost locations, such as China, while retaining innovative design in Taiwan and the US.

There is significant know-how at the interface of the design functions and the wafer fab functions. The IC fabrication process and resulting device specifications are captured in a sophisticated set of models that are provided by the wafer foundries. These models capture the detailed physics of the transistors so that the designers can simulate the operation of the circuit before fabrication. The successful wafer foundries have considerable expertise in making this interface user friendly with the aid of web-based tools for easy information transfer. Wafer fabrication takes the IC design and creates actual circuitry on a silicon wafer. Process tools, the capital equipment used by wafer fabs, embody most of the process technology. Thus, the process technology R&D is carried out by the process equipment firms, such as Applied Materials, Nikon and ASML. In terms of process R&D, the IDMs and foundries carry out the process integration from machine to machine and the interface back to design. Assembly and test function takes the chip and adds the packaging that allows the chip to interface with other electronic components and then test the packaged IC. Some firms do both processes, but many firms do solely assembly or testing. Marketing and distribution of ICs is an important function of the component value chain as these components have in some cases become brand names, such as Intel's CPUs. Specialized distributors also do the marketing and distribution function.

IDMs perform all five functions though they often outsource assembly and test. They attempt to do value-added processes in wafer fabs and capture systems design of products in silicon. Most IDMs are following a fab-light strategy that follows in line with the progressive abandonment of in-house assembly and test operations.

Foundries perform only the fabrication function. While much of the technology is captured in fab tools, foundries do have large and growing R&D departments for process technology and also capture value by being more efficient in fabrication due to their focus and flexibility. Competing with flexibility, multiple processes and multiple products share the same fabrication facilities and even the same wafer as in TSMC's multi-product wafer (MPW) production. Foundries also compete on the service elements of fabrication by trying to provide ever more detailed information about the timing and quality of production to their customers via the Internet. At the leading foundries, customers can receive real-time data on their wafers as they are being fabricated. The need for a design firm to reveal IP to foundries in order for the foundry to be able to fabricate the chips necessitates that foundries strive to protect customer IP in order to keep clients and attract new ones.

The electronics product value chain stretches from defining what the product is to marketing and distributing the product, which includes provision of services to end-users of the product. Product definition consists of trying to create a product concept that will sell in the market. This function requires both sophisticated knowledge of the market demands, both extant (market pull) and latent (market push) coupled with highly valued design engineering to define the product. Design is the creation of a product blueprint that matches the specifications of the product definition. Manufacturing and test turns these designs into the physical products and tests them. Marketing and distribution maintains brand image, identifies and creates consumers for the products and manages the complex logistics of delivering to them. Marketing and distribution has become one of the key value generating functions of the electronics product value chain as manufacturing know-how has spread and become increasingly commoditized. Large retail firms, such as Walmart, within the marketing and distribution function play a significant role by sending feedback to the firms in the product definition and product design functions as the large retailers send volume orders for products with certain specifications. Given that these large retail chains are dealing with products with very large volumes, commoditized products, and lack any R&D capability to generate new products based on new technologies, they are sending signals to the product design function for an evolutionary change. For example, the large retailer sends orders for a 2 mega-pixel digital camera with removable storage card. This feedback rarely results in a new product definition where the goal is to create new products differentiated from the competitors. The services provided to the end-user as part of the purchase of the product are becoming a critical value generator, which will be highlighted in the case studies.

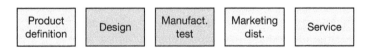

Figure 4.2 Electronics product value chain model

In the product value chain, large MNCs tend to be strong in product definition, marketing, distribution and service, which constitute the core activities of maintaining a brand. While these MNCs may constitute flagship enterprises (Rugman and D'Cruz 2000: 84; Ernst and Kim 2002:1422) in the sense of having extensive influence over the other activities in the chain, these branded firms do meet their match in terms of suppliers of critical, technology-intensive activities that exercise reciprocal influence with the flagship firm e.g. Qualcomm and cellular phone brands, or Intel and PC brands. Vertically integrated firms are now a rarity though some large firms are developing new business models in which they perform multiple functions that are not contiguous in the value chain. For example, there are companies that define products, market them and have a service component. Others attempt to straddle the component and product chains by defining products and then capturing the concept in silicon. Detailed design and manufacturing are often sub-contracted. ODMs do design and manufacturing in an attempt to add value through detailed design, and CEMs do just manufacturing.

The electronics value chain was not always organized into two distinct chains separating components and products. Often, the two chains were integrated within the firm. Macher and his colleagues note in *US Industry in 2000* that the so-called merchant IC firms, what would later be called IDMs, were a type of firm particular to the US and that IC firms in Europe and Japan tended to be within the vertically-integrated box manufacturers (Macher *et al.* 1999). Even in the US, a number of firms, such as IBM, were integrated in this fashion. A number of firms still contain many or all of the functions of these two chains within the firm even if they do not necessarily rely on their in-house activities. Given these historical roots, a significant number of firms try to straddle these two chains even as they react to pressures to focus.

The extent of modularization

How extensive has reorganization actually been? Using data on the IT industry from a joint study by BAH (Booz Allen Hamilton) and the IFC (International Finance Corporation), we have determined that over two-thirds of the value of the IT industry was vertically specialized by 2001. In value terms, US $322 billion was produced in a vertically specialized manner and only US $152 billion was produced in a vertically integrated or quasi-vertically integrated manner. These figures actually understate the amount of vertical specialization for two reasons: (1) evidence points to increased vertical specialization since 2001; and (2) even within the segments our estimates counted as vertically integrated, displays, DRAM (see Fuller *et al.* 2003) and OEM in-house manufacturing, had some of their value produced in a vertically specialized manner.

When examined across the activities along value chain, the rise of modularization is also evident. The spread of vertical specialization in ICs in the component chain will be examined as ICs are the most important component in terms of value, comprising almost one-third of the total IT industry value in 2001 (BAH IFC 2002), and arguably technologically as well. For product chains, the case of vertical specialization in the computer industry, including components, such as boards, is well known (Bresnahan 1999; Bresnahan and Malerba 1999) so the case of mobile handsets will be examined.

The rise of the pureplay foundry and the reorganization of the global IC components value chain

When the Taiwanese first started to create private IC firms in the early 1980s, the IC industry was dominated by IDMs that vertically integrated the production of ICs from the design segment to fabrication through to the test and assembly stages and by vertically-integrated firms that combined IC components and products in one vertically integrated firm, such as IBM, Philips or any of the large Japanese electronics firms. Led by a returnee from the US, Morris Chang, TSMC experimented with a new type of IC firm organization that took advantage of several emerging technological opportunities. Chang conceived of a firm that would focus on fabrication of the ICs, leaving the design and the test and assembly stages to other firms. While many IDMs had served as foundries for chip designers as a sideline to their own business, this new model was called the pureplay foundry model because it would focus solely on being a fabrication foundry for its customers and undertake no other activities. This decoupling of the IC design and fabrication functions was demonstrated initially by some university/DARPA projects in the US, and led to the formation of MOSIS, which essentially provided technical proof of the concept of a digital interface of design and fabrication. However, no one had proven that this concept would work in actual IC production. The decoupling of the IC design and fabrication stages was made possible by the ability to codify knowledge of device characteristics in computer models using CAD (computer aided design) technology. TSMC actually may have over-anticipated this trend by trying to use this model in the late 1980s while sufficient computer modeling of the interaction was not possible until about 1993–1994. Nevertheless, TSMC definitely reaped the advantages of being the first mover in this field as the technological trends justified this new type of fabrication-only firm, the pureplay foundry, and TSMC outstripped its Taiwanese rivals to become the largest IC producer in Taiwan in 1993. TSMC's sales revenues were US $475 million in 1993 and grew to almost US $10 billion in 2009. From the beginning of TSMC's invention of the pureplay foundry model, TSMC was the largest pureplay foundry and remains so today.

One example of how difficult it was to manage a fabless design house before the emergence of TSMC and its pureplay foundry model is the operational tightrope act that Crystal Semiconductor, one of the early American fabless design houses, had to carry out to ensure the fabrication of its chips. Crystal had to coordinate production done in the fabs of seven different IDMs in order to have access to the best foundry service for a particular product and to ensure that the fabless firm was not too dependent on a single IDM firm. The logistical nightmare that Crystal had to endure in a world without pureplay foundries points to the great opportunity for those firms that eventually figured out how to be pure providers of foundry services.

With the advent of foundries, the market share of fabless design houses has also exploded. By 2003, the fabless design segment had grown to over 16 percent of total IC revenue at almost US $20 billion, and this revenue did not count the large portion of IDM revenue that was outsourced to foundries as part of fabless revenue. Fabless growth was particularly prevalent in the US and Taiwan, the two countries which embraced the modular model the earliest. By 2009, global fabless sales were over US $56 billion and represented approximately 24 percent of total semiconductor sales. Taiwan's fabless sector has grown at the same fast pace as the global fabless sector over the past decade and has 20 percent of global fabless revenues (IEK 2005). As shown in the Table 4.1 below, fabless firms from Taiwan, Mainland China and Hong Kong have become major competitors with 24 of the top 150 global publicly listed firms being fabless firms from Greater China.

The pureplay foundry model succeeded not only because the trend of de-coupling led to the emergence of a large number of fabless design houses in search of fabrication services, but also due to the ability of pureplay

Table 4.1 Hong Kong, Taiwan and Mainland Chinese design houses among the global top 125 IC firms in 2006

Rank	Company	Revenue (USD)	Home	Rank	Company	Revenue	Home
40	Mediatek	1.6 b	Taiwan	97	Faraday	170 mln	Taiwan
54	Novatek	964 mln	Taiwan	101	Sitronix	138 mln	Taiwan
55	Himax	745 mln	Taiwan	102	ELAN	137 mln	Taiwan
58	VIA	658 mln	Taiwan	107	Richtek	132 mln	Taiwan
67	Phison	382 mln	Taiwan	109	Vimicro	128 mln	Mainland China
68	Realtek	381 mln	Taiwan	112	O2Micro	125 mln	Mainland China
72	Solomon Systech	322 mln	Hong Kong	113	Pixart	122 mln	Taiwan
73	Etron	322 mln	Taiwan	114	Holtek	119 mln	Taiwan
74	CoAsia	311 mln	Taiwan	116	Silan*	113 mln	Mainland China
85	SiS	243 mln	Taiwan	117	Silicon Motion	106 mln	Taiwan
95	Elite Memory	178 mln	Taiwan	120	Advanced Power	101 mln	Taiwan
96	Actions	170 mln	Mainland China	122	ALI	100 mln	Taiwan

Source: Fuller (2010), Table 10.3 p. 252 based on data from Hurtarte *et al.* (2007).

Note: *Silan has some IC fabrication capacity, but most of its revenue comes from IC design.

foundries to capitalize on the benefits of focus. Pureplay foundries devoted their energies to increasing the sophistication of their wafer production rather than having their energies and R&D budgets split between design innovation and fabrication process innovation. The pureplay foundry model was also ideal for firms that were technologically behind because they could learn from their customers primarily through customer feedback. While this type of learning through customer feedback continues to this day, the feedback mechanism and more direct demands and technology transfers were critical in the early stages to enable catch up to the process technology of advanced firms. For example, VLSI Technology transferred specifications for 1.2 micron technology to help TSMC upgrade to that level of process technology (Mathews and Cho 2000: 172).

The Taiwanese foundries, with TSMC in the lead, soon became world leaders in being able to produce multiple products with multiple processes within a single fab and in achieving extremely high production yields. By as early as 2001, there were credible reports that the leading Taiwanese foundries had taken their place among the industry leaders in process technology (Cataldo 2001). The yearly benchmarking done by the quasi-governmental ITRI saw Taiwan, represented by Taiwan's foundries, at the technological frontier along with the US and Japan in CMOS logic fabrication at .13-micron process technology (TSIA 2001). Not taking a back seat to other leading firms in creating the generation beyond .13-micron, TSMC has cooperated with other leading IC firms including members of the Crolles-2 alliance and NEC to align their next generation of process technology, .09-micron technology. In 2010 TSMC was even able to leap ahead of foundry rivals, such as the IBM Alliance members, Globalfoundries and Samsung, in process technology. However, it must be acknowledged that the Taiwanese foundries have also been able to take advantage of the trend toward embodying greater amounts of process technology in the capital equipment to keep up with the technological frontier.

With the rise of the foundries and the advent of expensive but efficient 300mm wafer fabs (estimated to cost between US $2.5 and $3.5 billion according to Taiwan's Market Intelligence Center), there are questions about the viability of any IDMs. There is no inherent technological difference between 300mm fabs and 200mm fabs, but they are much more expensive and much more efficient than 200mm fabs with cost savings of 30–40 percent over 200mm fabs, assuming 80 percent utilization. The answer according to the analysis of interview subjects, several investment banks and the Fabless Semiconductor Association is that only IDMs with large revenue streams and high profitability can meet the challenge of keeping 300mm production in-house, whereas small and unprofitable producers should outsource. Furthermore, leading IDMs may be wary to pass on leading process technologies to foundries that help their competitors. Many suggest the cut-off point of US $10 billion in revenue for IDMs to support 300mm fabs, but other analyses and interviews with IDMs suggest the bar is somewhat lower. TI and ST Micro are mainly retaining fabrication, but as large a firm as Freescale (formerly Motorola) clearly embarked on outsourcing as its main strategy for fabrication. Finally, those firms producing DRAMs cannot outsource their production efficiently for technical reasons (Fuller *et al.* 2003).

The strategies to deal with the high cost of 300mm fabs go beyond the stark in-house versus outsource dichotomy. Other strategies are partial owner-ship of fabs in conjunction with foundries or IDMS, guaranteed access to fab capacity by investment in foundries or swapping technology for fab space. TI began to outsource extensively keeping only analog chip production strictly in-house. ST Micro has taken a very similar approach to TI as they outsource some production to TSMC with the same concern for mitigating risk even while they are keeping much of the production in-house due to the ability to create a wide array of high margin products.

Mobile handsets and digital still cameras

Mobile handsets lagged behind computers in the extent of vertical specializa-tion, but within the last decade have rapidly begun to devolve to the vertical specialization model. This vertical specialization can be seen not only in the outsourcing of manufacturing by brands, but also in the use of independent design firms and the weakening link between lead firms and proprietary mobile handset chips.

The outsourcing of mobile handset manufacturing has accelerated rapidly in the last few years with even originally reluctant outsourcers, such as Nokia, pursuing this route. The major suppliers are both Taiwanese ODMs and contract manufacturers from elsewhere in the world, such as Singapore's Flextronics.[6] Major players in high-end smart phones, such as Research In Motion and Apple, do not have and never had in-house mobile handset manufacturing.

Manufacturing is not the only part of the value chain that is being outsourced. The established brands are beginning to employ outside design firms and new branded firms in the developing world, such as TCL, purchase modules designed by established brands and by new design firms. Exact figures on this outsourcing of design are particularly difficult to calculate due to the fact that the design firms are often new, unlisted firms with no requirements to make their financial information public. Interviews with mobile design firms and established brands confirm that this outsourcing of design is a growing trend. Finally, the independent chip vendors are crucial part of the value chain in this sector. Samsung is a vertically integrated mobile handset manufacturer but, as early as 2004, 43 percent of the firm's mobile handset production value came from outside suppliers, principally in the form of ICs (Morgan Stanley 2004). Even major handset brands that also have had in-house chip-making capacity, such as Motorola before it spun-off Freesacale as an independent semiconductor company, outsourced chips for much of their own mobile handsets rather than relying on in-house designs (Interview), and this

Table 4.2 Global handset outsourcing in 2004

Handset brand	Nation-ality	Tier 1 partners	Tier 2 partners	Handset units (millions)	Estimated out-sourced (%)
Nokia	Finland	Elcoteq	Celestica, Jabil, Solectron, Telson, Hon Hai	165	<20
Motorola	USA	Flextronics, BenQ, Pantech	Celestica, Compal, Solectron, Compal, Telson	65	<60
Samsung	Korea	—	—	65	0
Sony-Ericsson	Japan–Sweden	Flextronics	Elcoteq, Arima, LiteOn	29	100
Siemens	Germany	Flextronics, Sanmina-SCI	Quanta	27	>60
LG Electronics	Korea	—	—	25	0
Panasonic	Japan		Celestica	16	<25
NEC	Japan		Celestica, BenQ, Arima	14	<20
Mitsubishi	Japan		Solectron	11	<10
Kyocera	Japan	Solectron		10	<30
Alcatel	France	Flextronics	GVC	4	100
TCL	China	Unknown	Unknown	12	35
Other Asian	n/a			22	80
Other non-Asian	n/a			6	80
Total				470	25–26 average

Source: Morgan Stanley Equity Research (2004) "Asia/Pacific Handsets," February 25.

arrangement was true even before the plan to spin-off Freescale. Proprietary chip designs are being abandoned in some cases, such as the collaborative effort of ST Micro and Nokia in the mid-2000s, but are a key part of the strategy for some firms considered to be leading-edge product designers, such as Apple which uses its own processor for the iPhone and iPad.

The same phenomenon is occurring in the digital still camera (DSC) value chain. Manufacturing is being outsourced, but also design firms and component firms have begun to emerge. In the area of critical components, with the rise of Complementary metal oxide semiconductor (CMOS) image sensors as competitors to the Charge-coupled devices (CCDs), the tight links between Japanese CCD suppliers and Japanese camera makers has been put under pressure as CMOS image sensor design firms form elsewhere in the world offer a competing product outside the traditionally closed and cooperative Japanese DSC production networks. The vertical specialization in this area is displayed in the figure below.

The prevalence of modular over lead firm-led networks

This section delineates the specific characteristics of modularized production networks in electronics. First, the ephemeral nature of control and rent accrual within the modularized production chain is demonstrated. Second, the lack of a dense human interaction between modules is demonstrated. Finally, a brief description of empirical examples of different combinations of functions will show that new and established firms differ in their scope and that no modal combination of functions prevails.

There are three types of networks in this modular world of industrial production: (1) the global flagship model; (2) the cyclical model – foundries versus fabless design houses in the silicon cycle; and (3) decentralized networks with no one lead firm – the majority of industrial production in electronics. Global flagship networks are a minority among the production networks functioning under modularization. With modularity, there is enough codification of information to allow other types of vertical specialized but non-hierarchical production flourish. Here non-hierarchical is taken to encompass those situations in which one firm may have temporary advantage but often as not experienced temporary disadvantage, such as in the cyclical

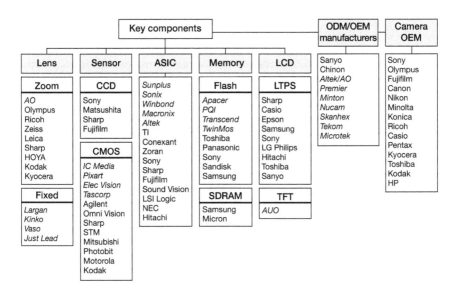

Figure 4.3 The modular DSC value chain
Source: Adapted from Morgan Stanley 2002.

model. To judge the role of a lead firm, one must measure the firm's ability to control the network's functioning (the control aspect) and its ability to reap incom-mensurately large rewards from the network (the rent aspect). If no one firm can be identified as having one or both of these characteristics, then the network cannot be said to have a lead firm.

The global flagship model still exists in certain parts of the IT industry, particularly in the telecommunications infrastructure equipment segment. In this area, firms such as Cisco and Ericsson are clearly lead firms that coordinate and control their networks of production. However, even in this area, this form of network management does not appear to be a necessity and these firms' networks may be vulnerable to competitors that choose the modular and non-hierarchical networks of production detailed below. Furthermore, with the rise of China's Huawei and ZTE in the telecommunication infrastructure equipment industry, it is clear that global flagships have only a tenuous perch on top of their industry's value chain.

The cyclical model is one where the reaping of economic returns varies between two parties depending on the industry cycle. The classic example is the silicon cycle's effect on whether the foundries or the designers receive a larger share of the economic returns from the IC industry. When the silicon cycle is at low ebb, the designers can squeeze the foundries on price and the weight of revenues shifts in favor of designers. Conversely, when the silicon cycle reaches its high point, foundries are able to demand a dispropor-tionate share of the revenues from the designers due to the full utilization of the fabs.

Corresponding to the accrual of rents, the control of the IC chain does not appear to be in the hands of one or the other party for long. Foundries have been known to remove fabless firms from their list of customers, but fabless design houses have also been known to second and third source despite the protests of their principal foundry source. Certain firms have made long term arrangements to smooth the cycle, but these arrangements often do not last. Even Mediatek, a former UMC subsidiary, chose to second source from other sources rather than rely solely on its mother company for fabrication. Control is diffuse and unclear in this sector, and to the extent that it exists, it does so only as the outcome of the industry cycle. While this chapter views the component chains as part of a larger whole, showing the shift in control and rent dynamics within part of the network of production shows that the models of lead firms and global flagships overstate the case for firm hierarchies of control and economic rent accrual.

The majority of networks appear to be operating with even more diffuse centers of control and rents. To take the most prominent example of the PC industry, the twin aspects of control and rents do not point to one single lead firm at any given time and geographic location. Intel accrues rent and exercises some control in the production chain through its near monopoly on branded microprocessors, but the firm does not exercise control over the end-product part of the chain where branded firms, such as Dell and Acer, and distributors, particularly in Europe, exercise power and have some rent accrual. While there is a clear subordinate section of the chain, the assemblers of the PCs, which suffer from lack of control and rent accrual, there is no clear driver of the chain. This duality of control and rent accrual is expressed by Stan Shih's Smile Curve in which the component firms and the marketing firms enjoy all the rents while the manufacturing firms accrue very marginal returns (Dedrick and Kraemer 1998: 156). To a lesser degree, this dualistic structure can be extended to other critical ICs and the end products they go into, such as the graphic chips of NVIDIA and ATI (subsequently bought by AMD) that are necessary for computers and game consoles.

Ernst and Kim (2002: 1421–1422) argue that there are two kinds of flagship firms, the brand leaders and the contract manufacturers, with their own distinctive GPNs and thereby sidestep the problem of the multiplicity of strategic firms within a single network. However, their own definition of a network flagship states that the flagship "is at the heart of the network, it provides strategic and organizational leadership beyond the resources directly under its management control" (Ernst and Kim 2002: 1422). The flagships that Ernst and Kim identify are only the leading firms if the production chain is spliced into narrow segments, which does not make sense given that the Intels and Dells of the world do influence each other through their connected chain of production.

The multiplicity of centers of control and rent accrual can be seen in the networks of new design-oriented firms. SMaL, a designer of DSCs and the critical component that defines their DSCs, CMOS image sensors, is at once in control and subject to other firms. When the silicon cycle is on the upswing, SMaL's foundry partners can squeeze SMaL on price and capacity and the reverse is true when the silicon cycle is in a downturn. However, the variation of control and rent accrual does not stop with the silicon cycle. SMaL at once can dictate the terms to its contract manufacturers, but also find itself under the thumb of distribution chains in the US or branded firms through which it sells in Japan.

Contrary to the expectations of Sabel and Zeitlin, the modularized production chain does not require intensive human interactions between modules in the chain. For example, the silicon intellectual property (SIP) vendors sell IP blocks, blocks of design, to fabless design firms around the world, but the sales forces they use to support their IP sales are quite small with one person being able to support a number of design clients. The design-to-foundry handoff is manageable by a single representative of the fabless design house co-located with the foundry. This low-level of co-located human interaction is one that even very small firms can meet. Likewise, product or component definition and the design of products or components are often continents apart without large dedicated forces to manage the information handoff. This ability to codify knowledge between modules explains why small enterprises not located in industrial districts covering the bulk of the production chain's activities can still enter the IT industry and thrive. Without this codification, the burden of co-locating substantial human resources with other modules of the chain would be too great a burden for most small enterprises to bear.

There is a clear difference between the new firms and established firms in their scope along the modular production chain. New firms generally do one or a narrow set of modules within the chain. The rise of fabless design houses is emblematic as these firms often do one function and at most three connected ones (component definition, innovative design and detailed design). Large established electronics firms do not usually devolve into one function or a narrow set of connected functions, but instead retain those functions in which they have core competencies or that they deem essential for maintenance of their core competencies.

Even among the large established firms, there are no modal models of modularization. Dell has concentrated on product definition and managing the marketing and distribution of computer products whereas HP in the same product area has re-defined its core competency as bundling business services with hardware. Both firms have dropped manufacturing and even most product design of computers.

Other established firms straddle the component and product chains. Hitachi has created a RFID tag with an entire system to link the tag to a computer system with a sophisticated database. The goal is to use this component to generate value through the service of operating the entire RFID tag system. Hitachi will not produce all the parts, concentrating on the tag itself and the service of managing the system. Another example is HP's inkjet printer. HP created inkjet print heads using a proprietary technology and these heads are the key component of the printer. HP sells own brand printers as well as selling inkjet heads to other printer makers, but the intermediate stages of manufacturing and even the design of the printers are not kept within HP.

Relocation

Modularity combined with better communication at lower costs opens up opportunities for vertically specialized, spatially dispersed activities. Relocation under modularity has several distinct features: no necessity to co-locate the production chain and human capital has become more significant as a driver of relocation due to the freedom from the previous necessity of co-location. In the past, only large vertically-integrated enterprises had the ability to spatially disperse their activities because hierarchy was needed to overcome the coordination and communication problems (Saxenian 2000: 259). Small firms at the very least needed to be in the vicinity of other firms to make use of the economies of scope, the industrial district model, because they did not have the capabilities to do everything in-house and they could not control outsourced activities at a distance. Today, fabless design houses around the world make use of the foundries of Taiwan, China and Singapore. Likewise, the branded electronics firms from the advanced economies make use of CEMs, manufacturing service firms, and ODMs, firms which offer both manufacturing and product design services, but the production facilities do not need to be near the contract manufacturer's headquarters nor near the branded firm.

What is strikingly different about the new relocation of the global IT industry is the role of small and new technology enterprises. Without the need to be tied to co-located economies of scope, new entrants seizing the opportunities afforded by the reorganization of the IT industry have pushed the geographic boundaries of the global IT industry to encompass more and more of the world. Generally, these new entrants occupying relatively high value-added functions along the value chain have placed their home location on the global electronics map rather than waiting for MNCs to take advantage of the opportunities of reorganization to promote new locations in the developing world. Traditional large MNCs tend to be first movers in those areas where they are looking to unload lower value-added functions, primarily product manufacturing, just as they were in past re-locations. New entrants are facilitated in the endeavor to relocate more highly value-added modules by transnational networks of co-ethnics (Saxenian 2002, 2006).

Along with modularity and better communications, the other new critical factor in determining location is human capital, the appropriate level of human capital for the function. Human capital has always been necessary to develop sophisticated technology-intensive products, but the interaction between the demands for ever more skilled personnel and the ability to utilize such personnel over great distances without necessarily paying the cost of setting up extensive operations in the distant locale is new. This interaction gives rise to a new pressing incentive to relocate and has given rise to new industries in new location, such as the software industry in Bangalore, and to the concentration of certain functions in old locations, such as the clustering of product definition and innovative design in certain places in the US and UK even as the rest of the value chain is located elsewhere.

Other old factors still play a role in shaping locational decisions in the new global IT industry. States still subsidize activities in order to encourage those activities within their borders. Lower labor costs still are attractive to firms making location decisions. Even with the WTO and ITA, trade barriers and regional trade pacts influence locational decisions. Managing geographic risk has always been a concern and has become even more of one now that activities are often located so far from the home base. The classic new IT industry example of this concern was the call for Taiwanese foundries to set up more operations outside of Taiwan in wake of the Taiwanese earthquake in 1999 despite the fact that the Taiwanese foundries were able to resume production within a few days.

The next subsection will provide data on the extent of relocation. The data on relocation will concentrate on areas other than low-end manufacturing because the relocation of low-end manufacturing to low wage locations is neither new nor what is starkly different about re-location under modularity.

Evidence of relocation

Other than low-end manufacturing, what else has moved to new locations in the world? The areas examined here will be technologically intensive fabrication, which is a form of high-end manufacturing, and various types of design operations.

As discussed earlier in the chapter, the pureplay foundry model was invented in Taiwan, but only grew to fruition in the 1990s as the possibility of transferring the design data digitally became available. Also discussed were the strong technical capabilities of the large pureplay foundries. Unlike the assembly of end-product boxes, IC fabrication remains capital intensive in both senses of the word. Modern IC fabs need expensive capital equipment, but they also need large numbers of technically educated engineers. Thus, the expansion of pureplay foundries cannot be construed as an expansion in search of unskilled labor, but rather the expansion of the industry to new areas with brains, skilled labor, in conjunction with vertical specialization.

The foundry model started by the Taiwanese and buttressed by the increasing modularization of the electronics value chain has begun to spread (see Table 4.3). The top five foundry firms hail from Greater China, and, more significantly, from other countries, such as the US, Israel and Singapore, in which there were existing wafer fabs but no major pure foundries until the last decade. The advanced economies also boast niche specialty fabs, such as X-Fab in Germany. Thus, modularization can even give rise to new industrial models in old centers of industry. New entrants in the developing world are becoming numerous. China's SMIC is the most well-known recent example as it became a top-five foundry in market share within three years of its founding. China's

Table 4.3 Top 15 foundries 2010

2003	Company	2010 revenue (USD millions)	Location
1	TSMC	13307	Taiwan
2	UMC	3965	Taiwan
3	GlobalFoundries	3610	Singapore/USA/UAE
4	SMIC	1555	China
5	TowerJazz	510	Israel
6	Vanguard	508	Taiwan
7	Dongbu Anam	495	Korea
8	IBM	430	USA (IDM)
9	Magna Chip	420	Korea (IDM)
10	Samsung	400	Korea (IDM)
11	SSMC	330	Singapore
12	X-Fab	320	Europe
13	Hua Hong NEC	295	China
14	TI	285	USA (IDM)
15	Grace	260	China

Source: IC Insights.

two other pureplay foundries, Huahong NEC and Grace, are among the top fifteen.

The IC design segment has also seen an expansion of geographic scope (Table 4.1). Originating in North America, design expanded to Taiwan in the wake of Taiwan's invention of the pureplay foundry model. This initial expansion beyond the US occurred before the SoC revolution that Ernst argues drove the process. Much of the expansion beyond Taiwan has coincided with waves of returnees from the centers of innovation to China and India but also to parts of the world with well-established IDMs, such as continental Europe and Korea, according to a list compiled by the Fabless Semiconductor Association in 2003.

The question of how much value is produced by different firms around the world is somewhat more complicated. Undoubtedly, North America still dominates in terms of revenue with still over 60 percent of worldwide fabless sales, but North American fabless firms have design operations in many other countries. In recent years, fabless companies have begun to set up operations in India and China. More importantly, some firms headquartered in the US are actually doing their design work almost entirely elsewhere. In China, one finds a similar phenomenon with the most innovative design firms being registered abroad, principally in the US, but with their core operations in China. The other companies doing design work in China are Taiwanese (see Chapter 7). In neither case would the design revenues generated by these firms' Chinese design operations be counted. Even with these limitations, one sees growth of certain markets, principally the growing amount of revenue coming from Greater China. Indeed, combined design revenue of Taiwan and China was equivalent to over one third of the design revenue of the US in 2004/2005 (Fuller 2007).

Another way to measure the shift in design activities is to look at the number of engineers employed in design in different countries. According to estimates by iSuppli, there were 40,000–50,000 designers in the US while there were 7,000 in China and 3,000–5,000 in India in 2004 (D. Clarke 2004). By 2011, Taiwan had 20,000 and China had 15,000 designers whereas the US still had 40,000–50,000 designers. However, the value generated by the designers in Taiwan and China was still only approximately half of that generated by American designers (Fuller 2012).

Product design activities have also spread to new areas of the globe outside the hierarchy of large MNCs. These new, small firms often have dispersed design activities, including design activities in the developing world. However, these firms often are not branded and listed so the exact size of their revenues is difficult to measure.

Conclusion

This chapter posits that the modularization of the electronics production has had a profound impact on the twin processes of reorganization and relocation of production. Reorganization has occurred, not under the constraints of the hierarchical networks controlled by lead firms, but under fluid and less clearly hierarchical conditions in which there are a number of points of control and rent accrual. Likewise, relocation occurs in other segments other than low-technology manufacturing and does not entail the building of vertically integrated giants with economies of scale and scope as some have suggested (Amsden and Chu 2003). Relocation to parts of the world previously bereft of anything but low-technology electronics assembly has occurred in design and technology-intensive manufacturing without requiring the emergence of vertically integrated giants. These twin processes of reorganization and relocation suggest new opportunities at the level of firm and nation (both developing and developed) to foster technology-intensive capabilities in the IT industry.

Greater China has been strategically placed to take advantage of these twin processes of reorganization and relocation. First and foremost, Taiwan in a symbiotic relationship with the US was at the forefront of much of reorganization, such as creation of the foundry model. Second, Taiwanese and Mainland Chinese more recently have gone (back) to China to replicate Taiwan's economic miracle and part of this replication process was bringing and further developing the industrial organization models they had employed in Taiwan and the US. The following three chapters each address different aspects, both positive and negative, of the Taiwanese impact on China's technological development.

Notes

1   This chapter draws heavily on Chapter 3 of Fuller (2005).
2   Pavitt (2003: 18) partially parted company with his fellow networked organization of production scholars by conceding that "recent advances in modularity have apparently shifted the balance in its favor in some industries . . ."
3   Ernst and Kim (2002) never state explicitly that the flagships capture more value, but they do state that the flagship controls the resources and capabilities for innovation and has power to pressure suppliers on price (p. 1422). Control of innovation and ability to squeeze suppliers present a picture of the flagship capturing a disproportionate share of the value-added.
4   Modularization could technically be made without digitization, but there would not be clean clearly defined interfaces so the costs of modularizing production would probably outweigh gains from focus on core competency (see endnote 2).
5   This prediction assumes vertical integration prior to the digitization that affords easy modularity. Thus, in those areas where social norms and historical institutional trajectory made de-verticalized industry the norm before digitization, such as the Third Italy, one would not expect modularity to have much effect on industrial structure though it would still have the profound effect of opening up the opportunity of sourcing or supplying certain functions from suppliers or to customers geographically distant from the industrial district. The digitization hypothesis makes no prediction about firms that for social normative reasons want to be modular. The area with the most modularized industry before digitization, the Italian and German industrial districts, is not a center of electronics so its experience

is out of the scope of our study, see Piore and Sabel (1984) *The Second Industrial Divide.*
6   Flextronics is Singaporean in stock listing only. The firm's functional headquarters is based in the US and most of its manufacturing is in Asia.

References

Amsden, A. and Chu, W. (2003) *Beyond Late Development: Taiwan's Upgrading Policies.* Cambridge, MA: MIT Press.

Asia Tech Strategy Team (2002) *Economics of a 300mm Fab.* Hong Kong: Credit Suisse First Boston.

Baldwin, C.Y. and Clark, K.B. (2000) *Design Rules.* Cambridge, MA: MIT Press.

Best, M. (2001) *The New Competitive Advantage: The Renewal of American Industry.* Oxford: Oxford University Press.

Booz Allen Hamilton, International Finance Corporation, June 2 (2002) "Electronics Manufacturing in Emerging Markets: Summary of Key Findings." Presentation. Washington DC/New York.

Borrus, M. (2000) "Exploiting Asia to Beat Japan: Production Networks and the Comeback of US Electronics," in Encarnation, D. (Ed.), *Japanese Multinationals in Asia.* Oxford: Oxford University Press.

Bresnahan, T. (1999) "Computing," in Mowery, D. (Ed.), *US Industry in 2000: Studies in Competitive Performance.* Washington, DC: The National Academy Press.

Bresnahan, T. and Malerba, F. (1999) "Industrial Dynamics and the Evolution of Firms' and Nations' Competitive Capabilities in the World Computer Industry," in Mowery, D. and Nelson, R. (Eds), *Sources of Industrial Leadership.* Cambridge, UK: Cambridge University Press.

Brown, C. and Linden, G. (2009) *Chips and Change.* Cambridge, MA: The MIT Press.

Brusoni, S. (2003) *Authority in the Age of Modularity.* SPRU Electronic Working Chapter Series, No. 101.

Cataldo, A. (2001) "Taiwan's foundry titans duel for .13-micron supremacy." *Semiconductor Business News.* www.eetimes.com/electronics-news/4100797/Taiwan-s-foundry-titans-duel-for-0-13-micron-supremacy. Accessed on January 8, 2013.

Chandler, A. (1977) *The Visible Hand: The Managerial Revolution in American Business.* Cambridge, MA: Belknap Press.

Chandler, A. (1990) *Scale and Scope: The Dynamics of Industrial Capitalism.* Cambridge, MA: Belknap Press.

China Economic News Service, January 9, 2001. "Chipmaker TSMC hits NT$ 166.3 in revenue in 2000." *The Taiwan Economic News.*

Christensen, C.M. (1997) *The Innovator's Dilemma: When New Technologies Cause Great Firms to Fail.* Boston, MA: Harvard Business School Press.

Christensen, C.M. (2001) "The Past and Future of Competitive Advantage." *Sloan Management Review* (Winter).

Clarke, D. (2004) "Another Lure of Outsourcing: Job Expertise." *Wall Street Journal,* April 12.

Dedrick, J. and Kraemer, K. (1998) *Asia's Computer Challenge.* Oxford: Oxford University Press.

East, W. (2003) "Introduction to ARM" by CEO Warren East, a chapter presented at IC China, Shanghai. March 25.

Ernst, D. (2004) (revised version). "Internationalization of innovation: Why is Chip Design Moving to Asia?" *East-West Center Working Chapters*, Economic Series No. 64.

Ernst, D. and Kim, L. (2002) "Global production networks, knowledge diffusion, and local capability formation." *Research Policy* 31, 1417–1429.

Fine, C. (1998) *Clockspeed*. Reading, MA: Perseus Books.

Fuller, D.B. (2005) "Creating Ladders out of Chains: China's Technological Development in a World of Global Production." Ph.D. dissertation, Department of Political Science, Massachusetts Institute of Technology.

Fuller, D.B. (2007) Sloan Industry Studies Annual Meeting. "Chip Design and Chindia: Implications for the United States." Conference Session: "Is globalization hurting US workers and innovation?" Boston, MA.

Fuller, D.B. (2010) "Government Neglect and the Decline of Hong Kong's Integrated Circuit Design Industry," In Douglas B. Fuller (Ed.) *Innovation and the Limits of Laissez-faire: Hong Kong's Policy in Comparative Perspective*, London: Palgrave.

Fuller, D.B. (2012) "Chip design in China and India: Multinationals, industry structure and development outcomes, Technological Forecasting and Social Change." http://dx.doi.org/10.1016/j.techfore.2012.10.025

Fuller, D.B., Akinwande, A. I. and Sodini, C.G. (2003) "Leading, Following or Cooked Goose?: Innovation Successes and Failures in Taiwan's IT industry." *Industry and Innovation*, 10 (2): 179–196.

Gereffi, G. (1996) "Commodity Chains and Regional Divisions of Labor in East Asia." *Journal of Asian Business*, 12, 1.

Gereffi, G., Humphrey, J. and Sturgeon, T. (2005) "The Governance of Global Value Chains." *Review of International Political Economy* 12(1): 78–104.

Hsieh, C. (2004) *China: Hype or Reality*. Hong Kong: ING Barings.

Hurtarte, J., Wolshiemer, E. and Tafoya, L. (2007) *Understanding Fabless IC Technology*. Oxford: Newnes.

IEK (Industrial Economics and Knowledge Research Center) (2005) Taiwan Bandaoti Nianjian [The 2005 Taiwan Semiconductor Yearbook]. Hsinchu, Taiwan: ITIS.

ITRI/IEK 2003. *Zixun Gongye Nianjian* [Information Industry Yearbook 2003]. Taipei, Taiwan: Market Intelligence Center.

Kawakami, M. (1996) "Development of Small-and-medium-sized Manufacturers in Taiwan's PC Industry." Chung-hua Institute for Economic Research, *Discussion Chapter Series*, No. 9606.

Langlois, R. (2003) "The Vanishing Hand: The Changing Dynamics of Industrial Capitalism." *Industrial and Corporate Change*, 12(2): 351–385.

Langlois, R. and Robertson, P. (1995) *Firms, Markets and Economic Change*. London: Routledge.

Lapedus, M. (2002) "How TSMC is expanding itself to serve up 90 nm." *Semiconductor Business News*, April 15. www.eetimes.com/electronics-news/4091079/Surprises-surface-in-top-25-CapEx-rankings Accessed on January 8, 2013.

Lapedus, M. (2003) "Surprises surface in the top 25 capex rankings." *Semiconductor Business News*, April 17. www.eetimes.com/electronics-news/4094958/How-TSMC-is-expanding-itself-to-serve-up-90-nm-chips. Accessed on January 8, 2013.

Lee, J. and Chen, J. (2000) "Dynamic Synergy Creation with Multiple Business Activities: Toward a Competence-based Growth Model for Contract Manufacturers," in: *Research in Competence-based Management Advances in Applied Business Strategy Series*. Volume 6A, Eds. R. Sanchez and A. Heene, Greenwich, CT: JAI Press.

Lester, R. and Sturgeon, T. (2003). "The New Global Supply Base: New Challenges for Local Suppliers in East Asia." *Industrial Performance Center Working Paper Series* (03-006).

Linden, G. and Somaya, D. (2003) "System-on-a-chip Integration in the Semiconductor Industry: Industry Structure and Firm Strategies." *Industrial and Corporate Change*, 12(5): 545–576.

Macher, J., Mowery, D.C. and Hodges, D.A. (1999) "Semiconductors," in: Mowery, D. (Ed.), *US Industry in 2000: Studies in Competitive Performance*. Washington, DC: The National Academy Press.

Macher, J., Mowery, D. and Simcoe, T. (2002) "E-business and Disintegration of the Semiconductor Industry Value Chain." *Industry and Innovation*, 9(3): 155–181.

Mathews, J.A. and Cho, D.S. (2000) *Tiger Technology: The Creation of a Semi-conductor Industry in East Asia*. Cambridge: Cambridge University Press.

McKendrick, D.G., Doner, R.F. and Haggard, S. (2000) *From Silicon Valley to Singapore: Location and Competitive Advantage in the Hard Disk Driver Industry*. Stanford, CA: Stanford University Press.

Morgan Stanley (2002) "Digital Cameras: Share the Moment" Report, September 20, 2002, p. 9.

Morgan Stanley Equity Research Asia/Pacific., February 25, 2004. Asia/Pacific Handsets. Hong Kong: Morgan Stanley.

Pavitt, K. (2003) "What are Advances in Knowledge Doing to the Large Industrial Firm in the 'New Economy'?" *SPR Electronics Working Chapter Series*, No. 91.

Piore, M. J. and C. F. Sabel (1984) *The Second Industrial Divide: Possibilities for Prosperity*. New York, Basic Books.

Rugman, A.M. and D'Cruz, J.R. (2000) "Multinationals as Flagship Firms, Regional Business Networks." Oxford: Oxford University Press.

Sabel, C. and Zeitlin, J. (2004) "Neither Modularity nor Relational Contracting: Inter-firm Collaboration in the New Economy: A Critique of Langlois and Lamoreaux, Raff and Tenin." *Enterprise and Society*, 5(3) in press.

Saxenian, A. (2000) "Networks of immigrant entrepreneurs," in: Lee, C., Miller, W., Hancock, M. and Rowen H. (Eds.), *The Silicon Valley Edge: A Habitat for Innovation and Entrepreneurship*. Stanford, CA: Stanford University Press.

Saxenian, A. (2002) "Transnational Communities and the Evolution of Global Produc-tion Networks: The Cases of Taiwan, China and India." *Industry and Innovation*, 9(3): 183–202.

Saxenian, A. (2006) *The New Argonauts*. Cambridge, MA: Harvard University Press.

Sturgeon, T. (2002) "Modular Production Networks: A New American Model of Industrial Organization." *Industrial and Corporate Change*, 11(3): 451–496.

Sturgeon, T. and Lee, J. (2005) "Industry Co-evolution: A Comparison of Taiwan and North American Electronics Contract Manufacturers," in: Berger, S. and Lester, R. (Eds.), *Global Taiwan*. New York: ME Sharp, in press.

TSIA (2001) Taiwan Semiconductor Industry Association, Overview on Taiwan semi-conductor industry. Available at www.tsia.org.tw.

Vernon, R. (1966) "International Investment and International Trade in the Product Life cycle." *Quarterly Journal of Economics*, 80(2): 190–207.

5 Divergent engagements

Comparing the roles and strategies
of Taiwanese and mainland
Chinese returnee entrepreneurs in
the IT industry*

Yu Zhou and Jinn-yuh Hsu

Introduction

Professionals and entrepreneurs returning to developing countries from developed countries play key roles in the technological 'catch-up' of their home countries, but they are rarely well-conceptualized by the theories of globalization. This is especially the case in Asia. The American-trained Chinese engineers who returned to Taiwan were instrumental in creating Taiwan's excellent semiconductor industry during the 1980s and 1990s. In a similar vein, since the late 1990s, Chinese professionals returning to the mainland have also emerged as the most innovative industrial and capital agents in the technological industry. In this chapter we compare the roles and business strategies of transnational entrepreneurs on the two sides of the Taiwan Strait in the information communication industry (ICT). While these Chinese returnees share striking similarities in their educational and personal trajectories, we identify major structural differences underlying their particular resources and commercial strategies. These empirical findings move beyond the assumptions of common behaviour by overseas Chinese, for they highlight the different political economic dynamics between Mainland China, Taiwan and the US in shaping the divergent engagements of these entrepreneurs in the emerging global technology industry.

It has become widely acknowledged in Asia that scientists and engineers returning from overseas play an instrumental role in the development of technology in the region. As skilled professionals return with expertise, experiences and connections after their education and extensive practices abroad, they create a new synergetic field upon which different regional economies and technology flows intersect. The transnational practices of returnees have produced major shifts in the patterns of transnational business, and have had significant impacts for technological changes in their homelands.

Despite a well-established recognition of the roles of overseas returnees and widespread policy mechanisms to attract them within developing countries, English-language literature has just begun to formulate a theoretical understanding of the forces underlying the transnational practices of these returnees. The globalization literature tends to regard large Western corporations and national and international regulatory bodies as the primary agents of globalization; the role of returnees is often included only as a footnote, if not ignored altogether (Saxenian 2007). Policy makers in developing countries, by contrast, are eager to capitalize on the return flow as strategic assets of the home countries. Yet, their policies rarely go beyond providing financial incentives to returnees, and frequently avoid addressing deeper structural problems for those have returned (Cao 2008). Though we appreciate the power of cultural affinity and social networking as major forces drawing overseas returnees back to their home countries, the highly varied patterns of returnees' practices over time and space indicate that a cultural explanation is insufficient. In this chapter we compare the business strategies of two significant streams of Chinese high-tech returnee entrepreneurs and professionals who spent time in the US before returning to Taiwan and Mainland China, starting in the 1980s. We show the prominent role of overseas returnees in creating the global articulation of the commodity chain within the information and communications technology (ICT) industries in both locations. More importantly, we argue that the patterns of returnees' activities and their success or failure are context specific, namely they depend on the convergence of global forces and the local formation of an institutional environment for returnee ventures. The findings suggest that, contrary to Kotkin's (1993) view, overseas Chinese are not an essentialized population with a predefined 'tribal-like' orientation to the homelands. Instead, we argue that uneven globalization processes and local geographical variations are critical variables in producing the returnees' divergent practices. Such differences are evident even among people from a similar cultural background within the ICT industry.

Transmigrants and the geography of flexible production and territorial grounding

The current literature on globalization has generally privileged the role of multinational corporations (MNCs), international organizations, treaties and national governments in structuring global commercial transactions and interactions. Sklair (2001: 5) argues that 'a transnational capitalist class based on the transnational corporations is emerging that is more or less in control of the process of globalization'. However, there is increasing recognition that transmigrants, namely those who develop and maintain multiple relations that span international borders – be they familial, economic, social, organizational, religious or political – are also agents of globalization. It is certainly possible to link transmigrants with transnational corporations, as the expatriate executive class exemplifies. The majority of transmigrants, however, do not necessarily enjoy privileged access to mainstream capital in the West. The host countries' dominant economic structure excludes or marginalizes many because of their immigrant or minority status. Instead, they may act as entrepreneurs, traders or professionals on their own initiatives. Drawing on and reworking the pre-existing notion of diaspora, scholars define transnationalism as a process in which migrants or diasporic populations build a social field that links their countries of origin to their countries of settlement (Pries 2001; Vertovec 2009). One can understand this decentralized transnationalism as an alternative form of globalization from below (Smith and Guarnizo 1998).

Transmigrants are in a better position and more highly motivated than MNCs to exploit the economic potential of countries located at different junctions in the global production chain. MNCs are keen to take advantage of world resources to advance their global interests, but the resources they use tend to be widely acknowledged, relatively mature, or 'visible' through the Western business media. The access that transmigrants have to social networks in several countries, by contrast, allows them to discover, mobilize and cultivate resources in their nascent stage. In this sense, it is precisely because transmigrants are often located on the margin or outside the mainstream in developed countries that they are more open to exploring or initiating changes in the global production system. It is often after their painstaking efforts to cultivate a resource enough for it to become 'workable' in the global division of labour that large MNCs start to take advantage of the resource. For instance, while China is widely acknowledged today as the 'factory of the world', its entry into the global division of labour was initiated by overseas Chinese entrepreneurs in Taiwan and Hong Kong during the 1980s – *before* MNCs viewed China as a viable option in the 1990s. Indian engineers working for large corporations in the US also initiated India's software industry (Saxenian 2007: 275) *before* India turned into a software-exporting powerhouse. In the end, the different globalizations that come from above or below are not contradictory. Rather, they *complement* each other, since transmigrants acting as entrepreneurs are constantly in search of ways to bring global capital to the countries on their residential itineraries.

Zhou and Tseng (2001) argue that patterns of transmigrant practices are grounded in territorial, political and economic complexes that are only effective if they create a powerful synergy between local and international spaces. Different locations are bound to give rise to distinct opportunities and constraints, and thus set off divergent strategies and patterns of growth.

The overseas Chinese are noted among transmigrant groups for their deep history and extensive geographical coverage in global production and trading networks, which have persisted for centuries (Marks 2007). They are recognized as central players in the flexible production networks around the Pacific Basin (Redding 1990; Huchet 1997; Ong and Nonini 1997; Yeung 2000; Choudhary 2001; Zhou and Tseng 2001). Lever-Tracy and Ip (1996) argue that the synergy between the specific skill sets of Chinese investors in labour-intensive export and labour management, and China's developmental local states were catalysts for China's rapid industrialization in the 1980s and 1990s. The cultural knowledge of overseas Chinese was also an indispensable factor because they were well versed in using propensities and social relations to get things done in a highly unregulated environment. As China's political and economic environment has become more established, some note that the importance of this particular form of synergy has declined (Smart and Hsu 2004). We argue that, as Taiwan and Mainland China have respectively entered an era of engagement with global technological development since the 1990s, new fields of synergy have emerged between the returning high-tech professionals in both places. In the following section we compare the trajectories of the Taiwanese and Mainland Chinese professional populations returning from overseas to their origins, and how they have influenced the ICT industry on both sides of the Taiwan Strait.

From 'brain drain' to 'brain circulation'

Post-World War II Chinese migration to the US started in 1965 following changes in US immigration law. From this point to the 1980s, scholars would study the movement of Chinese professionals to the United States within the framework of the 'brain drain', for the net flow of expertise was heavily unidirectional (Salt and Stein 1997). After completing their studies, most students who had arrived as graduates to pursue postgraduate degrees remained in the US as academics, government scientists, industrial engineers or researchers. Once committed to an American career, few returned home.

Since the 1980s, highly skilled engineers and professionals from Taiwan and Mainland China have been returning in growing numbers. Saxenian (2007) has noted the active engagement of Chinese and Indian engineers in technological start-ups in Silicon Valley, California, calling them 'the new Argonauts' when describing their roles of connecting technological spheres around the globe. Saxenian and others (Saxenian and Hsu 2001; Zhou and Tseng 2001; Wong 2006) have also shown that local ethnic associations in California that promote entrepreneurial endeavours in both host and home countries have institutionalized the international circulation of technical expertise. Their findings have led to the coinage of the term 'brain circulation' (Saxenian 2007; Saxenian and Sabel 2008), which describes the phenomenon of skilled immigrants becoming increasingly beneficial to both home and host countries.

The changing pattern of migration and circulation suggests that, beyond cultural affinities, which one can regard as more or less constant for the foreign-born generation of immigrants, political and economic forces bring about the major changes in the flows. In particular, while studies have shown that the circulation of professionals and institutionalized links can give rise to new models of the global division of labour, few studies have looked into the process of local institutional formation that supports transmigrant activities. We argue that the return flow can only be substantiated and sustained if transmigrant activities are firmly grounded in both countries' respective regional economies and supported by their local institutions.

To date, with the exception of Saxenian's work, most studies on trans-migrants have been country or region specific. In our attempt to elucidate what structural forces shape the returnees' practices, we focus on two groups of Chinese professionals in the ICT industry – those from Taiwan and those from Mainland China. The two Chinese groups are a good pair for comparison because they share similar cultural, linguistic and social backgrounds. Beyond sharing certain staple Chinese cultural traditions prior to their migration, both groups were composed of highly educated and selected people with a strong predisposition to careers in science and technology. The bulk of the returnees left their homeland at the time of authoritarian governments and returned to a more open, though not necessarily democratic, society, especially in the case of Mainland China. In the US, they generally received postgraduate educations and launched their careers in American high technology companies; some started their own companies in the US. Governments on both sides of the Taiwan Strait also actively courted them. For both groups, the return flows occurred during the economic boom in East Asia, but differed in important respects. For example, the two groups grew up in different societies – Taiwan was more Western oriented and capitalist, whereas Mainland China was isolated and communist during the 1960s and 1970s. Furthermore, they both returned to different political and economic contexts at different stages of globalization. The high-technology industry in Mainland China, though connected with Taiwan, is lower on the technology hierarchy, but with one of the world's largest growing markets. As a result, the returnees face very different sets of opportunities, resources and constraints, both globally and locally. In the following sections, we look at the life trajectories of Taiwanese and mainland Chinese professionals in the US and the factors informing their decisions to return to their homelands. We shall then examine their contrasting business strategies.

Outgoing flow of Chinese students

'Brain circulation' started earlier in Taiwan than on the mainland. The island, which has been a staunch US ally since World War II, has close ties with American political and economic establishments (Liu and Cheng 1994). Since the 1960s, going to the US has become a rite of passage for Taiwan's most elite students. According to one survey (NYC 1987), 21,248 students left Taiwan in the 1960s to advance their studies abroad, but only 1,172 (5 per cent) returned. Between 1970 and 1979, 33,165 students studied abroad and 5,028 or 15 per cent returned – a marked improvement, but still a low rate. The overwhelming majority of these students went to the US. Overall, the non-returnees in the two decades amounted to approximately 88 per cent of the student migrants. Science and engineering dominated the fields of study. In fact, more than 40 per cent of the graduates from the departments of mechanical engineering, electrical engineering, civil engineering, physics and chemistry at prestigious universities such as National Taiwan University (NTU), Tsinghua University and Chiaotung University went abroad.

As can be expected, better research facilities, promising career prospects, better professional opportunities, higher salaries and stronger job satisfaction were reasons that supported the student migrants' decision to stay in the US (NYC 1987). These conditions remained unchanged until the mid-1980s, when Taiwan's economy took off and the Taiwanese government started to recruit overseas talent for high-technological development (Chang 1992).

The flow of mainland Chinese students to America lagged behind Taiwan by about 20 years, but when it came it came as a torrent. China's international isolation under Mao's regime meant that virtually no mainland students went to the West between 1950 and 1980. Those who went to the Soviet Union in the 1950s returned in the 1960s. The 1980s saw about 34,000 mainland students go abroad, primarily to Western countries (Figure 5.1). Given the strict passport and visa controls, a significant portion of them applied for short-term government-sponsored study programmes. However, foreign universities were also paying for growing numbers of self-sponsored students on an extremely selective basis. With higher incomes in China in the 1990s and more relaxed passport regulations, the number of students travelling abroad soared to almost 150,000, and then leapt to three-quarters of a million between 2000 and 2006. Since the 1990s, the student body has become increasingly mixed with more and more private households able to afford foreign education. Government sponsorship has accordingly diminished. In the 2000s, self-sponsored students grew to constitute over 90 per cent of the total outgoing flow.

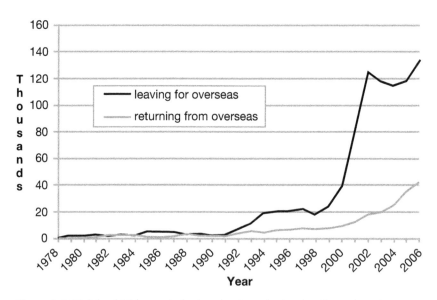

Figure 5.1 Mainland Chinese students going to and returning from abroad
Source: Cao (2008).

The US has always been the most favoured destination for mainland Chinese students. The US Institute of International Education (IIE 2008) reported that Mainland China was the leading sender of foreign students to the US throughout much of the 1990s – only in 2001 did India begin to exceed China; however, the latter has remained in second place, growing at a rate of more than 10 per cent every year. In 2008, there were 81,127 Chinese students in institutions of higher education in the US and 65.4 per cent of these were in graduate programmes.

For our focus on returnees, we concentrate on people who went abroad in the 1980s and 1990s. This is because those who left in the 2000s either are still abroad or, if not, were likely to be in entry-level positions at the time of the research. Their huge numbers indicate, however, that once they return to China in significant numbers – which is almost inevitable given their visa status – they will have a major and lasting demographic/social/economic impact on China's professional population. It is thus necessary to conceptualize China's return flow at the beginning stage.

Calls from home: the draw of high-tech industry

Taiwan

The significant return flow of professionals and entrepreneurs to Taiwan began in the 1980s, corresponding with the economic boom and political opening up. More precisely, the combination of a booming high-tech industry, the soaring stock market, and a ready supply of skilled engineers created a suitable entrepreneurial environment that enticed overseas talent to return in growing numbers.

In the late 1980s, Taiwan's PC industry got into its stride and entered a phase of rapid growth (Hwang 1995; III 1991). The sales revenues of local PC manufacturers reached US\$ 1 billion in 1985, 1.6 per cent of Taiwan's total GDP of US\$ 62 billion. At the same time, the skyrocketing stock market – fuelled in part by the real-estate boom after the mid-1980s – provided local financial options for higher-end technology ventures. The transaction value of the stock market then reached US\$ 650 million. Several small semiconductor companies founded by Taiwanese-Americans moved their bases to Taiwan to tap into the huge reservoir of capital on the island, and a number of major technological ventures went public on the stock market. The steady supply of skilled and less expensive labour was another attracting factor. In the late 1980s, American and Taiwanese universities flooded the island with graduates in computer and related fields, giving Taiwan a substantial pool of engineering talent (Liu 1993). These financial and manpower incentives, in addition to government subsidies in the PC and semiconductor industry, and a booming PC business, created a highly favourable climate to attract and support a large number of overseas talents. As president of ITRI (Industrial Technology Research Institute), a public and private research institute, Mr. Chin-Tay

Shih, observed, 'When the current of overseas technology and talent met the current of local capital and Taiwan's industrial base, it created multiplier effects. The two forces were complementary, and reinforced each other' (Chang et al. 1994).

The development of the semiconductor industry in particular shows the role of the Taiwan state in cultivating and encouraging return flows. Taiwan, a relative newcomer to the industry, decided to borrow technologies from foreign countries, especially the US. Many overseas Chinese worked in large semiconductor companies in the US, and Taiwan needed their expertise. Under the leadership of the Minister of Economic Affairs, a group of senior overseas Taiwanese electronics engineers provided advice and guidance to help nurture high-technology industries in Taiwan. The group later formed an informal Technical Advisory Committee (TAC),[1] which regularly met to discuss the progress of Taiwan's semiconductor industry. The following quote from Dr Wen-yuan Pan, head of TAC, summarizes Taiwan's strategy: 'to expedite the growth of Taiwan's electronics industries, the semiconductor industry should be targeted. The best way to develop it was to transfer technology from foreign companies, particularly the American companies, to save valuable time' (ERSO 1994: 5). Heeding this advice, the Taiwanese government targeted recruitment from US industries in particular. The strong political alliance between the US and Taiwan during and after the Cold War made the arrangement politically tenable. Taiwan dedicated more than US$ 10 million to the development of the semiconductor industry through a series of projects that successfully caused local semiconductor firms to take root, as discussed later.

After the initial stage of long-distance consultation from overseas, the state heightened investment in the industrial infrastructure, including public projects, in the hope of luring back overseas talent. For the semiconductor industry, the establishment of state labs, such as the ERSO (Electronics Research Service Organization) and the HSBIP (Hsinchu Science-based Industrial Park), were significant developments. The inflow into the HSBIP – the government established research park – shows the growth of returnees. In the early 1980s, the HSBIP attracted only a handful of returnees each year, cumulatively 422 by 1990. By 1997, however, the cumulative total had increased fivefold to more than 2850 – with an average of 350 returning each year. US-educated engineers started almost half the 97 companies in the HSBIP in 1997. The significance of these returnees went far beyond their number, as many of them had returned to Taiwan in mid-career after having accumulated considerable managerial or entrepreneurial experience in Silicon Valley (HSBIP 1998).

Mainland China

As in Taiwan, the significant upswing in the return flow of mainlanders came 20 years after the outgoing flow. As Figure 5.1 shows, the return flow increased much more slowly than the outgoing flow and a noticeable upward swing came after 2000. Given that the economy in Mainland China was less developed than in Taiwan during the 1980s and 1990s, and with an authoritarian and oppressive government, Mainland Chinese had little incentive to return after receiving their education in the US. Research in the 1980s and 1990s found extremely low interest among Chinese self-sponsored students to return home, though returning rates were much higher among government-sponsored students or scholars (Zweig and Chen 1995; Hertling 1997). Zweig and Chen reported that the leading reasons for students not returning to Mainland China in the early 1990s were political instability, restrictions on political freedom, lack of economic opportunities and low standards of living. In 1989, the Chinese government's violent crushing of peaceful student movements in Beijing shocked the world and hardened the students' resolve not to return home. Subsequent to the crackdown, political sympathy from the US government and the public allowed the rapid passing of the Chinese Student Protection Act in 1992, which gave all Chinese nationals – around 50,000 at the time – permanent residence in the US. Studying abroad in the 1980s and early 1990s for mainland students meant, practically, that they had a one-way ticket to stay in the US; meanwhile, going home was considered extraordinary, if not unfortunate. The cultural ties lay dormant.

Compared with the Taiwanese government, the Chinese government also had much more trouble enticing the return of overseas talent during the 1980 and 1990s. Given that Chinese students had lobbied and taken advantage of US governmental protection made it difficult for the Chinese government to command their political loyalty. In contrast with Taiwan, it was not until the late 1990s that the Chinese government could begin systematically to seek out the assistance and advice of the overseas Chinese population.

The situation began to change in the late 1990s during the heyday of the dot-com rush – and with little governmental initiative at the beginning. The internet boom in the US made China look like an untapped gold mine for prospective internet entrepreneurs. With the memory of the 1989 event gradually fading, a few Chinese professionals returned to the mainland to test the business waters. Some returnee-founded enterprises, such as Sohu.com, AsiaInfo.com, and UTstarcom, successfully drew foreign venture capital and achieved wealth and fame within a short period (Sheff 2002; Zhou 2008a). Their examples inspired a growing number of Chinese professionals to contemplate the possibility that China might at last be ready for private ventures in knowledge-intensive industries (Sheff 2002).

The internet bubble burst in the spring of 2000 as NASDAQ crashed. Yet the disappointment did nothing to moderate the return flow, which has actually intensified since 2000 (Figure 5.1). China's sustained economic growth since the 1980s proved crucial in attracting returnees. The rapid rise of income also significantly reduced the gap in standards of living between China and advanced countries. Sensing the growth of its return flow, China started to implement numerous governmental programmes to provide financial incentives for returnee entrepreneurs or professionals. In addition, local governments provided grants and preferential policies for high-tech start-ups by returnees in their science parks. Industrial aid has not, however, been systematic and policy changes aimed at easing travel restrictions, such as the multi-year visa for returnees, are unavailable. It is unclear how effective the state incentives have been in fostering the flow (Xiang and Shen 2009).

As in Taiwan, major science parks in large Chinese metropolitan areas like Beijing, Shanghai and Shenzhen worked hard to attract returnees, and they now host the lion's share of returnee entrepreneurs in the high-tech sectors. In 2000, Beijing's Zhongguancun Science Park, the earliest and largest high-tech zone in China, began keeping records on returnee-founded enterprises. These show a steady increase of roughly 500 firms every year (Zhou 2008a: 126–127). People returning from North America, who make up 46 per cent of the total, founded half the returnee enterprises. Returnees from Europe, Japan and other countries make up the remaining half. The vast majority of these enterprises in a range of technological areas are very small and undercapitalized (Saxenian 2007), yet their growth has helped the ZGC industrial ecosystem become more internationalized.

Besides the pull factors of the homelands, it is also important to acknowledge the push factors in the US for mid-career Chinese professionals. Hitting glass ceilings in American corporations was a common experience among Chinese from both the mainland and Taiwan (Zhou and Tseng 2001). After 15 to 20 years in the US, many of these professionals had finished studying and had already spent a decade in their careers. While there are a few high-profile Chinese executives in some leading high-tech companies, racial discrimination and cultural barriers have kept the vast majority out of the key corporate decision-making posts. A large number of technical professionals faced this 'glass ceiling' in corporations quite early on, coming to the sad realization that they had reached the peak of their career in their late thirties or early forties, with nowhere else to go in the American corporate world (Wong 2006). Many chose to settle in their current tracks, but the more ambitious and restless of them inevitably looked for new challenges and excitement. For them, Taiwan and Mainland China – their rapidly developing homelands – held irresistible appeal. Edward Tian, the founder of AsiaInfo, famously announced that his career choice had been between counting little white rats in the biology lab for the rest of his life or creating the internet in China (Sheff 2002).

In sum, despite the different political economies in Taiwan and Mainland China, there are striking parallels between the return flows. Both regions experienced about 15 to 20 years of brain drain, and both are seeing an accelerating rate of return after the significant local development of high-tech industry. While the Taiwan return flow has matured, it has only begun for the mainland. The much larger outgoing pools in the latter suggest that a broad scale and far more lasting circulation will be likely.

The role of the state has been much more coordinated and focused in Taiwan than on the mainland, even though the state in China is more centralized.

The state played an instrumental role in the early stage of returnee recruitment and technological upgrade in Taiwan. The Chinese state began active recruitment after the initial return flow, but its efforts lacked focus and their effects are unclear.

Business strategies in Taiwan: domestic capital and global market

Regardless of government efforts, the success and sustainability of professional returnees really depend on the convergence of global and local interests, particularly the configuration and maturation of the local industrial environment. This consists of the market, the industrial structure and capital provision. We make the following comparisons between Taiwan and the mainland.

Taiwan has an export-oriented economy. The returnees come from the high-tech sectors in the US, so have the precise combination of technical expertise and connections with the exporting market. Building on the success of electronic exports, the returnees made their most visible contribution to the semiconductor and venture capital industries. Compared with South Korea and Japan, Taiwan's high-tech industry has a unique business structure where smaller or medium sized enterprises (SMEs) play a strong role, in addition to large enterprises in most exporting industries. Such systems of highly specialized production through a subcontracting network was present in labour-intensive export industries, and was replicated in the later PC sectors as well as in the technology-intensive sectors such as Integrated Circuits (IC) sectors (Shieh 1992; Saxenian 2007). SMEs constituted diverse entry points to join the game, especially for those returnees who possessed new product technologies for start-ups, but did not have the large capital for major ventures.

In the process of new firm formation, the role of the government, along with the operation and movement of the production networks, was critical for the returnee to start up their businesses. Take IC design as an example. Despite a swarm of returnees setting up design houses, the real thrust for the IC boom came from a fabrication plant with state-of-the-art technology. The Taiwanese government initiated the TSMC (Taiwan Semiconductor Manufacturing Corporation) to concentrate on manufacturing chips for other companies, while not competing with them in the sale of the chips.[2] Today domestic foundries do more than 98 per cent of the fabrication work the independent design houses generate. In fact, design companies have emerged in abundance since the establishment of TSMC. There were fewer than five design houses in the HSBIP in 1987; afterwards there were more than 20, with 200 more founded in the 1990s. The establishment of made-to-order fabrication factories, pioneered by Mr. Zhang in Taiwan, is an exemplary case of how the knowledge, expertise and social connections of transmigrants can reshape the global IC commodity chain and attract more returnee enterprises.

The returnees also maintain ongoing collaborations and partnerships between specialist producers at different stages of the global supply chain, connecting

Silicon Valley with production in Mainland China. While Silicon Valley and Hsinchu are at different levels of development and have different specialisms, the interactions between the two regions are increasingly complementary and mutually beneficial. As long as the US remains the largest and most sophisticated market for technology products, which seems likely for the foreseeable future, new product definition and leading-edge innovation will remain in Silicon Valley. Taiwanese semiconductor SMEs, however, continue to enhance their ability to design, modify, adapt and rapidly commercialize technologies developed elsewhere. As local design and product development capabilities improve, Taiwanese companies are increasingly well-positioned to take new product ideas and technologies from Silicon Valley, to integrate them quickly and to produce them in volume at relatively low cost.

One of the key driving forces behind the burgeoning IC design houses has been the role of small venture capitalists. Since the early 1980s, the Taiwanese government has tried to promote the venture capital industry to imitate the Silicon Valley model. As mentioned earlier, the boom of Taiwan's stock market in the 1980s provided initial capital channels for firms in PC industries and then for the higher-end semiconductors industry. Later, returnees became a central player to bridge the domestic capital with technological expertise and establish connections with the global market. Taiwan's venture capital companies rose from 1 in 1984 to 27 in 1994. Some 97 per cent of their investments are concentrated in the ICT industries. The total amount of total venture capital investment reached US$ 5 billion in 2004. Some venture capitalists, like Champion Investment, and some securities companies, like Chien-Hong Securities, are becoming very important investors in high technology sectors. Saxenian (2007: 151) argues that Taiwan's venture capital industry reached the point of self-sustaining growth in the 1990s, which significantly improved entrepreneurial opportunities for returnees.

In sum, building on their success in labour-intensive exports, the Taiwan returnees help transformed the global chain of semiconductor production to make Taiwan an indispensable part. Returnees thrived on their transnational networks and experience with leading semiconductor firms in Silicon Valley. They also took advantage of Taiwan's indigenous capital market and highly skilled population. The state provided the initial crucial steps and helped to found the large capital-intensive ventures that anchored the growth of SMEs. Maturation of the industrial environment attracted even more returnees with experience and this further strengthened brain circulation.

One needs to note that this did not happen overnight. Collaboration among returnees, the state, local capital and multinational companies has being going on since the 1970s. A solid political alliance between the US and Taiwan, and decades of a thriving, export-oriented, SME-centred economy, also contributed towards the success. At this point, the return flow has become self-sustaining with broad international reach alongside close and ongoing links with the US and Mainland China.

Mainland returnees: global capital and domestic market

In sharp contrast to Taiwanese returnees, neither the opportunity to become involved in the global division of labour nor the availability of local capital initiated the recent return of Chinese entrepreneurs; it was the prospect of China becoming an immense market for high technology goods and services.

Market and industrial structure

When China became the 'factory of the world' in the 1990s, it started to develop a buoyant export industry, which the overseas Chinese (and technically the returnees) initiated. Chinese professionals in the US generally have little experience of labour-intensive manufacturing or of the export economy; China's domestic market potential attracted their attention.

In the late 1990s China entered the global scene as one of the largest and most rapidly growing high-tech markets in the world (OECD 2006). The internet, in particular, shows the promise of the world's largest population. By the mid to late 1990s, China had a nascent domestic ICT industry, but the state-owned enterprises dominated the key telecommunication sectors, and foreign companies dominated the PC and other key high-tech equipment markets. The non-state technological firms such as Lenovo and Huawei were just emerging between the two giants. They specialized in manufacturing, but were too weak financially and too inexperienced in R&D to engage in risky higher-end ventures in the 1990s (Zhou 2008a). The feverish pace of internet development in the US, by contrast, suggested the transformative potential of the internet for China. The first-generation mainland returnee entrepreneurs were younger and less experienced than their Taiwanese counterparts were. Edward Tian, the co-founder of AsiaInfo mentioned earlier, trained as a biologist. Charles Zhang, the founder of China's top internet portal, sohu.com, had a Ph.D. in physics; his only prior high-tech experience was in a dotcom company that his Harvard friend had founded. One of the most experienced of the returnees, the founder of Baidu.com, Li Hongyan, had worked in a number of high-tech firms but had not reached the middle management level before deciding to return to Beijing to work on his start-up. These entrepreneurs were interested in transplanting the start-up models from Silicon Valley to China and not in reconfiguring the global commodity chain.

There are reasons for their choices. Compared with other high-tech industries that require the formation of a complex industrial supply chain, the internet is a service industry directly interfacing with the end users. The returnees thought they could bypass China's relatively lagging commercial infrastructure, or at least avoid dealing with traditional sectors where they had few connections, but it did not take them long to realize how wrong they were. China's commercial soil is quite different from that of Silicon Valley. Regulation by state bureaucracies and the monopolies of the state-owned telecommunication giants turned internet development into an obstacle course (Zhang 2006).

Under-developed finance and logistic infrastructure slowed down the emergence of many necessary supporting services. Yet, these internet companies persisted with adaptations and innovations to meet the demand of a surging Chinese online population. By the mid-2000s, China had largely fulfilled its internet promise. Many start-ups, founded by returnees or locals, have emerged in almost all areas of the internet industry. The lack of a pre-existing monopoly and low technological barriers helped make the online industry the most hospitable space for small high-tech start-ups. Today China has the world's largest and fastest growing internet population and one of the largest internet markets. The pioneering work of returnees in probing and pushing for reforms in China's finance, logistics and other service sectors deserves considerable credit. China's online industries remain a key area attracting venture capital investments from overseas as the so-called TMT (telecom, media and technology) sectors (Li 2006).

Since 2000, more high-tech fields have opened up, together with return flows of more experienced professionals. Some joined large MNCs or state-owned companies; others started their own businesses. Mr. M[3] was among the earliest Chinese students to go to the US. He left in 1982 with a master's degree in engineering. He got a Ph.D. in the US and started to work for IBM in 1987, specializing in semiconductor physics and engineering. After a solid career at IBM, he took early retirement and returned to Shanghai to work for a major China–Japan semiconductor joint venture in 2007. Regular calls from his graduate colleagues, many of whom had already gone home to assume leadership positions in the company, prompted his decision to return. Mr. M was an athletic man in his early fifties and he moved to Shanghai to start a new career, not to enjoy retirement. Similarly, Mr H, in his early forties, had also had a long career in major IT companies such as Philips and IBM; he voluntarily relocated to work in the IBM Beijing R&D centre while leaving his family in the US. Most of the key engineers in major MNC R&D centres in China were returnees. They do not have much routine contact with local enterprises, but they often become role models by indicating that returning is a viable option for career development.

Those who came back to found their own companies, by contrast, have had a bumpier ride. The promise of China's mass market initially lured most of them, but many discovered that the Chinese market was not yet ready for the advanced technology to which they were accustomed in the US.

One returnee, Hu Hui, set up his company in Zhongguancun Science Park for US$ 150,000, which is too little for a venture in Silicon Valley but significant in China. Hu developed a software solution for remote medical diagnoses at Beijing's Zhongguancun, but he could neither find any buyers in China nor persuade Chinese venture capitalists (VCs) to invest in his firm. He donated the manufactured device with his software to Chinese hospitals during the SARS outbreak in 2003, but they never used the units. Relief finally came from the US: an American firm bought his company for the princely sum of US$ 18 million in 2004 (ZGC Administrative Commission 2004).

The returnee entrepreneurs commonly complained about the lack of a market and this reflects a key structural problem. Taiwan's export market suited returnees, but China's domestic market is entirely new. The overall low purchasing power and lack of experience with high-tech goods in the mainland suggest that China's mass market, namely one in which demands are increasing in both quantity and sophistication, has materialized in only a few areas. In other areas, returnee entrepreneurs will have a hard time. In addition, since most returnee companies are small and highly specialized, they need the maturation of the entire commodity chain to become a viable business. One entrepreneur interviewed in 2005 said that he spent eight months rethinking his business strategies after returning to China:

> The commodity chain in China is far from developed compared with America. If you just specialize in your technological niche, it will be impossible to survive here. You have to extend your work up or down the chain. It might be enough for me just to do software in the US, but here I have to make it into a piece of hardware, so it is a so-called product. Otherwise, the clients do not recognize the value of your technology. To make these adjustments, I have to have considerably more capital and some business partners.

We followed up with him again in 2008, and it was only then that he was finally able to locate a niche incorporating his chips with surveillance cameras makers.

Concentrations of returnee firms have begun to emerge in areas with reasonable commodity chains. Mobile phone and IC design are the clearest examples. These sectors relate to both the development of China's manufacturing capacity for the world market and its unique consumer demands (Zhou 2008a and 2008b). As in Taiwan, China's IC designers tie up with the PC and mobile phone industry. Vimicro, a company a Chinese returnee from California founded in 1998, has been one of the most successful fabless[4] IC design houses in China, specializing in PC and wireless phone cameras. Most of Vimicro's engineers are mid-career returnees from Intel, Lucent Kodak and elsewhere. The company became established by supplying PC camera chips to PC manufacturers, and it claims it had 60 per cent of the world market share in 2006 (company website). The path of Vimicro is thus similar to many Taiwan IC design houses in its strategy of tapping into the global manufacturing chain. The company's ambition, however, is to serve China's domestic market for third-generation wireless phones rather than to supply to global production (Zhou 2008a: 133).

China's largest IC designers are concentrated in Shanghai, though Beijing and Shenzhen also have sizable clusters. Returnees who had worked with the major chip manufacturers founded many of the chip design houses and software companies. As in Taiwan, the establishment of the large foundry manufacturer, Semiconductor Manufacturing International Corporation (SMIC), which is a student of and rival to TSMC, facilitated the rise of mainland Chinese design houses. A China–Japan joint venture – Huahong–NEC – also located in Shanghai and had been in the business for decades.

A 2008 study by Obukhova (2008) at MIT on the IC design industry in Shanghai suggests that these design houses did not grow explosively between 2004 and 2008 as such businesses did in Taiwan in the 1990s. Many firms are yet to become profitable, but the returnee-founded companies have a better chance of survival. This suggests that although IC design is an area with a strong returnee presence, it might be misleading to expect the mainland to replicate the success of Taiwan in exactly the same sector. The Taiwan semiconductor industry had a substantial lead and it continues to progress. In addition, much of its designing capacity has moved to the mainland, so there is little cost advantage for the mainlanders. In addition, there has been a reduced rise in the demand for IC chips in the West since the 2000s, which has slowed the industry down, especially since the start of the recession in 2008. The best strategy for mainland returnees' firms might lie in collaboration rather than competition with Taiwanese firms. In fact, such collaborative patterns have already emerged among Taiwan firms relocated in China. The case of *Shanzhai* cellphone is particularly illustrative. *Shanzhai* is a new Chinese term describing knockoff phones. Such phones mostly follow the prototypes of the branded products, such as Nokia or the iPhone, but with additions or modified functions in order to meet local demands. It is estimated that more than 150 million *Shanzhai* mobile phones (*Shanzhaiji*) were sold in 2008 in China and even exported (Lin 2008; Barboza 2009). *Shanzhai* phones are one-third of the branded price and their core component is the GSM chip, which is the product of MediaTek (MTK), a Taiwanese IC design house. MTK, which collaborates with mainland mobile phone makers and dealers, has successfully created new low-priced mass markets with many segments.

If the Chinese market fails to materialize for high-tech products, the returnees have another business strategy: this is to focus on advanced markets, using China primarily as an R&D site, while keeping an eye on the Chinese market potential for their products. This is often an involuntary choice. After failing to locate a local market in a short time, many returnees have realized that their best hope might still be abroad. Focusing on the advanced market is a relatively simpler operation on the China end of returnee enterprises. Local engineers may lack experience, but they are fast learners and are more willing than their American counterparts are to put in long hours and at one-tenth of the cost. Chinese entrepreneurs involved in start-ups in the US or Japan might consider moving part of their R&D operations to China so that their capital can stretch further. For those companies, the main office is typically still in Silicon Valley and the Chinese operation consists of back-office R&D. Operating in China also gives entrepreneurs the opportunity to observe and experiment with the Chinese market. Software export is an example in this area. Returnee enterprises have a natural advantage – they speak English well, they have overseas social contacts and they have been the main founders of such enterprises, often through collaborating with companies abroad. For example, Mr. Z returned to China from Texas in 2003. He originally hoped to provide his software to China's logistics industry, but later switched to software export with partners in California. The California companies receive orders and he provides software support with his employees in Beijing. Even though China is far behind India in this sector, the software outsourcing industry is growing quickly, over 50 per cent a year since 2000 (CSIA, multiple years). Compared with India though, China started decades late and lacks large, well-recognized firms. To overcome their size limitations, small firms have engaged in establishing alliances with each other to share work. Overall, given the much weaker English-language facilities in China, it is unlikely that China will be as competitive as India in software outsourcing for English-speaking countries, even if this sector continues to grow.

In short, mainland returnees have made significant inroads in sectors targeting the Chinese market and are increasingly moving into the international markets. Nevertheless, returnee enterprises are still in the initial stages, with sizeable returnee firms only beginning to emerge in 2002. Thus far, the online industry remains the most successful area for returnees, though, like very successful non-returnee companies such as Alibaba, it has become highly localized. Smaller clusters of IC design and software export have also emerged, but without the transformative impact of Taiwan or India on the global division of labour.

Given the early stage of return flow, we cannot be certain that the lack of rapidly growing clusters of returnee enterprises, besides the internet, is a permanent phenomenon; we also cannot determine whether the lack of clusters is necessarily a bad thing. China's policy is to increase the overall technology level of many sectors by incorporating returnees rather than creating returnee enclaves. We make two observations. First, the patterns and dynamics of returnees in the ICT industry in the mainland have failed to replicate the export-oriented development in Taiwan, with China's domestic market the primary attraction. ICT might possibly even be the wrong area in which to look for additional returnee breakthroughs. For example, returnee companies have become global leaders in the alternative energy industry. Suntech, for instance, which returnees founded, has become the largest maker of solar products in the world.

Second, in comparison with Taiwan, returnee ventures on the mainland need to make many more adjustments to fit in with China's market and economic system. This is hardly surprising given China's general weakness in supporting SME entrepreneurship, which is a sharp contrast to Taiwan's long history of SME-dominated growth. Below, we examine in more detail the problem of capital provision on the mainland.

Mainland returnees: capital

China has a centralized financial system with mostly state-owned banks. As is well known, this system discriminates against non-state enterprises and

SMEs, to which returnee companies largely belong. High-tech start-ups may have valuable intellectual property, but they are often low in the kinds of assets that might serve as collateral for bank loans. A few selected returnee firms were able to raise substantial investment from Chinese banks, but that is more the exception than the rule. For the vast majority of returnee enterprises, support from the government is available but limited; it comes mostly in the form of state-sponsored business incubators, small start-up grants, bank guarantees for small loans, rent breaks and other limited subsidies. These are helpful at the beginning stages of the start-ups but are of little use for sustaining further development. In Beijing's Zhongguancun Science Park, the administrators have done local experiments to help firms with a good credit history. Overall, however, the situation has not changed fundamentally (Zhou 2008a). China's stock market has one of the largest market values in the world, but it has been unfriendly to small innovative companies. In 2009, China started to establish a NASDAQ style stock market to encourage innovation and this has generated a considerable amount of excitement.

Given the obstacles of China's financial system, it is not surprising that overseas venture capital from the US, Hong Kong and Japan supported the first waves of returnee enterprises. China's population and its sustained economic growth provided global capital with ample room for imagination. Global capital, with its deep pockets, has been willing to fund – at first rather tentatively but later on more lavishly – potential Chinese entrepreneurs hoping to gain inroads into this vast potential market. This was different from Taiwan where local capital was the main source of funding for high-tech firms.

Since the mid-2000s, the venture capital industry, which foreign capital interests in China's online ventures mainly fuels, has grown rapidly in China. By 2001, China and Hong Kong together accounted for 30 per cent of Asia's private equity investment, overtaking Japan for the first time. By 2002, the total venture capital pool in Mainland China reached US$ 7.15 billion (Batjargal and Liu 2004). There was a brief dip between 2001 and 2003 due to the after effects of the NASDAQ crash, but growth has accelerated since 2003 as a series of Chinese companies, including the telecom provider China Netcom, the online gaming company Shenda, the semiconductor company SMIC and others have gone public in the US or Hong Kong. The rush of venture capital reached a feverish pace around Baidu's IPO at NASDAQ in 2005. On its first listed day Baidu's share price more than quadrupled, which set a first-day record for any foreign firm ever listed on the US stock market and any firm in the previous five years (Barboza 2005). Since 2004, large amounts of mainstream US venture capital have entered China, with new capital injection reaching over US$ 4 billion in 2005, far exceeding the total of the previous three years. According to a report by British USB Wealth management, issued in August 2007, China has overtaken Britain as the second largest destination of venture capital in the world (Arnold 2007). With the robust growth of China's economy in the global recession, it is certain that more venture capital will target China as a fertile field for innovative ventures.

Returnees have been key agents in the venture capital industry. For example, Hong Chen, the chair and CEO of a major Chinese venture capital company, Hina Group, was the founder of two technology companies in California. One of the largest and most influential of the Chinese high-tech business associations, the Hua Yuan Science and Technology Association (HYSTA) in Silicon Valley, has more than three thousand members, with chapters in Beijing and Shanghai. The three former chairs of the HYSTA were all entrepreneurs in the valley, and each is now involved in the venture-capital business in China (Du 2007).

It is important to note that China *does* have an indigenous venture capital industry, with government-sponsored VCs established since the late 1990s. These organizations are, however, mostly affiliated with state-owned financial institutions, which have little experience and expertise in the venture capital industry. In addition, since China's own stock market could not work as an exit for venture capital funds, foreign VCs financed the lion's share of projects, for they are the experts in bringing innovative companies to foreign stock markets. This, however, will change with China's own 'NASDAQ' taking shape in October 2009. Already, in the second quarter of 2009, domestic VCs grew by more than 70 per cent and for the first time invested in more cases than foreign VCs, mostly in anticipation of this new public option (Ye 2009). It is clear that the weakness of China's financial provision has been the crucial inhibiting factor for the growth of returnee firms, a weakness that foreign VCs can only partially compensate. To make the venture capital industry sustainable, China has to connect its huge accumulation of capital to the professional investment and industrial expertise in the high-tech sectors, as done successfully in Taiwan. The new NASDAQ style market can potentially be a game changer on that.

In sum, the success of returnees in Taiwan's semiconductor and China's internet industries suggests that these are two clusters in which the synergy of capital and markets through global and local sources has emerged, but with different combinations. The global market and local capital ensured the success of Taiwan's semiconductor industry, whereas the domestic market and international capital formed China's internet industry. The slow development in other returnee clusters in the mainland points to an immaturity of the local industrial structure, a stagnant global market, or both. The experiences of mainland and Taiwan returnee firms suggest that the development of returnee businesses is not that different from the development of SMEs in general. They both require a local supporting structure of fair financial systems, less monopoly, and better information channels and services. Taiwan returnees benefited from a friendlier environment for SMEs, while mainland returnees had to battle against a more hostile one. Returnees coming from well-established business environments may be more demanding or more vulnerable if such local ecosystems are not in place.

Conclusion

In this chapter, we have demonstrated that returnee professionals and entrepreneurs are critical agents reshaping the map of high-tech global production and service in the Pacific basin. Even though mainland and Taiwan returnees from the US share similar personal attributes and life trajectories, their commercial strategies reflect the different intersections and synergy of global forces and local conditions. The concentration of Taiwan returnees in the semiconductors sector – a Taiwanese specialism in the global market – contrasts with the concentration of mainland returnees in the internet and telecommunication sectors, which focus on the domestic market. Both have utilized their technological experiences and personal connections in America. Taiwanese returnees, however, have deeper technological accumulation, better-focused technological fields and more success in establishing a self-sustaining entrepreneurial environment. Mainland returnees are only emerging, and they attract more attention from global capital and are involved in broader fields of technology. They also face considerably more difficulty in adjusting to a developing domestic market, which involves overcoming weakness in finance and commodity chains, and working with an uncertain regulatory framework. Despite these problems, the mainland returnees have shown perseverance and business shrewdness in creating an online industry. Given that the flow of returnees only really gathered momentum in 2002, more profound changes may occur in the future. Given the much larger and more diverse economy of the mainland, it is entirely plausible that the returnee ventures may be less concentrated than the more specialized Taiwanese equivalents.

The experiences of returnees on both sides of the Taiwan Strait show that technology expertise and personal trajectories are only the beginning of building a sustainable return flow. The Mainland China state has been actively constructing financial incentives to attract returnees. Its most important task is to address the totality of the local environment with a view to lowering barriers to non-state firms and SMEs in general, especially with respect to capital, the market, business services and information channels. If China can create a more hospitable environment for non-state SMEs, there is little doubt that the returnee enterprises will thrive.

Acknowledgements

This research benefited from the financial support from National Science Foundation, Chiang-Ching Kuo Foundation for International Scholar Exchange, National Science Council (Taiwan), and research funds from Vassar College and the Program for Globalization Studies of the Institute for Advanced Studies in Humanities and Social Sciences at National Taiwan University.

Notes

* An earlier version of this chapter appeared in *Global Networks*, 11(3), 398–419.

1   TAC has three groups within it: a Bell Labs group, an IBM group and a university group. They meet four times a year with ITRI and ERSO personnel in Taiwan (Meaney 1991).
2   As Mr. James Dykes, the first president of TSMC, argued, 'the idea of a pure foundry is unique. Other semiconductor companies can utilize our resources without fear that we will take their technology and run to the market' (*Electronics*, 5 March 1987).
3   We use people's real names if the sources are published elsewhere. For interviews with middle level managers of larger firms or executives of small firms, we use only the initial of the last name to protect the interviewee's identity.
4   A fab is a facility that produces its own silicon wafers. A fabless facility is one that outsources the production of silicon wafers. Fabless companies focus on design and development.

References

Arnold, M. (2007) 'China overtook the UK as the world's second-biggest destination for venture capital investments last year', *Financial Times*, 23 August.

Barboza, D. (2005) 'Baidu turns up spotlight on Chinese web stocks', *New York Times*, Business, 8 August.

Barboza, D. (2009) 'In China, knockoff cellphones are a hit', *New York Times*, 27 April.

Batjargal, B. and M. Liu (2004) 'Entrepreneurs' access to private equity in China: the role of social capital', *Organization Science*, 15, 159–172.

Cao, C. (2008) 'China's brain drain at the high end: why government policies have failed to attract first-rate academics to return', *Asian Population Studies*, 4(3): 331–344.

Chang, S. (1992) 'Causes of brain drain and solutions: the Taiwan experience', *Studies in Comparative International Development*, 27(1): 27–43.

Chang, P., Shih, C. and Hsu, C. (1994) 'The formation process of Taiwan's IC industry – method of technology transfer', *Technovation* 14(3): 161–171.

Choudhary, B. (2001) 'Role of foreign direct investment in the Chinese economy with special reference to the overseas Chinese: its implication for India', *China Report*, 37(4): 463–474.

CSIA (China Software Industrial Association) (2000). *Annual Report of China's Software Industry*. Beijing: CSIA.

Du, Chen (2007) *Returning from the Silicon Valley*. www.ceocio.com.cn/store/detail/article.asp?articleId=13356&Columnid=3049&adId=10&view=ed (in Chinese).

ERSO (Electronics Research Service Organization) (1994) *Wind, Rain and Sunny Shine – The Developmental Trajectory of ERSO 1974–1993*. Hsinchu: ERSO. (In Chinese.)

Hertling, James (1997) 'More Chinese students abroad are deciding not to return home', *Chronicle of Higher Education*, 43(29): 151–153.

HSBIP (Hsinchu Science-based Industrial Park) (1994) *Annual Report of Hsinchu Science-based Industrial Park*. (In Chinese.)

Huchet, Jean-Franscois (1997) *The China Circle: Economics and electronics in the PRC, Taiwan and Hong Kong*. Washington DC: Brookings Institution Press, 254–289.

Hwang, C. (1995) *Taiwan – The Republic of Computers*. Taipei: Commonwealth Publishing. (In Chinese.)

IIE (Institute of International Education) (2008) *Open Doors 2008*, Country fact sheets, http://opendoors.iienetwork.org/?p=131583.

III (Institute for Information Industry) (1991) *An Overview of Taiwan's Personal Computer Industry*. Taipei: Institute for Informatics Industry. (In Chinese.)

Kotkin, J. (1993) *Tribes: How race, religion, and identity determine success in the new global economy*. New York: Random House.

Lever-Tracy, C. and Ip, D. (1996) 'Diaspora capitalism and the homeland: Australian Chinese networks into China', *Diaspora*, 5(2): 239–273.

Li, N. (2006) VC, 'The expansion and urges for action of VCs', *IT CEO & CIO China*, Vol. 189/190, www.ceocio.com.cn/12/93/148/224/6006.html.

Lin T. (2008) 'Shanzhai products roll up China', *United Daily*, 2 November (in Chinese).

Liu, C. (1993) 'Government's role in developing a high-tech industry: the case of Taiwan's semiconductor industry', *Technovation* 13(5): 299–309.

Liu, J. M., and Cheng, L. (1994) 'Pacific Rim development and the duality of post-1965 Asian immigration to the United States', in P. Ong, E. Bonacich and L. Cheng (eds) *The New Asian Immigration in Los Angeles and Global Restructuring*. Philadelphia, PA: Temple University Press.

Marks, Robert B. (2007) *The Origins of the Modern World*. New York: Rowman & Littlefield.

Meaney, C. (1991) 'Creating a competitive niche: state policy and Taiwan's semiconductor Industry', paper presented at the Center for Chinese Studies, University of California, Berkeley, 27 April.

NYC (National Youth Commissions) (1987) *A Helping Hand to Overseas Scholars for their Service at Home*. Taipei: National Youth Commission.

Obukhova, E. (2008) *IC design industry in Shanghai, 2004–2008*, MIT Sloan School of Management, http://web.mit.edu/obukhova/www/fabless/2008%20Shanghai%20fabless% 20EO%20.pdf.

OECD (Organization for Economic Cooperation and Development) (2006) *OECD information technology outlook: information and communication technologies*. Paris: Organization for Economic Cooperation and Development.

Ong, A. and Nonini, D. (1997) *Ungrounded Empires: The cultural politics of modern Chinese transnationalism*. New York: Routledge.

Pries, L. (ed.) (2001*) New Transnational Social Spaces: International migration and transnational companies in the early twenty-first century*. New York: Routledge.

Redding, G.S. 1990. *The Spirit of Chinese Capitalism*. Berlin/New York: Walter De Gruyter.

Salt, J. and Stein, J. (1997) 'Migration as a business: the case of trafficking', *International Migration*, 35(4): 467–494.

Saxenian, A. (2007) *The New Argonauts: Regional advantage in a global economy*. Cambridge, MA: Harvard University Press.

Saxenian, AnnaLee and Hsu, Jinn-Yuh (2001) 'The Silicon Valley-Hsinchu connection: technical communities and industrial upgrading', *Industrial and Corporate Change*, 10(4): 893–920.

Saxenian, A. and Sabel, C. (2008) 'Venture capital in the 'periphery': the new Argonauts, global search, and local institution building', *Economic Geography*, 84(4): 379–394.

Sheff, D. (2002) *China Dawn: The story of a technology and business revolution.* Vol. 1. New York: HarperBusiness.

Shieh, G.-S. (1992) *Boss Island: The subcontracting network and micro-entrepreneurship in Taiwan's development.* New York: Peter Lang Publishing.

Sklair, L. (2001) *The Transnational Capitalist Class.* New York: Blackwell.

Smart, A. and J. Hsu (2004) 'The Chinese diaspora, foreign investment and economic development in China', *The Review of International Affairs*, 3(4): 544–566.

Smith, M. P. and L. E. Guarnizo (eds) (1998) *Transnationalism From Below.* New Brunswick, NJ: Transaction.

Vertovec, S. (2009) *Transnationalism.* New York: Routledge.

Wong, Bernard P. (2006) *The Chinese in Silicon Valley: Globalization, networks and ethnic identity.* New York: Rowman & Littlefield.

Xiang, B. and W. Shen (2009) 'International student migration and social stratification in China', WP-09-70, Centre on Migration, Policy and Society, University of Oxford.

Ye, L. (2009) 'Initiating actions in VC market Board', *IT CEO & CIO China*, Vol. 272, www.ceocio.com.cn/12/93/522/565/44461.html.

Yeung, H. (2000) 'Organizing "the firm" in industrial geography I: networks, institutions and regional development', *Progress in Human Geography*, 24(2): 301–315.

ZGC Administrative Commission (2004) Touzi Zhongguancun: 'Huhui Xianxiang' yantaohui shilu (Investment in Zhongguancun – Huhui phenomenon) discussion panel transcript. 2004 [cited 7 July 2005]. Available from http://gov.finance.sina.com.cn/zsyz/2004-07-20/16782.html.

Zhang, J. (2006) 'Market transition, state connections and Internet geography in China', *China Review*, 6(1), 93–124.

Zhou, Y. (2008a) *The Inside Story of China's High-tech Industry: Making Silicon Valley in Beijing.* Lanham, MA: Rowman & Littlefield.

Zhou, Y. (2008b) 'Synchronizing export orientation with import substitution: creating competitive indigenous high-tech Companies in China', *World Development*, 36 (11), 2353–2370.

Zhou, Yu and Yenfen Tseng (2001) 'Regrounding the "ungrounded empires": localization as the geographical catalyst for transnationalism', *Global Network*, 1(2): 131–154.

Zweig, D. and Chen, C. (1995) *China's Brain Drain to the United States: View of overseas Chinese students and scholars in the 1990s.* Edited by J. Sandstrom. Berkeley, CA: Institute of East Asia Studies.

6 Spatial clustering and organizational dynamics of trans-border production networks

A case study of Taiwanese IT companies in the Greater Suzhou region, China*

You-Ren Yang and Chu-Joe Hsia

Transborder investment by Taiwanese IT companies has driven the development of a new industrial space in the Greater Suzhou region (GSR) of China over the last ten years. In this chapter we aim to explore some characteristics of this expansion from the perspective of the organizational dynamics of global production networks. We found that foreign brand-name companies have played a key role in propelling this wave of investment in the GSR by Taiwanese IT companies. At the same time, their business strategies have influenced the mechanisms governing these Taiwanese companies' supply chains and have forged the dynamics of spatial agglomeration. We argue that the transborder extension of the production networks is interwoven with the exercise of power between enterprise organizations. Our findings suggest that interdependence among firms in close geographical proximity is inseparable from the asymmetrical power relations embodied in global commodity chains; a point emphasized by economic geographers as the main reason for transborder production shifts that result in the formation of new industrial spaces in developing countries. However, if these production networks can respond collectively to such a strict environment through instituting suitable organizational governance, then their competitive advantage will be enhanced, while also benefiting the host region's development through localization.

Introduction

Since the 1990s Taiwan has been recognized as one of the most important exporters of IT-related hardware in the world. However, the regional division of labor in the Taiwanese IT manufacturing sector has changed significantly since 2000. Taiwan's IT manufacturing total output value in 2000 was less than 50 percent of world output. By 2002 Taiwan's IT manufacturing output value had decreased to 36.3 percent of the world output, and, in contrast, China's portion has increased to 46.9 percent (Ministry of Economic Affairs 2004). The fact that China has surpassed Taiwan in the total output value of the IT industry seems like the latest trend, and this in turn also signifies China has replaced Taiwan as the most important global IT hardware production base.

In the mid 1990s Taiwanese IT manufacturers began to establish a new industrial cluster in the Yangtze River Delta of east-central China, especially in the cities of Suzhou, Kunshan, and Wujiang. The commuting intervals between these areas are less than one hour, and supply chains have been gradually built up. This area is known as the Greater Suzhou region (GSR) (Figure 6.1). It may be regarded as a region that is rising in importance as the result of an outward-oriented economic development policy. The important development zones include the Suzhou–Singaporean Industrial Park, the Suzhou New District, and the Kunshan and Wujiang Economic Development Area. In addition to city-level and county-level governments concentrating on enticing foreign capital by providing cheap land and infrastructure services,

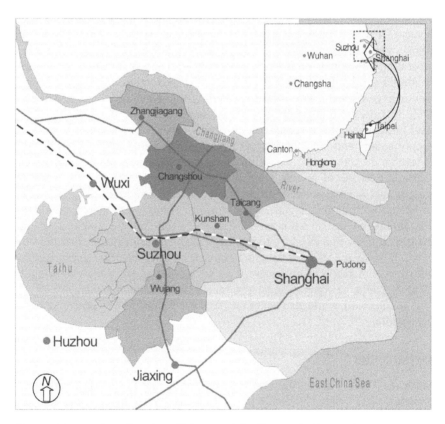

Figure 6.1 Location of northern Taiwan and the Greater Suzhou region

many town-level governments have been quick to enter this race for foreign investment too. Moreover, the most important product of Taiwan's IT industry, the notebook computer, has also become the principal product in this wave of transplantation. After 2002 the proportion of notebooks made in China surpassed that made in Taiwan, greatly enhancing the output value of China's IT industry.

The formation of this IT cluster in the GSR raised some interesting questions. For example, Wei (2002) argued that the orthodox Sunan model centered on the development of township and village enterprises (TVEs) has become inadequate to account for the recent development and restructuring in Kunshan: its spatial development was a complicated process incorporating the roles of state, local development conditions, and foreign investment. Building on this idea, we attempt to investigate some characteristics of the GSR derived from transborder investment over the last ten years, as well as to propose an explanation for the formation of such a cluster.

Essentially in this chapter we echo Dicken and Thrift's (1992) argument that studying the organizational behavior of enterprises is relevant for the study of geographical industrialization. We take the spatial agglomeration of IT companies in the GSR as a given, and attempt to propose an explanation based on the interorganizational dynamics of global production networks, especially the dynamic relations among Taiwanese IT-system manufacturers, their major clients (large MNCs), and component suppliers. In other words, the central object of this paper is to investigate "network embeddedness" (Henderson *et al.,* 2002) in the process of the geographical extension of production networks, and its implications for geographical configuration.

Methodologically, the empirical data supporting this study were collected through firm-level surveys and face-to-face interviews with Taiwanese IT manufacturers and their component suppliers located in the GSR, in the period from March to December 2002. We visited twenty-eight system manufacturers who were producing notebook PCs, desktop PCs, LCD monitors, mother-boards, personal digital assistants (PDAs), scanners and digital cameras, as well as twenty-seven component suppliers that were producing printed circuit boards, passive components, casings, keyboards, cable connectors and other electronic materials. The total number of employees of the sampled companies exceeded 90,000. These sampled companies were carefully and systematically selected, as the first author of this paper is a consultant of COMPUTEX TAIPEI (the world's second largest IT exhibition) and another exhibition held by the Taipei Computer Association (TCA) in Suzhou, eMEX. In other words, these sample companies are highly influential and credible. For example, ten of the top-twelve system manufacturers, occupying over 60 percent of the total PC-related industrial output value in Taiwan, were included. These companies are Asustek, Benq, Compal, Wistron, Quanta, Inventec, Foxconn, FIC, Arima and Microstar. The component suppliers we visited were also important companies in their respective product categories, such as Delta, Yageo, Darfon, Catcher, Gold Circuit Electronics, Ji-Haw, Sumida and Ralec. Furthermore, we interviewed staff at sixteen branding companies at the international procurement offices (IPOs) in Taipei, who were in charge of outsourcing business from May to August 2004; these IPOs include DELL, HP, IBM, Toshiba, Fujitsu, Hitachi and IngramMicro. The people interviewed included managers of the purchasing, marketing, manufacturing and quality-control departments, as well as factory directors, vice general managers and general managers. In addition to oral interviews, the interviewees were also asked to answer a questionnaire designed for this paper. In this fieldwork, our roles were consultants of eMEX, the largest IT exhibition in China, held by the TCA and the Suzhou city government. Through organizing seminars, forums, and exhibitions and sourcing services, we built solid partnerships with these interviewees.

In the second section we critically review hypotheses that explain the industrial cluster, and elaborate on our analytical thesis, which highlights the power relations within global production networks. In the third section we explore the influence that the business strategies of brand-name buyers have on the spatial behavior of Taiwanese IT companies. In the fourth section we analyze some characteristics of the IT cluster in the GSR. Finally, in the fifth section we investigate the governance mechanism of local industrial clusters. By analyzing the formation of these governance mechanisms we further explore the economic and geographical meanings of local agglomeration of global production networks and the implications these have for the development of the regional development.

Organizational mechanisms behind the industrial cluster: the resurgence of power relations

The starting point of this section is to expound on the dynamic relationship between industrial organizations and geographical configurations (Dicken and Thrift 1992; Markusen 1996; Sabel 1989; Storper and Scott 1992). For example, the theory of industrial districts is concerned with the phenomenon of industrial clusters from the perspective of the dynamics of industrial organization. The major characteristics of industrial districts are the cooperation of specialized local companies and socio-cultural elements that support interfirm cooperation. Furthermore, researchers at the California School of External Economy have pointed out that the dynamics of spatial agglomeration are derived from a reduction in transaction costs. In order to reduce risks and enhance competitiveness firms adopt specialization strategies and vertical disintegration, thus resulting in frequent interfirm interactions that are more complex and unpredictable. Mutual trust plays an important role in these interactions, as it can reduce transaction costs in the absence of temporary contracts (Scott 1993; Storper 1997).

However, we thought that not all industrial clusters are "Marshallian" nodes (Amin and Thrift 1992). The approaches mentioned above focus mainly on interfirm cooperation and organizational networks internal to the industrial agglomeration. The perspective of global commodity chains greatly differs from interfirm networks, requiring focus on linkages external to the industrial agglomeration (Gereffi and Korzeniewicz 1994; Hopkins and Wallerstein 1986). Thus, the theory of global commodity chains influenced us in two dimensions. First, this theory proposes that in addition to the element of interfirm interdependence, the exercise of power relations is also an aspect of global production networks. Second, it argues that characteristics of leading companies, which are driving the commodity chains as well as governance mechanisms, will influence development of the territory in which the commodity chains are embedded (Gereffi 1999; Bair and Gereffi 2001).

Although many scholars have noted the significance of transborder investments for regional development (Hardy 1998; Pavlinek and Smith 1998; Rutherford 2000), few have paid enough attention to the organizational dynamics of the transplantation process. In this paper we define the term "governance mechanism" as the rules and conventions of coordination and interactions between different economic organizations in the organizational network. For example, Powell (1990) distinguished modes of interaction between economic organizations into three different prototypes: markets, hierarchies and networks. The basic operational logics of these three prototypes are all different. Distinguishing the three prototypes of governance of economic organizations is helpful for investigating the organizational relations within transborder production networks. We suggest that exploring the way the governance mechanisms of commodity chains are transformed in the process of transborder investment can illuminate the relationship between industrial organizations and geographical configurations. But first we have to define "networks".

According to Powell (1990), the first definition of a network is the mode of economic governance, as mentioned above. The second definition of a network is a configuration of organizations, such as Thorelli's (1986) concept of several nodes and links among economic actors. In this paper we refer to the second definition as "network structure". We perceived the governance mechanism of the network structure to be complex, thus the way the governance of the production network was transformed during its geographical extension is our major concern, particularly the dynamic relationship between the power structure and the network.

The contribution of the social-network approach to organizational studies is that it reveals how the governance mode of the network facilitates the efficiency of interorganization transactions and how trust-based interactions enhance the survival of organizations (Gulati 1996; Uzzi 1997). However, we found that discussions of the effect of power relations within organizations upon networking interactions are still limited to the sphere of economic sociology, and few are suitable for exploring transborder production networks, for which the dimension of "power at a distance" is relevant (Dicken *et al.* 2001). For example, the resource dependency approach (Pfeffer and Salancik 1978) and exchange-network studies (Skvoretz and Zhang 1997; Walker *et al.* 2000) deal mainly with dual-organization relations. Few of those studies explored the ways that power is exercised beyond single relations of its extension through industrial networks.

The global-commodity-chain perspective is an exception (Gereffi and Korzeniewicz 1994; Gereffi *et al.* 2005). However, this perspective tends to highlight that asymmetrical power is exerted by leading firms in commodity chains. We think that this concept of power inscribed on the major agents is only one type of power influencing the organizational behavior of production networks. We find that Allen's (1997) discussion of the concept of "collective" power may be helpful, especially his emphasis on the way resources are mobilized producing certain outcomes. Following this argument we propose the idea of power as "the ability of an organization to reflexively and collectively respond to changes faced by actors in the network and thus enhance the resources they could access." In this view the concept of "dominance," emphasizing the asymmetrical nature of the relationship between two parties, is only one type of power. The spatial reach of this commanding power is limited, as more effective organizations may generate other types of power which are more collective, diffuse, and less coercive in their impact, achieving far-reaching goals in complex environments. Thus we distinguish between two dimensions of power relevant to the governance of production networks. The first one is "systemic power" inherent in the network structure, inscribed to brand-name "giant" buyers who play a leading role in the market channels. The second dimension is "networked power," which is related to the collective dynamics in the network structure that unfold through instituting new rules and conventions for transactions, as well as by forming new organizational linkages and governance patterns (that are competitive according to changes in the broader environment), enhancing the competence of the actors in the network structure.

We propose that the geographical extension of production network is interwoven with the exercise of power among enterprise organizations, manifested in the colliding of "systemic power" and "networked power," which to a certain degree influences the governance of production networks. Using such an analytical framework we attempt to investigate the way power is exercised during the process of the geographical extension of production networks, and explore its influence on the characteristics of the GSR. These aspects, we believe, are significant for the study of industrial clusters.

Influence of brand-name buyers' strategies on the spatial behavior of Taiwanese IT companies

In respect to "systemic power" in the global IT production networks, the strategies of major-brand-name companies are relevant. Since the 1990s, in response to severe competition, Compaq initiated the trend to outsource, and other branding companies followed this strategy. The business model of OEM/ ODM (original equipment manufacturing/own designing and manufacturing) thus flourished. Accompanying this strategy, the branding companies also launched the production models of produce to order (PTO), build to order (BTO), and configure to order (CTO). The essence of the PTO model is that OEM/ODM partners set up fore factories in low-cost locations that produce the "bare-bones" system with the motherboard, power supply and floppy drive in the casing. After they receive an order they assemble the bare-bone components with other key components in their rear assembly factories near the potential market. This pattern has gradually been transformed to BTO and CTO models (Figure 6.2). The BTO model refers to the way that system manufacturers provide particular components and modules according to the possible demands of the final customers, and the CTO model means that system manufacturers provide all possible assemblage of components and completely configure them according to the demands of the final customers.

Strategies for adopting the BTO/CTO model from the perspective of the brand- name companies are (1) to glean diversified demands; and (2) to avoid the risk of high-valued inventories by outsourcing some outer businesses (such as manufacturing). Except for Toshiba, Fujitsu-Siemens and Sony, the proportion of outsourcing by most of the top-ten global notebook brand-name companies is very high (Table 6.1).

Outsourcing contracts from foreign IT brand-name companies has become an important business for Taiwanese system manufacturers who lack the marketing channels to reach end customers, and business models of OEM and ODM emerged in system products in the mid-1990s. The operation of these models, from the perspective of Taiwanese system manufacturers, is illustrated in Figure 6.3.

In this chapter, we deal mainly with the process after an RFQ (request for quote). Basically RFQ refers to outsourcing contracts between brand-name buyers and system manufacturers. An RFQ serves two major functions. The

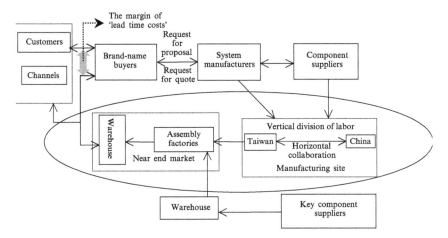

Figure 6.2 Illustration of the global logistics model of build to order/configure to order

Table 6.1 Outsourcing proportion of the top-ten global notebook brand-name companies in 2003

Company	Percentage of outsourcing	Taiwanese OEM/ODM[a] manufacturers
HP	90	Inventec, Arima, Quanta
Dell	90	Quanta, Compal, Wistron
Toshiba	15	Compal, Inventec
IBM	90	Wistron, Quanta
Fujitsu-Siemens	15	Quanta, Compal, Wistron
acer	100	Quanta, Compal, Wistron
NEC	80	Arima, FIC, Wistron, Mitac
Sony	20	Quanta, ASUS
Apple	100	Quanta, Elitegroup

Source: The ITIS project of the National Bureau of Economic Development in Taiwan (2004).

Note: a OEM/ODM – original equipment manufacturing/own design and manufacturing.

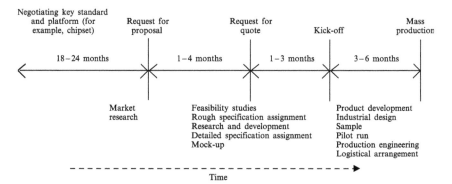

Figure 6.3 The process of the original equipment manufacturing/own design and manufacturing business in the IT industry

first is the consignment of specifications of key features and functions of the product; the second is to define terms on timing, quantity, quality and price of the outsourcing business. During RFP (request for proposal), the initial specifications of the product are defined, which include the whole system specification. Taiwanese system manufacturers then carry out a basic system framework in response to clients' demands, and propose this back to the clients. In the initial process, both brand-name buyers and system manufacturers try to search for potential cooperators, and through a certain process of qualification screening conducted by the brand-name buyers, some system manufacturers may be included in the AVLs (approval lists). Afterwards, the RFQ is released to companies on the AVL, and a series process of bidding begins. Those companies that receive the contracts then start the subsequent processes of product development, industrial design and so on, followed by mass production.

The process of RFP/RFQ has the same purpose as that pursued by the BTO/CTO model. However, one main obstacle to the entire system is the presence of lead time. Lead time refers to the time needed for a firm to prepare materials, produce a product and deliver it. We propose a concept of "lead-time cost" to signify the stock cost derived from the time lag between the production end – including preparation of components and materials that are time-variant in their values – and the marketing end (see Figure 6.3).

Empirically, the lead-time costs are inherent in the production models of OEM/ODM, as a major characteristic of these models is "producing to forecasts." The manufacturers have to arrange their logistics according to the future-market forecasts of brand-name customers, but inaccuracy always exists, as a result of uncertainty in the downstream market. Theoretically, the lead-time cost indicates limitation in the flexibility of the production mode to respond to the fluctuation in downstream market, as the components that need to be gathered for production have their own material values, and it is impossible to release these values, which become a burden on the suppliers, through instantaneous market exchange. Smoothing the production process requires temporal–spatial strategies to compress lead-time cost, otherwise the lead-time cost will increase to such a degree that it might disrupt the whole production system. Thus, determining how to diminish lead-time costs has become a very important issue, and this requires substantial coordination in the supply chains. In contrast to orthodox economists' views of cost in terms of pure market architecture, we try to illustrate our contention that considerable bargaining occurs in such a coordinating process. The way lead-time costs are defined and shared in transactions reflects the power structure of global production networks.

Our fieldwork has shown that foreign brand-name companies are utilizing their "systemic power" to negotiate with their OEM/ODM partners. This process unfolds in their predominant roles instituting the RFQ with Taiwanese system manufacturers, which demands that these OEM/ODM companies shorten lead times by all means in order to reduce their stock costs. In other words, when they promote such operation models as "global logistics" and institute new transaction rules, brand-name buyers have transferred the risks inherent in lead time to Taiwanese system manufacturers. According to the model of global logistics, it appears that the cooperation between Taiwanese system manufacturers and foreign brand-name buyers stretches from manufacturing to global delivery and global services, but the costs and risks for Taiwanese system manufacturers increase at the same time. The implication of engaging in global services (after-sale services) is that the repair costs of products are borne by the OEM/ODM partners (a so-called penalty). As the purpose of global delivery is to supply the market just in time, system manufacturers have to set up warehouses or assembly factories near the final markets. In other words, Taiwanese OEM/ODM partners have to absorb the stocking costs of components and products.

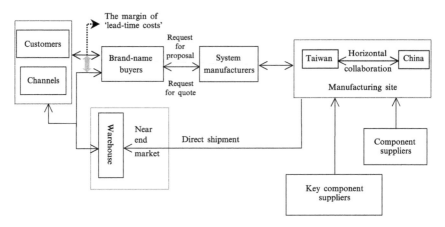

Figure 6.4 Illustration of global logistics model of Taiwan direct shipment/China
         direct shipment

In order to respond to the customers' demands and shorten delivery as well
as lead times, Taiwanese system manufacturers have transformed their global
logistics model. Taking notebook computers as an example, Taiwanese
notebook manufacturers now apply a "Taiwan direct shipment" model of
logistics, or "China direct shipment." On the basis of integrated and localized
supply chains, these models adopt ways of pinpointing direct shipments by
airline, which is suitable for high-value, low-volume products. Compared with
the BTO/CTO models mentioned above, according to these models, system
manufacturers have to set up only one inventory center (a hub) at the manufacturing base; they do not have to set up other rear assembly factories near
the market. This way inventory risks can be reduced. For example, Inventec
closed its assembly factories in Europe and adopted the China direct shipment
model. As Figure 5.4 shows, the margin of lead-time costs is compressed in
the new model.

Two interrelated conclusions may be drawn at the end of this section. First,
the logistics issue is very important in the geographical expansion of production
networks, especially with regard to effectively diminishing lead-time costs.
Second, we propose that under the new global logistics model adopted by
Taiwanese system manufacturers, the GSR, far from being the site of rear
assembly, is an important manufacturing base for Taiwanese IT companies.

Analysis of the spatial agglomeration of Taiwanese
IT manufacturers in the GSR from an organizational
perspective

To further address characteristics of the GSR from the perspective of
interorganizational dynamics, we focus our investigation in four directions.

Retention of the OEM/ODM models

First of all we would like to examine whether Taiwanese IT system manufacturers transformed their business models from OEM/ODM to OBM during the process of recent transborder investments in the GSR. In this business model, OBM – own branding and manufacturing – companies establish their own brand name and engage in directly exploiting the customer's end market. We aim to look into the implications of transborder investments that Taiwanese IT manufacturers have made for their position in the network structure of global commodity chains.

Among the twenty-eight system manufacturers we interviewed, only two companies indicated their business models had significantly changed to OBM after their trans- border investment in China. Table 6.2 shows that fourteen companies chose to develop their own-brand names, yet these companies had adopted such a strategy way before their transborder investments in China. However, another fourteen system manufacturers are set to pursue the OEM/ODM models. They have not developed a strategy of creating their own marketing channels in China. Therefore, we can say that most Taiwanese IT system manufacturers still retain the OEM/ODM business model in their recent transborder investments in China.

One implication of retaining the OEM/ODM model is that the outsourcing relations between large MNC clients and Taiwanese IT system manufacturers are of essential concern during recent transborder investments in the GSR. Our survey results showed that "client demands" was the leading reason for transborder investments made by Taiwanese IT system manufacturers, and what really mattered is keeping "costs down." Although our survey results also showed that "exploiting the Chinese market" was the second major reason for transborder investment, in reality few companies have been able to easily enter the Chinese market so far. Outsourcing orders from brand-name multinational corporations (MNCs) are still the primary business of Taiwanese IT system manufacturers who make transborder investments.

Table 6.2 Spatial division of labor of twenty-eight Taiwanese IT system manufacturers (units are number of firms, unless otherwise specified)

	Northern Taiwan	*Greater Suzhou area*	*Existent*	*Non-existent*
Brand name			14	14
Marketing/sales	28	12		
Research and development	28	15		
Purchasing (%)	30.6	69.4		
Pilot run	22	28		
Mass production	16	28		
Global delivery			28	
Global services			26	2

Source: Calculated from firm-level surveys for this study.

Under such a structure, the element of "systemic power" derives from collaborative relations with outsourcing businesses and is manifested by large MNC clients manipulating price competition to demand their OEM/ODM partners engage in transborder investments in China as a way to lower costs. The notebook PC industry is a perfect illustration. Owing to the fact that Taiwanese notebook manufacturers have expanded their investments in China resulting in oversupply of the market, the bargaining power of large MNC clients has increased.

The employment of external supply chains

The next issue is how Taiwanese companies respond to brand-name buyers' strategy of fostering price competition. Among the twenty-eight system manufacturers we interviewed, nineteen system companies have not chosen to increase the extent of their internal production. In this sense, utilizing external production networks is still an important strategy for Taiwanese IT system manufacturers engaged in recent trans- border investments in China. Another nine had increased the degree of internalization of certain work procedures or the production of some materials; however, the increase in the degree of internalization is not much. According to our survey, the average was about 10 percent.

Moreover, our survey results show that for component suppliers, "following the decision of system manufacturers" is the most significant reason they gave for transplanting to the GSR. For system manufacturers, "the integrity of local suppliers" was not really an important reason for them to choose the GSR as the location for transplanting, and neither was the reason of "direct command of foreign buyers." This indicates that Taiwanese system manufacturers have considerable autonomy in choosing the location to which they transplant. In other words, these companies are able to create "locational capacity" through the shepherding of those of their component suppliers engaged in mutual transborder investment (Storper and Walker 1989).

The strategy of employing external supply chains resulted in a geographical configuration of spatial agglomeration of system manufacturers and component suppliers in the GSR. Although its logic still requires further investigation, we found this spatial-organizational strategy beneficial for frequent coordination regarding unforeseeable problems in the production process. As one desktop manufacturing director put it:

> If there is a problem, you just have to make a phone call, and they will arrive in five minutes. After working together through the night, the problem is solved on time. If your vendor is in Taiwan, communication can be a big problem. Also, refinement of the mold and shipping take at least three or four days; after custom clearances, a week has passed already [translated from Chinese].

In addition, it seems that, even though the frequent coordination of upstream and downstream firms located nearby is based to some extent on trust relations derived from previous transactions and social ties, it is not the only mechanism of interorganization governance. As a desktop manufacturing director put it, "We transplanted here, hoping our [component] suppliers would follow, giving us more choices. Take the floppy as an example: we now have five or six sources, and with each supplier's quality being almost the same, costs become a major issue" (translated from Chinese).

In other words, the system manufacturers also apply a "market" governance mode as discussed below.

The localization of supply chains

Third, we elaborated on a method to investigate general circumstances of supply-chain localization and decentralization of purchasing power to local branches. Data was collected through firm-level surveys and corporate interviews of twenty-eight system manufacturers, including nine for notebooks PCs, two for desktop PCs, four for motherboards, seven for LCD monitors, two for PDAs, two for scanners, and two for digital cameras. These companies were asked to rate the following nine alternatives from 0 to 10 according to the proportion of the "value" of their product components in each mode. Those answering the questionnaire directed the procurement business of their companies, and included procurement managers, factor directors, vice general managers and general managers. Besides, the scores in each alternative reflected the proportion of procurement values, so these scores could be considered as continuous variables.

X_1: The headquarters take charge of sourcing materials that are imported from Taiwan.

X_2: The headquarters take charge of sourcing materials that are imported from areas outside Taiwan and China.

X_3: The headquarters take charge of sourcing materials that are produced in China.

X_4: The local branch takes charge of sourcing materials that are imported from Taiwan.

X_5: The local branch takes charge of sourcing materials that are imported from areas outside Taiwan and China.

X_6: The local branch takes charge of sourcing materials that are from former foreign vendors that have transplanted to the GSR.

X_7: The local branch takes charge of sourcing materials that are from former Taiwanese vendors that have transplanted to the GSR.

X_8: The local branch takes charge of sourcing materials, which are from new Taiwanese vendors that have transplanted to the GSE and with whom they have never had business with in Taiwan.

X_9: The local branch takes charge of sourcing materials from new mainland vendors located in the GSR.

We calculated the relative weight as:

$$W_i = \frac{X_i}{\sum\limits_{i=1}^{9} X_i}$$

We then defined the related indices as follows:

Localization of the supply chain index (*L*-index) $= W_3 + W_6 + W_7 + W_8 + W_9.$

The *L*-index indicates the proportion of a component's value of products procured in the GSR.

Purchasing power decentralization index (*P*-index) $= W_4 + W_5 + W_6 + W_7 + W_8 + W_9.$

The *P*-index indicates the proportion of a component's value of products sourced by branches in the GSR.

Opening of the supply chain index (*O*-index) $= W_8 + W_9.$

The *O*-index indicates the proportion of a component's value of products sourced from new vendors in the GSR.

Dependence of components on Taiwan index (*D*-index) $= W_1 + W_4.$

The *D*-index indicates the proportion of a component (by component value) consisting of products imported from Taiwan.

Mainland companies adoption index *(M*-index) $= W_9.$

The *M*-index indicates the proportion of a component (by component value) which has been sourced from mainland Chinese companies in the GSR.

Results are shown in Table 6.3. We found that the average of the *L*-index was 0.556; this shows that for these seven products, more than half of their components can be sourced in the GSR. Moreover, the average of the *P*-index of these twenty-eight companies was 0.694; this indicates besides certain key components that are the purview of the Taiwan headquarters, local branches are gradually taking charge of other components.

Decentralization of purchasing power also reflects that an increasing number of system manufacturers are applying a method of processing imported materials (in Chinese: *jinliao jiagong*), rather than processing supplied materials (in Chinese: *lailiao jiagong*). Basically, processing supplied materials means customers assign all materials to manufacturing partners, and a batch of goods is sent into the factory, then the entire batch goes out with the product.

Table 6.3 Related indices of Taiwanese IT manufacturers' supply chains in the Greater Suzhou region

Company/product	L-index	P-index	O-index	D-index	M-index
Average of the sample system manufacturers	0.556	0.694	0.191	0.183	0.066
Coefficient of variation of the sample system manufacturers	0.239	0.222	0.497	0.523	0.741
Average of notebook companies	0.53	0.62	0.13	0.17	0.03
Average of LCD companies	0.58	0.70	0.20	0.15	0.05
Average of motherboard companies	0.53	0.71	0.23	0.26	0.11

This pattern is very common in the Pearl River Delta region of southern China, and it usually means headquarters in Taiwan take full charge of the purchase of materials. Nevertheless, the pattern of processing imported materials is more common in the GSR. The difference is that materials can nimbly be switched among different production projects, and materials purchased for specific projects can be used for other projects. In other words, the pattern of processing supplied materials enhances the purchasing power and scope of maneuvering by local branches.

Furthermore, in terms of the production process of design, purchasing, manufacturing and sales, decentralization of purchasing power is important to develop the research and development (R&D) capacities of local branches. If a product is designed and produced by a local branch, the purchasing of related components is usually the responsibility of the local branch. This indicates that as more products are designed in the GSR, a greater proportion of purchase activities will become the responsibility of local branches. This way, the extent of the decentralization of purchasing power partially reflects a progression of the capacity for local branches to carry out R&D.

Horizontal collaboration between northern Taiwan and the GSR

Last, we would like to investigate the tendency for territorialization of trans-border production networks in the GSR from the perspective of spatial division of labor between Northern Taiwan and the GSR. The term "Northern Taiwan" refers to the "Hsinchu–Taipei corridor" (Hsu and Saxenian 2000; Hsu 2005), the most important IT cluster in Taiwan, in which the commuting interval between the cities is less than one hour.

From the point of value chain, at the stage of R&D, fifteen branches of the twenty- eight system manufacturers we interviewed have R&D functions. As for the fifteen system manufacturers that have set up their own R&D departments in the GSR, the division of labor of R&D activities between local branches and home companies can be generalized into three patterns. The first pattern is that the R&D departments of local branches do not work independently; they are just auxiliary to their counterparts in Taiwan. The second pattern is that the practices of R&D departments are allocated according to the technological level of products: local branches concentrate on modifications and development of existing, low-end products, whereas departments in Taiwan work on the high-end products. In the third pattern, R&D departments of local branches are capable of independently developing new products in parallel to departments in Taiwan. We found that a trend toward the third model is growing and is becoming the goal of most system manufacturers.

As for the stage of key-component purchases, although local branches have gradually taken charge of the purchase of most components, it seems that the headquarters still dominate purchasing power of certain key components. These key components (such as DRAM and CPUs) are usually characterized by high value fluctuations and high price fluctuations, and a specific strategy of the "initial purchase" is required. This type of purchase is similar to a futures transaction, and the requirement is for high sensitivity to product trends and market fluctuations. Because the related risks are relatively high, senior purchase managers who are able to obtain the target price, quantity and delivery time, always govern the initial purchase. Moreover, purchasing certain key components also needs to occur in collaboration with the R&D department to accommodate the specifications of modules and products. In this sense, Northern Taiwan has an advantage over the GSR in the initial purchase of key components, because more key component agents, market informants, senior purchase managers and related R&D departments are gathered there.

Finally, with respect to the manufacturing stage, all of the twenty-eight system manufacturers we interviewed have established departments for pilot runs and mass production in the GSR. The yields have surpassed those of Taiwan, and the GSR has become the main mass production base. However, this does not mean branches in the GSR have replaced production functions of Taiwan. Twenty-two and sixteen of these twenty-eight system manufacturers maintain departments for pilot runs and mass production, respectively, in Taiwan. Moreover, new products developed by R&D departments often go through a pilot run in Taiwan, where mass-production departments have the advantages of specialization in high-end products and fast market response.

From the above discussion it is clear that the R&D capacity in the GSR has gradually improved. Moreover, the tendency toward local sourcing is obvious. We also found that Northern Taiwan still retains pilot runs and mass production of some high-end products. Thus it appears that the spatial division of labor and the functional integration between Northern Taiwan and the GSR are being transformed from a vertical division of labor to horizontal collaboration.

Governance mechanisms of transactions in the local industrial cluster

So far we have inspected the influence of the strategies of branding buyers as well as basic characteristics of the GSR IT cluster. Next, we try to combine the organizational dynamics and geographical configuration from the perspective of governance mechanisms and propose an explanation for their interrelations. As we argued above, lead-time costs within the global production network are inevitable and they significantly influence profit margins of related companies. In this section we investigate how companies in production networks transform their governance mechanisms in an attempt to eliminate lead-time costs.

The governance mechanisms for transactions between Taiwanese IT system manufacturers and their component suppliers in GSR have several character-istics. The first characteristic is a structure of "buyer-side zero stock costs." This governance mechanism is derived from the fact that local component suppliers have to deliver goods according to the forecasts from system manu-facturers. Shortening delivery time and forecast accuracy are top priorities, so frequent communication between suppliers and their customers based on spatial proximity is very important. However, as a result of fluctuations in downstream markets and the uncertainty of the transborder logistics of certain key components, system manufacturers' predictions are not always accurate, and component suppliers themselves have to constantly keep an eye on the cost of their stock.

The interfirm governance mechanism of "buyer-side zero stock costs" reflects the pursuit of the "Just in Time" (JIT) strategy by IT system manu-facturers. Basically, for component suppliers, determining whether to engage in JIT is a dilemma between consolidating business relations and absorbing stock costs. Our fieldwork shows that some component suppliers have pushed themselves to become the "hub" for their customers, and have adopted the models of vendor-managed inventory (VMI) and supplier-owned inventory (SOI). These models mean that the suppliers have set up a warehouse inside the customers' factories or located nearby, all the material and components are owned and managed by the suppliers, and these goods are not charged until the customers actually use them. The prerequisite of this strategy is acceptance of customers' demand for "zero stock costs" and the provision of goods based entirely on customers' forecasts; in the meantime, however, suppliers must assume risks associated with fluctuations in the market. This challenges them to upgrade their inventory-management systems. As one general manager of a system manufacturer put it,

> Once upon a time, forecasts imposed the liabilities on those who issued the orders. But now I can say [to a supplier] that I don't want the liability. If you want this order, you have to take the risk. Or I will simply cancel it [translated from Chinese].

Furthermore, many IT system manufacturers located in the GSR have adopted a purchasing strategy of fostering price competition. They introduce more vendors (including companies from Mainland China) into their approval lists and launch price competition among vendors. Moreover, they sometimes weed out some original Taiwanese vendors, who are unable to reduce costs or accept the rules set by the system manufacturers, especially the rule of "buyer-side zero stock costs." The strategy of competitive purchasing is to cooperate with the mechanism of buyer-side zero stock costs. Its purpose is to increase organizational resources by increasing the number of negotiable suppliers in order to diminish the lead time of system manufacturers and avoid the awkward situation of being short of supplies. In our fieldwork we observed that local branches of system manufacturers in the GSR are in charge of such strategy execution; this also illustrates the decentralization tendency of purchasing power within Taiwan system manufacturers.

Accompanying concern about lead-time cost, there are also other mechanisms to facilitate the operation of production networks. Component suppliers must be qualified as candidates in the system companies' AVL through a specific approval system. Applications of IT components are highly related to the characteristics of the products, such as concerns over the issue of safety, and they are not as interchangeable as regular industrial materials. System manufacturers will set up certain specifications for properties of components that their suppliers must follow. Samples are strictly surveyed and tested before transactions proceed, and the more strategic the component, the stricter the approval process.

This governing mechanism, based on the approval system, can be interpreted as a mechanism of "institutional trust" (Shapiro 1987). Basically, IT system manufacturers establish a trust-based relationship with their suppliers through objective appraisals, and do not rely solely on social-characteristic trust based on personal relationships. This type of governance mechanism has two implications. First, it helps develop long-term transaction collaboration. The existing transaction relationship will influence subsequent purchasing behaviors. Second, this kind of approval system, and the related specifications, has certain influences over the suppliers' technological trajectories. It opens up opportunities to joint technology development between suppliers and their customers. From this point of view, the opening of supplier networks in the GSR will facilitate proliferation of localized technology, as suppliers are able to receive diverse knowledge from different customers.

Furthermore, Taiwanese IT system manufacturers still pay much attention to the quality of their component suppliers, and this fact is reflected in the establishment of the system of vendor quality assurance (VQA). The emphasis is on controlling quality during component production at the vendors' facilities. Such a system of quality assurance forms a fourth governance mechanism between system manufacturers and their component suppliers, and is usually a part of the approval system. It can be argued that such a governance mechanism indicates certain elements of cooperation and collaboration between system manufacturers and their component suppliers, and assistance from the VQA departments of the system manufacturers is also one of the sources of technological upgrade.

The fifth transaction governance mechanism between IT system manufacturers and their component suppliers under pressure to cut costs is mutual trust formalized by certain organizational monitoring mechanisms. This can be regarded as a mode of "institutional trust." For example, many component suppliers check the credit conditions of their customers. For customers with low credit (especially companies from Mainland China), cash transactions are required. Yet, for customers with good credit, transactions of a long usance are acceptable. Fieldwork showed that the payment terms Taiwanese system manufacturers offer their component suppliers often are four to five months. Compared with the usual sixty days in Taiwan, the longer payment terms in the GSR reflect the pressure of price competition from the downstream market, and this pressure is passed on to component suppliers step-by-step.

From this discussion it seems that the transaction governance mechanisms between Taiwanese IT system manufacturers and their component suppliers in the GSR are interwoven with hybrid modes of mutual trust, collaboration, hierarchical controls and market competition. Furthermore, it can be argued that price competition and hierarchical control do not completely supplant respect for trust-based relations, which is transformed into institutional trust through certain regulations. Although it seems to be disadvantageous for component suppliers to handle their business under such transaction governance mechanisms, it is apparent that some suppliers are developing reactionary strategies of specialization or becoming the appointed suppliers of brand-name buyers through technological innovations. Furthermore, the business environment is becoming stricter, providing opportunity for component suppliers to upgrade themselves, and this is manifested in management of the shop floor and inventories. In other words, component suppliers are also adjusting their practices under these governance mechanisms.

We argue that Taiwanese system manufacturers are trying to transfer lead-time costs to their upstream component suppliers, and that a set of JIT transaction conventions which is composed of the related interfirm governance mechanisms we described above, is taking shape. Clustering of upstream and downstream IT companies in the GSR can be interpreted as a spatial strategy to pursue the goal of diminishing lead-time costs. Therefore we can examine the influence of brand-name buyers on transaction-governance mechanisms, as well as the dynamics of spatial agglomeration in the GSR's industrial cluster. But from another angle, we can also show how Taiwanese IT companies have collectively responded to the problem of diminishing lead-time costs and enhanced their capability in face of new challenges. In other words system manufacturers are exercising their networking power to absorb lead-time costs with their component suppliers by instituting the complementary governance mechanisms described above.

Conclusion: the formation of the Just in Time cluster

As already discussed, we observed that during this wave of Taiwanese IT production networks' transborder investment in the GSR, business models of OEM/ODM were retained, and external supply chains were employed. We also observed a tendency to localize Taiwanese IT production networks in the GSR, especially increasing procurement and R&D functions there. Combining the spatial-organizational formation of the governance mechanisms of Taiwanese transborder production networks and efficient local custom systems, a highly competitive industrial cluster is beginning to take shape. Currently in the GSR, the time interval between receiving an order to export is compressed to fewer than 120 hours. We refer to this highly efficient and flexible production base as the Just in Time cluster.

Through empirical investigation of the issues surrounding lead-time cost we propose an explanation for the formation of such a cluster and the localization of production networks. This wave of transborder investment by Taiwanese IT companies is driven by the major brand-name-buyers' strategy of fostering price competition, and the process also reinforces the market structure of oversupply. This situation gives foreign brand-name buyers additional "systemic power" to dominate the terms of outsourcing contracts as well as to exploit lead-time costs against their OEM/ODM partners. To respond to such challenges, system manufacturers under the OEM/ODM model have transformed their logistics pattern, and consequently instituted governance mechanisms of "buyer-side zero stock costs" as well as price competition in the supply chains. That is to say, the Taiwanese system manufacturers are strategically reproducing these global power relations with their suppliers in the GSR through the socio-spatial constitution of a set of institutional arrangements to collectively absorb lead-time cost. This organizational dynamic explains the localization and territorial embedding of supply chains to some extent. Moreover, as system manufacturers begin to work with new local Taiwanese vendors, as well as those from Mainland China that can accept the new transaction rules, the trend toward establishment of local production networks will enhance localized technology diffusion. In other words, the Taiwanese IT system companies are performing a bridging/learning function for Mainland China, and this process of exercising "networked power" is relevant to the domination by Taiwanese IT supply chains of the global outsourcing market.

Recently, implications for regional development of the relations between upstream and downstream firms under particular modes of production (for example, JIT) have received much attention in the sphere of economic geography (Mair 1993; Frigant and Lung 2002; Larsson 2002). In this paper we have echoed this theoretical interest and further explored the formation of the localized JIT mode of transaction from the organizational dynamics in the global production networks. This paper indicates that the transaction governance patterns between Taiwanese IT system manufacturers and their component suppliers are interwoven with various modes of trust relations, mutual cooperation, hierarchical controls and market competition. Among these patterns, the most significant one for spatial agglomeration is "buyer-side zero stock costs." Although our fieldwork did not refute the argument of the "California School of Externality" that the dynamics of spatial agglomeration derives from reductions in transaction costs (Scott, 1993), by digging deeper into the issue, we point to the emphasis on governance mechanisms dominated by the buyer's side, and the significant influence of demand for JIT deliveries on the pattern of spatial clustering in the GSR.

On the basis of this case study of the GSR, we reveal the way that systemic power is exercised beyond geographical boundaries and how it has influenced the development of local production networks through the formation of the modes of transaction governance described above. However, this does not mean that the systemic power of brand-name buyers could alone drive the global production networks. Meanwhile, a dynamic of networked power has also emerged, and manifested in the transformation of logistics, interfirm collaboration and institutional trust, through certain regulations in response to a stricter business environment. Thus, echoing the argument that networks are essentially relational processes (Dicken *et al.* 2001), we proposed a perspective that this process is also a dynamic process of power exercising, such as the interplay of systemic power and networked power we have revealed in this study, which may result in hybrid governance patterns in different sociospatial contexts.

Finally, we conclude this paper with three arguments. First, for new industrial spaces in developing countries shaped by transplantation of global production networks, the interdependence characterizing the industrial district's interfirm relationships is by no means separate from the asymmetrical power relations inherent in global commodity chains. On the other hand, and second, it is important to emphasize that, if production networks collectively can respond to strict demands by instituting suitable organizational governance, then the competitive advantage of the production networks will be enhanced, and localization of production networks will also benefit the host region's development. Third, we criticize mainstream economic sociology for its insensitivity to the influence of power relations within organizations upon a network mode of interactions. We argue that distinguishing the network mode of governance from complex and dynamic interorganizational interactions is not enough to understand real-world, sociospatial, economic activities. It is necessary to re-embed these governance patterns back into their broader sociospatial context and re-explore their logic of interaction. We believe this apparently messy suggestion could, actually, enhance our understanding of how global economic activity really works.

Notes

* An earlier version of this chapter was published in Environment and Planning A 2007, volume 39, pages 1346–1363. Reproduced with permission of Pion Ltd, London. www.pion.co.uk and www.envplan.com

References

Allen, J. (1997) "Economies of power and space," in R. Lee and J. Wills (Eds.) *Geographies of Economies*. London: Arnold, pp. 59–70.

Amin, A. and Thrift, N.J. (1992) "Neo-Marshallian nodes in global networks." *International Journal of Urban and Regional Research*, 16: 571–587.

Bair, J. and Gereffi, G. (2001) "Local clusters in global chains: the causes and consequences of export dynamism in Torreon's blue jeans industry." *World Development*, 29: 1885–1903.

Bradach, J.L. and Eccles, R.G. (1989) "Price, authority, and trust: from ideal types to plural forms." *Annual Review of Sociology*, 15: 97–118.

Dicken, P. and Thrift, N. (1992) "The organization of production and the production of organization: why business enterprises matter in the study of geographical industrialization." *Transactions of the Institute of British Geographers*, 17: 279–291.

Dicken P., Kelly, P.F., Olds, K. and Yeung, H.W.C. (2001) "Chains and networks, territories and scales: toward a relational framework for analyzing the global economy." *Global Networks*, 1: 89–112.

Frigant, V. and Lung, Y. (2002) "Geographical proximity and supplying relationships in modular production." *International Journal of Urban and Regional Research*, 26: 742–755.

Gereffi, G. (1999) "International trade and industrial upgrading in the apparel commodity chain." *Journal of International Economics*, 48: 37–70.

Gereffi, G. and Korzeniewicz, M. (Eds.) (1994) *Commodity Chains and Global Capitalism*. New York: Praeger.

Gereffi, G., Humphrey J. and Sturgeon, T. (2005) "The governance of global value chains." *Review of International Political Economy*, 12: 78–104.

Gulati, R. (1996) "Does familiarity breed trust? The implications of repeated ties for contractual choice in alliance."*Academy of Management Journal*, 38: 17–30.

Hardy, J. (1998) "Cathedrals in the desert? Transnationals, corporate strategy and locality inWroclaw." *Regional Studies*, 32: 639–652.

Henderson, J., Dicken, P., Hess, M., Coe, N. and Yeung H.W.C. (2002) "Global production networks and the analysis of economic development." *Review of International Political Economy*, 9: 436–464.

Hopkins, T.K. and Wallerstein, I. (1986) "Commodity chains in the world-economy prior to 1800." *Review*, 10: 157–170.

Hsu, J.Y. (2005) "A site of transnationalism in the `Ungrounded Empire': Taipei as an interface city in the cross-border business networks." *Geoforum*, 36: 654–666.

Hsu, J.Y. and Saxenian, A. (2000) "The limits of *guanxi* capitalism: transnational collaboration between Taiwan and the USA." *Environment and Planning* A, 32: 1991–2005.

Larsson, A. (2002) "The development and regional significance of the automotive industry: suppliers parks in Western Europe." *International Journal of Urban and Regional Research*, 26: 776–784.

Mair, A. (1993) "New growth poles? Just-in-time manufacturing and local economic development strategy." *Regional Studies*, 27: 207–221.

Markusen, A. (1996) "Sticky places in slippery space: a typology of industrial districts." *Economic Geography*, 72: 293–313.

Ministry of Economic Affairs (2004) *Information Industry Yearbook*. Taipei, Taiwan: Ministry of Economic Affairs, ExecutiveYuan, (in Chinese).

Pavlinek, P. and Smith, A. (1998) "Internationalization and embeddedness in East-Central European transition: the contrasting geographies of inward investment in the Czech and Slovak republics." *Regional Studies*, 32: 619–638.

Pfeffer, J. and Salancik, G. (1978) *The External Control of Organizations*. New York: Harper and Row.

Powell, W.W. (1990) "Neither market nor hierarchy: network forms of organization." *Research in Organizational Behavior*, 12: 295–336.

Rutherford, T.D. (2000) "Re-embedding, Japanese investment and the restructuring buyer-supplier relations in the Canadian automotive components industry during the 1990s." *Regional Studies*, 34: 739–751.

Sabel, C.F. (1989) "Flexible specialization and the reemergence of regional economies," in P. Hirst and J. Seitlin (Eds.) *Reversing Industrial Decline? Industrial Structure and Policy in Britain and Her Competitors*. New York: St Martin's Press, pp. 17–70.

Scott, A.J. (1993) *Technopolis: High Technology, Industry and Regional Development in South California*. Berkeley, CA: University of California Press.

Shapiro, S.P. (1987) "The social control of interpersonal trust." *American Journal of Sociology*, 93: 623–658.

Skvoretz, J. and Zhang, P.D. (1997) "Actors' responses to outcomes in exchange networks: the process of power development." *Sociological Perspectives*, 40: 183–197.

Storper, M. (1997) *The Regional World: Territorial Development in a Global Economy*. New York: Guilford Press.

Storper, M. and Scott A.J. (Eds.) (1992) *Pathways to Industrialization and Regional Development*. London: Routledge.

Storper, M. and Walker, R. (1989) *The Capitalist Imperative: Territory, Technology and Industrial Growth*. Oxford: Basil Blackwell.

Thorelli, H.B. (1986) "Networks: between markets and hierarchies." *Strategic Management Journal*, 7: 37–51.

Uzzi, B. (1997)"Social structure and competition in interfirm network: the paradox of embeddedness." *Administrative Science Quarterly*, 42: 35–67.

Walker, H.A., Thye, S.R., Simpson, B., Lovaglia, M.L., Willer, D. and Markovski, B. (2000) "Network exchange theory: recent developments and new directions." *Social Psychology Quarterly*, 63: 324–337.

Wei, Y.D. (2002) "Beyond the Sunan model: trajectory and underlying factors of development in Kunshan, China." *Environment and Planning* A, 34: 1725–1747.

7 The cross-strait economic relationship's impact on development in Taiwan and China

Adversaries and partners across the Taiwan Strait*

Douglas B. Fuller

Introduction

This chapter assesses the impact of trade and investment across the Taiwan Strait on the economic development of Taiwan and China,[1] and finds that the benefits for each side have outweighed the costs thus far. While there have been fears of hollowing out of manufacturing in Taiwan with the opening of trade with China following WTO accession, this chapter argues that Taiwan has adjusted remarkably well to the increasing trade with and investment in China. For the Taiwanese, even for some sectors, such as manufacturing employment, where one might expect severe economic dislocation and adjustment, the effects have been relatively minor. From China's vantage point, there have been charges that foreign investors, including Taiwanese,[2] have come to dominate China's economy, particularly its export sector, even as these foreign investors have brought little actual technology and knowledge to China.[3] This chapter will provide evidence that Taiwan has in fact played a critical role in boosting China's technological development, despite the charges to the contrary. Nonetheless, the gains from integration are not the only story in the cross-strait economic relationship. There were also costs to this increasing integration and disappointments in areas where benefits were expected.

First, the chapter will present the historical development and general statistics of the cross-strait economic relationship. Then, it will examine the economic impacts of integration on Taiwan and China. Finally, the conclusion will consider the sustainability of current trends.

The historical development and current magnitude of cross-strait economic ties

The initial reaction of Taiwan's government to the beginning of reforms in China was to ban completely imports from and exports (even indirect ones) to the People's Republic of China. Over the course of the 1980s, the Taiwanese government gradually loosened restrictions on investment and trade even as China continued to open up its economy to trade and investment. In 1985, indirect exports channeled through Hong Kong were legalized and unofficial Taiwanese tolerance of small-scale investments in mature industries emerged. With the lifting of martial law in 1987, Taiwanese were permitted to visit China for the first time since the end of the civil war in 1949. This new regulation, combined with capital outflows in the context of the appreciation of the New Taiwan dollar following the 1985 Plaza Accords, opened up significant investment and trade opportunities with China. As always, the legalization trailed the actual trade and investment flows so indirect trade, investment and technical cooperation were only permitted in 1989.

With growing investments in China, the Taiwanese government in 1990 decided to increase its supervision of flows of technology and capital to China by requiring all investments over US $1 million to register with the Ministry of Economic Affairs' (MoEA) Investment Commission. Investors were prohibited from investing in certain "valued" industries and a list of prohibited lists was created. In 1996, in the face of continuing investments in China including investments from Taiwan's prized electronics sector, President Li Denghui in 1996 announced his *jieji yongren* ("no haste be patient") policy that introduced new regulatory hurdles for investment in China. Investment was capped at US $50 million and technology sector investments had to be approved on a case-by-case basis, which was simultaneously a liberalizing move (items were moved off the prohibited investments list) and a constraining one in that investments still had to be vetted by the Investment Commission. These regulations established a pattern that would be repeated time and again. In face of growing investment in China, the Taiwanese government would grow alarmed and then try to gain some control over China-bound investment, but due to demands from the business community, the regulations were never strict enough to slow very significantly the cross-strait economic relationship.

This cycle repeated itself once again when Chen Shuibian came to power precisely in 2000 because the sectoral shift of investment (Figure 7.2) worried the government. Whereas in the early years of legal investment a mix of sectors invested in China, in more recent times the electronics industry came to dominate the investment in China. More worrisome for the Taiwanese government was the increasing investment in higher value-added parts of the electronics industry from the late 1990s onward.[4] Even the notebook computer segment began to move production to China despite specific Investment Commission prohibitions against the manufacture of notebooks in China. While these prohibitions were still in force, this author visited a number of major Taiwanese manufacturers' plants in China where notebooks were being produced.[5]

The government was alarmed and yet the business community demanded greater access to investment in China because of competitive pressures pushing Taiwanese manufacturers to make use of China's relatively cheap labor.[6] Chen, after convening a conference with business leaders, announced his *jiji kaifang,*

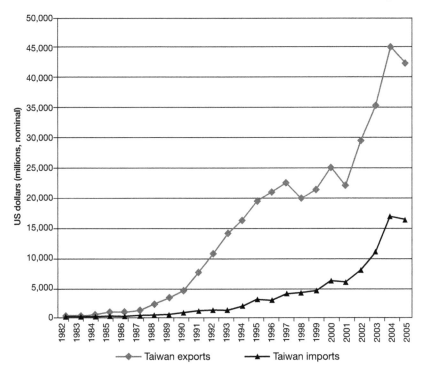

Figure 7.1 China–Taiwan bilateral trade

Source: Mainland Affairs Council, ROC based on statistical data from the People's Republic of China and Taiwan, available at www.mac.gov.tw/big5/statistics/em/ and accessed on February 27, 2006.

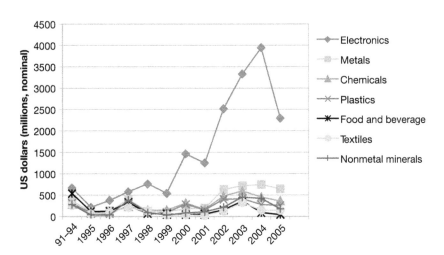

Figure 7.2 Investment by sector

Source: Investment Commission, MoEA, ROC at www.moeaic.gov.tw/ and accessed on February

youxiao guanli ("active opening, effective management") policy toward economic integration in China in August 2001. The liberalization measures announced were substantial: the US $50 million investment cap was scrapped, direct investment was permitted, the bar to require investment approval was raised to US $20 million, the investment cap was lifted to 40 percent of a firm's total worth and the prohibited investments list was reduced. However, some of the measures took a year to implement and it was not clear which prohibited items would be legalized. Conflicts between government and business over the details played out across several sub-sectors of electronics.[7] The end result was the same: partial liberalization with continued restrictions or clarifications of restrictions. This compromise gave the business community some of what it wanted while partially assuaging the government's concerns about hollowing out.

The cycle of increased integration followed by generally ineffective state attempts to manage the cross-strait economic relationship continued in President Chen's second term. At the beginning of 2006, President Chen announced a change in economic policy by scrambling the words of his previous policy. The new policy was *youxiao kaifang, jiji guanli* ("effective opening, active management") and promised a tightening up of actual supervision of Taiwanese investment in China. And yet, when President Chen convened an economic summit between his administration and business leaders in Taiwan, no breakthroughs were made in terms of further regulation as hoped for by Taiwanese independence supporters or further liberalization as pushed for by Taiwanese businessmen. In short, the cross-strait economic policy debate had reached a stalemate.[8]

While the sheer volume of investments and trade demonstrate the increasing importance of China to Taiwan's economy, the investments from Taiwan also have been a large part of China's increasingly large FDI inflows. In nominal terms reported by China's government, Taiwan's is the fifth largest source of FDI in China. However, this data seriously underestimates Taiwan's role for two reasons. First, much of Taiwan's investment has flowed through Hong Kong, which helps to explain why Hong Kong's quite small economy has contributed by far the largest amount of FDI. Second, as Taiwanese investors, especially those investing in items on the prohibited list, came under increasing scrutiny from the Taiwanese government, they began to move their indirect investments through the discreet offshore banking locations in the Caribbean.[9] This movement of Taiwanese funds through the Caribbean also explains why such minor economic powers, such as the Cayman Islands and the British Virgin Islands, have been among the top-ten largest investors in China over the reform period (see Figure 7.3). When one accounts for the Taiwanese FDI to China coming through these other regions, it is likely that Taiwan is actually the second largest source of China's FDI after Hong Kong. Taiwan probably accounts for over 10 percent of China's cumulative US $610 billion in FDI and some estimates place Taiwan's contribution as high as US $150 billion.[10]

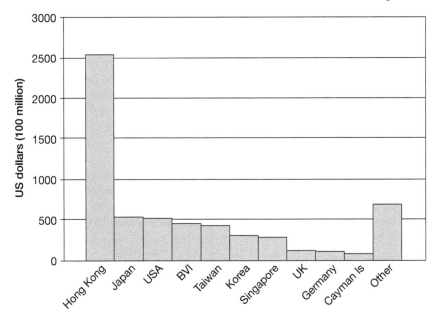

Figure 7.3 China's cumulative realized FDI 1979–October 2005

Source: Mainland Affairs Council, ROC based on People's Republic of China data at www.mac.gov.tw/big5/statistics/em/156/29.pdf and accessed on February 27, 2006.

Even with such large flows of trade and capital, the question remains as to what the impact these flows have on each economy. The next two sections address that question for Taiwan and China, respectively.

The impact of economic integration in Taiwan: triumphs of adjustment

In evaluating Taiwan's economic integration with China, three issues are paramount: the extent of hollowing out of its industrial base and employment, Taiwan's successful industrial adjustment and the disappointment of Taiwanese business in pursuing the "China Dream"[11] of conquering China's potentially huge market.

The absence of hollowing out in Taiwan

Fears of hollowing out of domestic industry are precisely fears of the loss of manufacturing jobs. Thus, one needs to examine industrial employment to look for evidence of hollowing out. What is most striking about the Taiwanese case is how small a negative impact integration with China has had on industrial employment (defined in Taiwanese statistics as manufacturing, mining, utilities and construction employment). For it is precisely in these areas where one would expect cheap low-skilled Chinese labor to displace less-educated

Taiwanese workers through Chinese imports and Taiwanese investment in manufacturing capacity in China. In fact, Taiwanese industrial employment has actually risen slightly in absolute numbers comparing 1991 to 2005 and industry has only experienced a slight decline in overall share in the economy. Even with the increasing employment of guest workers in the industrial sector from 1992 onwards, there has been a less than 1 percent decline in the number of locals employed in industry between 1992 and 2005. Indeed, the only year where more locals were employed in industry than 2005 was 1992. All of this evidence suggests fears of hollowing out of Taiwan's industry and employment have been highly exaggerated.

Separating manufacturing employment out from the broader category of industrial employment, the same pattern of robust employment holds. Manufacturing employment peaked at 2.8 million[12] workers in 1987 well ahead of the shift of manufacturing plants to China. The gentle decline in manufacturing jobs did however coincide with the revaluation of the New Taiwan Dollar, which took place from 1985 to 1987 in the wake of the Plaza Accords. In 2005, Taiwan still had 2.7 million manufacturing jobs, which was higher than any year after 1989. When taking into account the foreign laborers,[13] 2.55 million

Table 7.1 Employment in Taiwan, 1991–2005 (unit: thousands of workers, unless otherwise noted)

Year	Total employment	Foreign total	Local total	Industry	Industry %	Foreign industry	Local industry	Service total	Service %
1991	8439	n/a	n/a	3370	39.93	n/a	n/a	3977	47.13
1992	8632	16	8616	3419	39.61	15.27	3403.73	4148	48.05
1993	8745	98	8647	3418	39.08	90.07	3327.93	4323	49.43
1994	8939	152	8787	3506	39.22	137.54	3368.46	4456	49.86
1995	9045	189	8856	3504	38.74	170.15	3333.85	4587	50.71
1996	9068	237	8831	3399	37.49	205.37	3193.63	4751	52.39
1997	9176	248	8928	3502	38.17	207.75	3294.25	4795	52.26
1998	9289	271	9018	3523	37.92	216.53	3306.47	4944	53.23
1999	9385	295	9090	3492	37.21	219.22	3272.78	5118	54.54
2000	9491	327	9164	3534	37.23	219.48	3314.52	5220	54.99
2001	9383	305	9078	3377	36	190.82	3186.18	5299	56.48
2002	9454	304	9150	3332	35.24	180.34	3151.66	5413	57.25
2003	9573	300	9273	3334	34.83	176.01	3157.99	5543	57.9
2004	9786	314	9472	3446	35.21	179.85	3266.15	5698	58.23
2005	9942	327	9615	3558	35.79	179.84	3378.16	5793	58.27

Source: Council of Labor Affairs, Republic of China at www.cla.gov.tw for the foreign labor employment by sector and Directorate-General of Budget, Accounting and Statistics, Republic of China at www.dgbas.gov.tw for the overall employment by sector. Both websites were accessed on February 27, 2006.

domestic workers were still employed in manufacturing in 2005, higher than any year since 1992. Contrast this with Hong Kong's experience where manufacturing employment collapsed as factories moved to China.[14]

As for overall employment, despite the twenty-fold increase in foreign guest workers between 1992 and 2005, the ability of Taiwan to employ almost 1 million more local workers in 2005 over 1992 (an almost 12 percent increase in numbers of Taiwanese employed) is impressive. Most of the employment increase was in the service sector, but that is to be expected in a maturing economy.

Employment is only part of the story. One also needs to examine trends in income distribution across the population to see if economic integration has led to declining wages for industrial workers despite the overall robust levels of employment. Integration has not been entirely painless for Taiwanese workers despite Taiwan's excellent employment performance. As should be expected when an economy with higher wages integrates with another with generally lower wages, Taiwan has experienced increasing wage inequality in recent years as it integrates more fully with China. As measured by the Gini index (a lower number in the Gini index signifies more equality in income distribution), a widely accepted measure of income inequality,[15] Taiwan's inequality has increased from a low of 27.7 in 1980 to 33.8 in 2005. However, it must be noted that Taiwan's high point of inequality in recent years was in 2002 in the wake of the Internet bubble bursting when Taiwan's Gini index was 34.5. Thus, increasing trade with China cannot be the only culprit in terms of Taiwan's increasing inequality of income distribution. Indeed, the decline in equality started before trade with China did and the recent years of heightened integration have witnessed a relatively stable income distribution. Moreover, Taiwan's Gini index places its level of income inequality roughly in the middle of the advanced economies in recent years. Indeed, despite an incomplete welfare state, Taiwan's inequality is still lower than that of the major neoliberal Anglo-American economies if still higher than that of the social democratic welfare states of Northern Europe.[16]

Overall, Taiwan's purported hollowing out seems more myth than reality. Industrial employment remains high. Income inequality has been relatively stable and moderate when compared to the rest of the advanced industrial economies precisely during the period that more Taiwanese manufacturing has moved to China and Taiwan has opened up its economy as mandated under its WTO entry agreement. This trend of stable income distribution sustained over time combined with continued high levels of industrial employment suggests that Taiwan is neither hollowing out nor simply preserving industrial employment by lowering wages of industrial workers.

Public and private initiative in Taiwan's industrial adjustment

The fact that Taiwan has run a large and generally growing trade surplus with China (see Figure 7.1) helps to explain why Taiwan's industrial employment has not declined in the face of increasing economic integration with China, but it still begs the question of how Taiwan has accomplished this feat of exporting manufactured goods to the "workshop to the world," China. This feat is all the more impressive when one considers that the core of Taiwan's industry, the electronics industry,[17] has seen manufacturing move to China. For example, manufacturing of PCs, the heart of Taiwan's electronic end-products sector, has moved completely out of Taiwan except for pilot production (author interviews).

Taiwan has avoided many of the adverse consequences of manufacturing moving offshore because it has been able to create new competitive advantages in certain segments of electronics and maintain existing competitiveness in one key component, semiconductors. Even in less technology-intensive and more labor-intensive industries, such as auto parts and bicycles, Taiwan has been able to maintain its competitive edge. In technology-intensive sectors, Taiwan's government has played a key role in the process of industrial adjustment so this section will examine both private and public initiatives in this process.

To understand Taiwan's ability to adjust in the key electronics sector, this section will examine three industry segments (semiconductors, AMLCDs i.e. flat panel displays[18] and mobile devices) and the new policy to attract multinationals' (MNCs) research activities to Taiwan. These cases demonstrate that, through a mix of private and public initiatives, Taiwan's electronics sector has been able to shift to new competencies and maintain existing strengths despite the move of computer manufacturing offshore, principally to China.

Since 2000, when two groups of Taiwanese semiconductor engineers announced plans to create foundries (firms that fabricate but do not design their own semiconductor chips) in China, the Taiwanese government has been alarmed by the prospect of China threatening one of the most technology-intensive areas in which Taiwan has developed competitiveness. Indeed, Taiwan has for years dominated the international foundry industry, routinely representing over 70 percent of the global foundry market.[19]

One of the two new foundry start-ups in China, Semiconductor Manu-facturing International Corporation (SMIC), has been quite successful in ramping up production, increasing sales revenue and its market share since production started in 2002.[20] However, SMIC has not threatened the com-manding position of Taiwan's foundry giants, Taiwan Semiconductor (TSMC) and United Microelectronics (UMC). These firms continue to increase their revenues and command imposingly large shares of the global foundry market (see Figure 7.4). Moreover, the global foundry market continues to grow as more and more semiconductor firms outsource their production to foundries. Thus, SMIC's gain has not been TSMC and UMC's loss. Instead, SMIC has displaced the perpetual and distant follower of UMC and TSMC, Singapore's Chartered, as the third largest foundry. Grace, the other Taiwanese-run, China-based foundry, and China's domestic champion, Huahong NEC (HHNEC), are still very small players in the global foundry market.

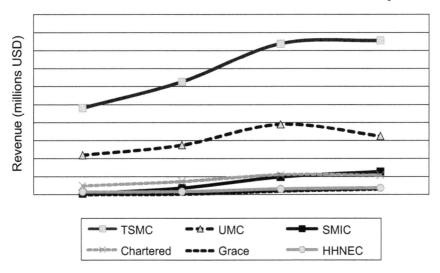

Figure 7.4 Foundry revenue 2002–2005
Source: IC Insights data provided by an interview subject.

Given the skill-intensive demands of semiconductor fabrication and the developed competencies in Taiwan's large engineering community, there has not been much incentive to replicate the rapid shift overseas of Taiwan's computer manufacturing. SMIC appears to have developed a successful model of bringing skilled Taiwanese engineers to China to train locals (see Section 3), but the fact remains that TSMC and UMC each have only one fabrication facility in China. Indeed, when TSMC and UMC have set up fabrication plants overseas, they generally have gone to advanced industrial countries where skilled engineers are located. TSMC has its own plants or joint ventures in Singapore and the US. UMC has its own plants or joint ventures in Japan and Singapore. These facilities have more total capacity than these firms have in China. Furthermore, most of their production capacity remains in Taiwan.

Although the Taiwanese state originally created both TSMC and UMC, the continued competitiveness of Taiwan's semiconductor fabrication has had little to do with government policy beyond preferential tax treatment. On the contrary, the one recent government initiative in semiconductor fabrication technology was undermined and ultimately abandoned because of the refusal of TSMC and UMC to take part.[21] Nevertheless, in moving into new segments of the electronics industry, Taiwan's government has continued to play a critical role. In particular, the quasi-governmental research institute, Industrial Technology Research Institute (ITRI), has continued to diffuse new technologies to industry, which then blossom commercially. ITRI's approach to technological diffusion and upgrading has been to master advanced foreign technologies in its own labs and then diffuse them to industry. This diffusion typically takes one of two paths. ITRI either spin-offs researchers from these labs into new commercial ventures or it transfers the technologies (often along with staff) to existing firms which supported or collaborated on the research. This so-called ITRI model of technological upgrading has been well documented,[22] but its continued effectiveness has been questioned. Fortunately for Taiwan, the cases of AMLCDs and mobile technologies prove that the ITRI model still works.

For AMLCDs, ITRI was less of a major force than has been typical in the past. Most of the Taiwanese AMLCD firms received their technology directly from Japan rather than from ITRI. ITRI did however play an active role in training engineers in AMLCD manufacturing techniques.[23] Consequently, Taiwan grew from being a nonentity in the global display industry in 2000 to become the largest producer of AMLCDs in the world today.[24]

What is interesting about the distribution of this relatively new Taiwanese industry is how quickly production has moved to China. As early as 2001, Taiwanese producers were building back-end LCD module plants in China. However, this distribution of the industry has been to Taiwan's advantage. The back-end module assembly part of the process is the labor-intensive part of the process. The actual making of the liquid crystal display is capital- and skill-intensive and remains in Taiwan. From the perspective of creating high wage employment with the potential of creating technological spillovers, this type of cross-strait distribution of production is just what Taiwan should want.

In mobile technologies, ITRI has led the way in acquiring and transferring mobile technologies, such as cellular phone technology, to local firms by training local engineers in these technologies under its Computer and Communication Research Laboratories (CCL). In fact, many of the computer firms, such as Quanta, Acer and Compal, were able to benefit from ITRI's technology transfer to become major producers of mobile phones.

In contrast to ITRI's success in diffusing IT knowledge to Taiwanese firms, the ITRI research units not connected to IT have been less successful in spurring local innovation. Instead, those mature manufacturing industries that have managed to stay competitive in the face of cross-strait integration, such as bicycle and auto parts manufacturing, have done so with little effective state support.

While the bicycle industry has moved some production of mass-produced bicycles to China, the higher value-added custom bikes are kept in Taiwan. Production of these bicycles relies on a dense network of specialized suppliers co-located in central Taiwan. In essence, the bicycle industry follows the Italian industry district model based on a network of small and medium enterprises (SMEs) with focused competencies and this is much harder to replicate in China. Thus, it is not surprising that much of the industry remains in Taiwan.[25]

After-market auto parts (i.e. replacement parts) have been the driving force behind Taiwan's auto parts success story and have had virtually no government technological help or guidance. In contrast to Taiwan's heavily protected and inefficient auto assembly industry, the after-market auto parts makers are focused on overseas markets. This focus has forced them to be efficient. Unlike auto assemblers, the barriers to achieving technological independence have not been high as these parts are often readily reverse engineered. Yet, Taiwanese manufacturers have still been able to distinguish themselves from Southeast Asian and Chinese auto parts makers relying solely on cheap labor because they have developed skills in electronic data exchange with their key retailers, primarily in the US, to receive, process and track orders.[26] Despite the heavy reliance of Taiwan's domestic assemblers on imported parts and falling protectionist barriers with Taiwan's 2002 entry into the WTO, Taiwan was still able to run a substantial trade surplus in parts because of its competitive after-market auto parts in 2005. Taiwan's surplus was over US $1 billion despite having over US $2.5 billion worth of imports.[27]

Taiwan's most recent economic development plan, the "Challenge 2008" Six-Year Development Plan (2002 to 2007), continued tax breaks for established technology sectors, such as AMLCDs and semiconductors, but it also embarked on policies heretofore unseen in Taiwan. Breaking with historical practice of eschewing tax breaks to lure MNC R&D activities,[28] Taiwan has initiated a new aggressive push to recruit MNCs as well as local firms to establish R&D centers to Taiwan. From virtually no MNC R&D activities in the 1990s, a number of renowned technology firms, such as Intel, Sony and IBM, have established 31 R&D centers even while subsidies for these centers have been kept in check. These trends indicate this policy has been at least moderately successful thus far.[29] This program was heavily influenced by Taiwan's economic bureaucracy in terms of planning as well as execution since the program spanned presidential terms. Thus, even if Chen had lost the 2004 presidential election, the plan would have remained in place.

Taiwan's frustrated China dream

Taiwan's integration with China has not been without its setbacks. First and foremost, like many others, the Taiwanese have been gripped by the "China dream" of capturing a market of over one billion customers. And like most of those seized by this dream, the Taiwanese have often been disappointed.

Unlike many others, the Taiwanese are in some sense more dependent on and possess special advantages for realizing the China dream. Taiwan is more dependent on realizing this dream because Taiwan's home market is quite small. This small home market has inhibited the development of globally competitive Taiwanese brands.[30] Thus, geographic and cultural proximity dictate that China is the logical "home" market of significant size for the Taiwanese to use to develop brands backed scale and scope. The same geographic and cultural proximity also may serve as Taiwan's competitive advantages in utilizing China as its home market. These potential advantages only make realizing the China dream more critical for the Taiwanese as there are not any realistic alternative home markets.

Several Taiwanese brands have been very successful in China. Giant Bicycle is the largest bicycle brand in China. Taiwan's Kang Shifu and President Group dominate the large instant noodles market in China and have extended their reach into other food and beverage products, such as bottled tea. Kang Shifu's success is particularly impressive because this firm was a small-scale supplier of inputs for Taiwan's instant noodle firms before it set up its own instant noodle manufacturing operations in China. In contrast, President Group and Giant have simply extended their prevailing business operations to China.

The success of Taiwan's food and beverage firms in China illustrates the advantage that cultural proximity gives Taiwan in certain product areas. In media as well as food, cultural knowledge is critical. Unfortunately, outside of the food and beverage business, Taiwan's success in culture-intensive industries has been limited because the PRC strictly prohibits majority ownership by non-domestic Chinese firms in its media sector. While Chinese audiences like Taiwanese pop stars, the Taiwanese media companies have little opportunity to take these cultural products and craft them into large media businesses given China's regulations.

The record of Taiwanese brands in China's electronics market is abysmal given the strengths of Taiwan's large electronics industry. While Taiwanese electronics manufacturers grew through manufacturing products for other bands, a number of these firms have had dreams of creating their own brands in the Chinese market. Acer, the one well-known Taiwanese computer brand, has tried to become a major player in China for almost a decade. For all its efforts, the firm still commands only a small slice of the Chinese market. Until 2005, regulations prevented foreign firms from setting up their own retail distribution networks in China,[31] but protectionist measures were only part of the problem. Major international brands, such as IBM, Hewlett Packard and Dell, were able to gain market share in China despite the retail restrictions. However, the position of these firms in the global industry has been quite different from Acer's. They offered higher-end models justified by their globally renowned brands whereas lesser-known Acer had to compete on price with local brands, such as Lenovo and Founder.

In mobile phones, the other IT end-product where Taiwanese have become major international players, the restrictions have been more stifling. China's Ministry of Information Industry (MII) restricted the number of foreign brands that could sell their mobile phones in China until 2005 when MII installed a more open system that allowed over thirty more firms to obtain rights to sell their own brand mobile phones. Originally, only one Taiwanese maker, Dbtel, was able to sell its own brand of phones in China. China's regulations clearly have not shown any favoritism to their Taiwanese compatriots as all the major international brands had licenses to sell in China while the Taiwanese were still kept out. To add insult to injury, Taiwan's Korean rivals, LG and Samsung, enjoyed licenses under the restrictive regime.

Thus far, the dream of the China market has been somewhat of a disappointment for Taiwanese firms that hoped to build a global brand from a major presence in China. The future does not look very promising either. The restrictions in the media appear to remain in place and China's openness to foreign brands means there is not much space to develop those from Taiwan.

True compatriots: how China benefits from cross-strait economic integration

Given the relative size of their economies, China's public debates about the economy are far less concerned about Taiwan than Taiwanese debates are about China. Still, commentary on Taiwanese investment has often been critical. Huang's *Selling China* sees investment from the ethnic Chinese economies, a category including Taiwan, as bringing little technology or new knowledge to China. Taiwanese investors have often been accused of relatively egregious labor practices compared to other foreign investors in China.[32] This section will weigh the evidence of the impact of integration with Taiwan and show that on balance Taiwan has made an overwhelming positive contribution to China's development, especially in the area of technological development.

Given that 34 percent of Taiwan's reported investment in China is in IT[33] and the actual figure is likely to be higher because much of IT investment is officially restricted, examining the impact of Taiwan's IT investments in China is critical. Taiwan's investment has contributed dramatically to China's development because the investment has a significant technology component ignored by some of the critics of Taiwan's FDI, such as Yasheng Huang. This technology can be seen through two sets of data. First, the Taiwanese semiconductor industry is training significant numbers of engineers in China. Second, Taiwanese IT firms are beginning to produce many US patents from China.

Turning to the semiconductor industry, we will look at the design and fabrication parts of the industry as these segments are more technologically intensive than the assembly and packaging process. As more and more firms focus on design and outsource fabrication to foundries, such as TSMC and UMC, the design segment has blossomed. In fact, fabless design houses (i.e. design firms without their own fabrication facilities) in the last twenty years have gone from producing 0.3 percent of global semiconductor revenue to producing 14 percent.[34] The spectacular growth of Taiwanese fabless design firms has made Taiwan into the second largest center of fabless design after the US. Taiwan's share of global fabless revenue was 28 percent in 2004 and had doubled since 1996.[35]

With this strong competitive position in fabless design, one might think Taiwan would not need to expand to China, but the growing demand for design engineers forced Taiwanese fabless firms to look abroad. Except for a few brave pioneers in the late 1990s, the first wave of Taiwanese design firms invested in China in 2000. The year 2000 was critical because Taiwan experienced an Internet boom that lured many engineers away from chip design. The shrinking supply of engineers available to design firms at a reasonable price forced them to explore sources of engineers abroad. In addition to geographic and cultural proximity, China has been producing large numbers of engineers[36] so the Taiwanese firms decided to explore this market.

Based on interviews with 58 design firms[37] in China employing approximately half of China's total design workforce[38], the Taiwanese design firms were extremely active in training local designers. Taiwanese firms trained one-third of the local designers who were trained in actual design skills rather than in reverse engineering. The Taiwanese firms generally reported that local engineering graduates require more training than their Taiwanese peers, but they also found local engineers to have a good basic engineering education so they were highly trainable. At least seven of the top-ten largest Taiwanese design firms have design centers in China. Two others may have centers in China, but Chinese subsidiaries of Taiwanese design firms are often hard to locate given the efforts Taiwanese design firms in China make to hide their identities from the Taiwanese authorities due to continued restrictions on investments in semiconductor design.[39]

In semiconductor fabrication, the established Taiwanese foundries have made only a moderate contribution to training China's engineers because they each have only one factory in China. Instead, experienced Taiwanese chip engineers left these firms to set up new foundries in China. The two most prominent, Grace and SMIC, were founded in 2000 and have become two of the largest semiconductor manufacturers in China. SMIC is now the third largest foundry globally (see Figure 7.2). What SMIC and Grace really have contributed is workforce training because most of the engineers at these firms are local. From 2001 to 2003, SMIC trained 800 local engineers to complement the 400 engineers it brought from Taiwan and elsewhere.[40] In contrast, the largest domestic Chinese firm, Huahong NEC, remains reliant on Japanese engineering expertise.[41]

Table 7.2 Taiwanese design centers in China

Revenue rank among Taiwanese design firms	Name	China design team
1	Mediatek	Yes
2	VIA	Yes
3	Realtek	Yes
4	Sunplus	Yes
5	Novatek	No
6	ALI	Yes
7	Elan	Unknown
8	Elite	Unknown
9	Faraday	Yes
10	Holtek	Yes

Source: Interviews.

In research and development of IT products, the important contribution of Taiwanese firms is also evident. Of the 939 corporate IT US utility patents of MNCs, large Chinese firms and Taiwanese firms originating from China, 689 are from Taiwanese firms, including Grace and SMIC.[42] More importantly, the Taiwanese firms show a much larger share of their patents coming from China than other foreign firms. Among non-Taiwanese foreign firms, only Microsoft can claim to have even 1 percent of its US utility patents originating from China. Five Taiwanese firms (Hon Hai, Inventec, UMC, Winbond and SMIC) are in the top-ten US IT utility patent holders from China and all have at least 1 percent of their patents from their Chinese operations.

Several Taiwanese companies have explicitly embraced using China as a major base of operations beyond manufacturing. Inventec, a major computer manufacturer, calls its strategy the "Twin Towers" approach, with one tower in Taiwan and the other in China. Hon Hai, a major component and computer producer, has gone so far as to list its Chinese assets on the Hong Kong stock market in order to circumvent continued restrictions on total investment in China. Both Hon Hai and Inventec derive a large percentage of their US utility patents from China, 18 and 32 percent respectively. Hon Hai has a very large US patent portfolio of almost 3,000 patents (comparable to the portfolio of mid-sized US technology company, Seagate) proving its commitment to research in China is not trivial.

Taiwan's contribution is not limited to training local engineers and pursuing R&D activities in China. Taiwan's venture capitalists have also contributed to China's technological development. Major Taiwanese-backed venture firms, such as Acer Venture Capital, Investar, China Merchant & Fortune Venture and Sino-Century, have invested in numerous technology start-ups based in China.

From interviews with eight local Chinese, five Taiwanese and nine foreign venture capitalists, it is clear that the Taiwanese firms are making a qualitative difference in spurring technological development through their selection of investment targets. The local venture capitalists are primarily state-owned financial vehicles with little experience or competence in selecting promising start-ups or fostering their growth. To the extent that they have been able to contribute effectively to technology entrepreneurship in China, they have done so by following the lead of foreign and Taiwanese investors. In other words, they allow foreigners and Taiwanese to select and help manage the investment targets while they co-invest in the selected start-ups.

The foreign venture capitalists, which are primarily American venture firms, look at China and see a place bereft of technology because they inevitably compare it to Silicon Valley, the heart of the American technology venture capital business. The Taiwanese with their experience in building up technology enterprises in a relatively technology backward economy have not been daunted when confronted with a similar task in China. Consequently, while the American firms have been concentrating on technology-light but profitable services, such as Internet and wireless services, the Taiwanese have been primarily investing in firms attempting to create technology in semi-conductor and wireless segments.

Where the Taiwanese have failed to contribute to Chinese development is in Taiwan's traditional area of strength: manufacturing. While Taiwanese firms have been helping China develop capabilities in the human capital-intensive manufacturing sector of semiconductors, the traditional Taiwanese assemblers of electronics and other products have not contributed much to China's development because of their closed manufacturing networks. When Taiwanese firms move to China, they tend to move the entire cluster of suppliers as well. Thus, they do not help to cultivate a supply base of local Chinese firms. Yang and Hsia's study of Taiwanese production networks in the Yangtze River Delta found that local Chinese suppliers were limited to furnishing 6 percent of total production value to the Taiwanese electronics network located in that area.[43] The author of this chapter's own interviews with seven electronics Taiwanese manufacturers in the Pearl River Delta also uncovered that overwhelmingly these assemblers relied on foreign-invested (including Taiwanese-invested) firms. None of these firms reported procuring more than 5 percent of the value of their inputs from local Chinese firms. Five of these firms had been in China for more than five years at the time of interviews, suggesting that even with time there had been little progress in developing local suppliers. The same pattern of closed supplier networks was found by Hsieh[44] in her investigation of Taiwan's traditional industries production in China. The one positive note found in the author of this chapter's interviews of manufacturing plants is in a large, decade-old complex where a significant number of plant executives were localized in contrast with the typical situation in which the management is almost entirely Taiwanese. Still, with Taiwan's other large contributions to China's technological development, the failure to build up Chinese manufacturers should count as a singular disappointment rather than the definitive feature of China's experience with cross-strait economic integration.

Sustainability of trends

Can Taiwan continue to integrate with China without sustaining high costs of adjustment with its lower-wage neighbor? The good news for those concerned about hollowing out from increased trade with China is two-fold. First, Taiwan's few heavily protected sectors pre-WTO, such as auto assembly, employ only a small fraction of Taiwan's manufacturing workforce so WTO-mandated opening up will not cause widespread unemployment. Second, China's labor cost advantage may be shrinking as there is increasing evidence of rising wages amidst *mingonghuang* (labor shortages).[45] Furthermore, the government's efforts to transform Taiwan from a manufacturing to knowledge-based economy are succeeding as evidenced by the growing number of foreign R&D centers and Taiwan's increasing international patent portfolio.[46]

The downside is that China's massive investments in education[47] could place significant downward pressure on Taiwanese white-collar wages[48] in the future if several conditions apply. First, Taiwanese white-collar workers are unable to avoid direct competition with Chinese white-collar workers by occupying different sectors or niches. Second, the global demand for such workers as Taiwan and China produce does not increase faster than the global supply, a condition which in part depends on what sectors or niches exist in the global marketplace. Finally, all of this assumes that China can create equally productive white-collar workers controlling for cost i.e. Chinese workers produce as much value per dollar of wages as their Taiwanese counterparts.

Given Taiwan's reliance on overseas markets, the danger of downward pressure for Taiwanese educated workers exists even if Taiwan chose to avoid integration with China. Richard Freeman has examined such a declining wage scenario for US engineers in the face of competition from engineers in China and India and argues that such a scenario is plausible.[49] If Taiwan is still trying to compete in the US and other marketplaces, Taiwan will face Chinese competition regardless of Taiwan's level of direct economic integration with China although without Taiwanese investments in China the process of training China's human capital would likely take much longer.

One must keep in mind the legitimate warning free trade advocates always have for those worried about the costs borne by workers in certain sectors. Free traders invariably point out that there are always new industries and niches we cannot anticipate. This observation suggests possibilities for new unanticipated sources of demand in the same sector for what would otherwise be displaced workers and entirely new fields of industrial activity that could absorb these workers. The trick of course is to encourage those activities to spring up in one's own economy and to ensure that one's own workforce is able to seize these opportunities. ITRI's track record in cultivating new activities, Taiwan's high level of entrepreneurship and sound educational system for technologists suggest Taiwan should be able to sidestep China's competition through developing new and/or niche activities that China does not possess. And this possibility is in addition to Taiwan's current ability to stay at least one step ahead of China in the similar areas of technology.

As for China, Taiwan will continue to contribute significant amounts of technological progress to China if three conditions hold: (1) China's growth areas match Taiwan's strengths; (2) China's maldistribution of finance continues; and (3) China's enforcement of intellectual property rights (IPR) does not significantly improve. All three conditions are likely to hold true for the medium-term.

Taiwan's strengths match some of China's growth areas. One of China's industrial growth engines is IT and this sector is precisely where Taiwan is strongest. If China continues to follow the path other Asian developers, IT will likely remain a major driver of growth.[50]

China's maldistribution of finance, through its support for inefficient state-favored firms and neglect of small, private and entrepreneurial firms, has been a drag on China's innovation. Thus, the Taiwanese have played an outsized role in part due to the constraints on domestic innovation in China. Will finance continue to play such a role in China? With high rates of savings and a healthy fiscal situation, China is under little pressure to change its current system of subsidizing its inefficient banking system as it still prefers to control the commanding heights of the economy.[51] Moves to reform the financial system have been baby steps compared to the thorough reforms needed.[52]

China's lax IPR regime does not deter Taiwanese technology firms from investing because they have been accustomed to operating in environments with relatively lax intellectual property enforcement. In contrast, many MNCs are more cautious of placing valuable activities in China due to the opaque environment.[53] For example, in IC design, American MNCs have placed quite sophisticated activities in India where the English legal structure is relatively (for a developing country) sound and transparent as well as familiar to American firms, whereas the same firms place only unsophisticated layout activities in China.[54] With MNCs scared off by China's lack of transparency, the Taiwanese have played a relatively outsized role in bringing technology to China. China's legal structures are improving but most likely it will take a long time before the IPR regime is strong enough for the comfort of MNCs.

Notes

* Copyright 2008 by The Regents of the University of California. Reprinted from *Asian Survey*, Vol. 48 No. 2, pp. 239–264, by permission of the Regents.

1 In this chapter, the Republic of China will be referred to as Taiwan and the People's Republic of China will be referred to as China for no other reason than these terms are convenient short-hand for these two economies.
2 The investors from Taiwan, Hong Kong and Macao are treated as their own category of investors separate from both domestic and foreign investors in the Chinese government's statistical data, but for most important purposes, such as tax breaks and sectoral restrictions on investment, they are given treatment equivalent with foreign rather than domestic firms.
3 Yasheng Huang, *Selling China* (New York: Cambridge University Press, 2003).
4 Douglas B. Fuller "The Changing Limits and the Limits of Change: The State, Private Firms, International Industry and China in the Evolution of Taiwan's Electronics Industry." *Journal of Contemporary China* 14: 44 (2005), pp. 483–506.
5 Some firms tried to justify their production of notebooks through a loophole in Taiwanese law. The law defined Taiwanese notebook computer generations by the central processing unit (CPU) used e.g. Intel Pentium 2. Some firms claimed to manufacture notebooks without placing the CPUs in them in China. However, this author's observations in plants in China indicate that these CPU-less notebooks were not the only Taiwanese notebooks produced in China.
6 Michael Chase, Kevin Pollpeter and James Mulvenon, "Shanghaied? The Economic and Political Implication of the Flow of Information Technology and Investment across the Taiwan Strait," RAND Technical Report 133 (July 2004). This report covers the wage pressures to move production to China historically (pp. 3–9) and in recent years (pp.13–14 and 71–72).

7 For the semiconductor case, see Chyan Yang and Shiu-wan Hung, "Taiwan's Dilemma Across the Strait: Lifting the Bar on Semiconductor Investment in China," *Asian Survey* 43:4 (2003), pp. 681–696.
8 Hwee Hwee Ong, "Taipei Economic Forum Fails to Reach Consensus," *Straits Times*, July 29, 2006.
9 Witness for example the case of Semiconductor Manufacturing International Corporation (SMIC). This Taiwanese-invested firm built a 200mm wafer fabrication facility (a plant for manufacturing semiconductor chips) in China when it was still illegal to do so under Taiwanese law. The firm registered in the Caribbean to place itself beyond the reach of Taiwanese authorities. The Taiwanese government has since threatened the founder, Richard Chang, with arrest if he enters Taiwan.
10 Ong, "Taipei Economic."
11 The phrase "China Dream" denotes the dream of selling billions of products to China's large population and has been used by a number of commentators on China's economy and business environment. For example: Joe Studwell, *The China Dream: The Quest for the Last Great Untapped Market on Earth* (Boston, MA: Atlantic Monthly Press, 2002) and James McGregor, *One Billion Customers: Lessons from the Front Lines of Doing Business in China* (New York: Free Press, 2005), p. 2. The Taiwanese have also used similar phrases to denote the same "China Dream." See for example, "Xijin Taojinmeng Sui, Taishan Xian Huiliu Qushi ["Go West Gold Rush Dream Broken, Now a Trend of Taiwanese Businessmen Returning Home"]," *DaJiYuan* [The Epoch Times], October 6, 2005, www.epochtimes.com/gb/5/10/6/n1076694.htm and accessed on May 22, 2007.
12 Manufacturing employment data in this paragraph were from the Statistical Yearbook of the Republic of China, available online at http://eng.state.gov.tw/public/data/dgbas032/bs2/yearbook-eng/y0251.pdf and accessed on July 9, 2007.
13 Data on foreign laborers in manufacturing was taken from Council of Labor Affairs, ROC, available at http//:statdb.cla.gov.tw/html/year/d11030.pdf and accessed on July 9, 2007. Given that the data prior to 2001 on foreign workers cited in this chapter does not separate out manufacturing employment from other types of industrial employment, the assumption used here is that the pattern of over half the foreign industrial workers working in manufacturing during 2001 to 2005 also holds true for the earlier years.
14 Stephen W.K. Chiu and Ching Kwan Lee, "After the Hong Kong Miracle: Women Workers under Industrial Restructuring," *Asian Survey* 37: 8, p. 56 shows that Hong Kong's manufacturing employment fell by more than half between 1987–1995. According to Hong Kong's government, it more than halved again between 1995 and 2005 and was just 5.3 percent of total employment in 2005. Government data available at http:// censtatd.gov.hk and was accessed on May 22, 2007.
15 Using the Gini index is superior to looking at average wage levels when examining the problem of hollowing out for two reasons. First, the Gini index captures the distribution of income across the population rather than simply the average of all wage earners. Second, hollowing out would predict increased inequality (precisely what the Gini index measures) as lower educated manufacturing workers become disproportionately unemployed, but because average wage rates do not necessarily provide data on such inequality, wage data cannot capture hollowing out-driven inequality.
16 The comparison of Taiwan and other advanced countries is based on data from John Weeks, "Inequality Trends in Some Developed OECD Countries," OECD Department of Economics and Social Affairs (DESA) Working Paper, No. 6, October 2005.

17 Fuller, Douglas B., Akintunde I. Akinwande, and Charles G. Sodini. "Leading, Following or Cooked Goose: Explaining Innovation Successes and Failures in Taiwan's Electronics Industry," *Industry and Innovation* 10:2 (2003), pp. 179–196.
18 Technically, AMLCDs are only one type of flat panel displays, but the media often use flat panel displays to refer specifically to AMLCDs.
19 Fuller, "The Changing Limits."
20 For a case study of SMIC, see Douglas B. Fuller, *Creating Ladders out of Chains: China's Technological Upgrading in a World of Global Production*. Ph.D. dissertation (Massachusetts Institute of Technology, 2005).
21 See Fuller, "Changing Limits," and Fuller *et al*. "Leading."
22 Dan Breznitz, *Innovation and the State* (New Haven, CT: Yale University Press, 2007); Mathews, John A. 2002. "Origins and Dynamics of Taiwan's R&D Consortia," *Research Policy* 31(2002), pp. 633–651; Fuller *et al.*, "Leading."; and Fuller, "Changing Limits."
23 This brief synopsis of the development of Taiwan's AMLCD industry relies heavily on the account in Fuller *et al.*,"Leading."
24 "Taiwan Dogs Korea for LCD Share," *Business Week*, June 14, 2006.
25 This section is based on Michelle Hsieh, *The East Asian Miracle Revisited: The Taiwan-South Korea Comparison based on a Case Study of the Bicycle Industry*. Ph.D. dissertation. (Department of Sociology, McGill University, 2005.)
26 Cunningham, Lynch and Thun "A Tale of Two Sectors: Diverging Paths in Taiwan's Automotive Industry," in *Global Taiwan*, Eds. Suzanne Berger and Richard K. Lester (Armonk, NY: M.E. Sharpe, 2005).
27 This data was provided by Mr. Chih-yen Tai of Industrial Economics and Knowledge Center (IEK), a unit of ITRI.
28 For Taiwan's past refusal to lure MNCs with incentives, see Douglas B. Fuller, "Globalization for Nation-Building: Taiwan's Industrial and Technology Policies for High-Technology Sectors," *Journal of Interdisciplinary Economics* 18 (2007): 203–224.
29 Fuller, "Changing Limits."
30 Fuller *et al.*, "Leading."
31 China was supposed to open distribution in December 2004 according to its WTO commitments. Instead, China opened them only in 2005 according to the US-China Business Council, http://uschina.org and accessed on February 27, 2006.
32 Anita Chan, *China's Workers under Assault* (Armonk, NY: M.E. Sharpe, 2001).
33 Government of the Republic of China, Mainland Affairs Council, http:// mac.gov.tw and accessed on February 27, 2006.
34 Shelton, Jodi. 2003. "FSA Update: What's on the Mind of FSA CEOs?" Fabless Semiconductor Association (FSA), http:// fsa.org and accessed on February 27, 2006.
35 Ibid.
36 Fogel, Robert. "Why China is Likely to Achieve Its Growth Objectives." Presented at Institute of Government and Public Affairs Seminar. University of Illinois at Chicago, 2005.
37 One of these firms has sold its design operation in China and five other firms had only sales operations.
38 This estimate is based on an I-Suppli estimate of total Chinese designers and the numbers of engineers employed as reported by each firm during interviews.
39 For example, many Taiwanese firms use different names for their Chinese subsidiaries. Design investments are no longer banned, but there are restrictions on the level of sophistication of design (measured in terms of the lithography width of fabrication process) allowed to be done in China. Furthermore, many of the firms set up shop in China before it was legal to do so and therefore face legal

problems if they report their activities to the Taiwanese Investment Commission now.

40 This figure is based upon interviews and an internal report from China's Ministry of Science and Technology.

41 Fuller, *Creating Ladders.*

42 The US Patent Office awards utility and design patents. Design patents are for the exterior appearance of a product and thus are not technology-intensive so they were excluded. Most patents are invented and held by individuals. Corporate means those patents funded and owned by corporations. The patent data was accessed on May 9, 2006 at US Patent and Trademark Office's database website, http://patft1. uspto.gov/netahtml/PTO/search-bool.html.

43 Yang, You-Ren, and Chu-Joe Hsia "Local Clustering and Organizational Dynamics of Trans-border Production Networks: A Case Study of Taiwanese IT Companies in the Greater Suzhou Area, China." *Environment and Planning A* 39 (2007): 1346–1363.

44 Hsieh, 2005.

45 Wang Yue-sheng, "Mingonghuang shi dui di chengben moshi de ziwo jiaozheng ["The labor shortage is a self-correction for the low labor cost mode,"] *Ershiyi Shiji Jingji Baodao* [Twenty-First Century Economic Herald], March 13, 2006.

46 Donald Floyd and Paul Meyer, "Global Patent Trends 2001,"Lehman Brothers Report, June 17, 2002.

47 Fogel, "Why China."

48 Here we define white-collar workers as university-educated workers.

49 Richard Freeman. "Doubling the Global Workforce." Presented at Centre for Economic Performance. London School of Economics, 2004.

50 Henry S. Rowen, Marguerite Gong Hancock, and William F. Miller (Eds.). *Making IT: The Rise of Asia High Tech* (Stanford, CA: Stanford University Press, 2006)

51 Margaret M. Pearson, "The Business of Governing Business in China." *World Politics* 57 (2005), pp. 296–322.

52 Nicholas Hope and Fred Hu, "Reforming Chinese Banking: How Much Can Foreign Entry Help?" Presented at Fourth Annual Conference on Chinese Policy Reform, Stanford Center for International Development, September 30 to October 1, 2005.

53 Xiaohong Quan, *Multinational Research and Development Labs in China: Local and Global Innovation.* Ph.D. dissertation (University of California at Berkeley, 2005) argues that MNCs have placed R&D activities in China primarily because they have been able to segment the R&D value chain so control of valuable knowledge is kept in the home base of the MNC.

54 Fuller, *Creating Ladders.*

Conclusion

Douglas B. Fuller

Many of the recent trends documented in this volume appear to continue apace and some are even picking up steam. Transnational technology communities of ethnic Chinese technologists have been reinforced by increased movement of R&D activities to China by MNCs from the Triad of the Japan, the EU and North America over the last decade as demonstrated by the increase in China-based patents generated both by MNCs and by firms embedded in these ethnic Chinese transnational technology networks (Fuller, 2013). The Economic Cooperation Framework Agreement (ECFA) recently signed by Taiwan and Mainland China points to cementing the current trade links even if the agreement is short on specifics on deeper economic integration across the Taiwan Strait. The geographic reach of cross-Strait integration within Mainland China is also expanding. Taiwanese production networks in places like Suzhou and Dongguan have begun moving farther into Mainland China's interior.

Despite evidence of increasing interaction and flows of knowledge across the Taiwan Strait and the Pacific, a note of caution is in order. One does not want to ignore the possibility that we are at the end rather than the middle of an era of hyper-globalization and that suggesting these trends are self-sustaining and self-reinforcing places one in the position of Norman Angell, who, right before World War I broke out, celebrated the economic integration that would maintain world peace. Political and social factors could easily upset and reverse the increasingly intensive and equitable economic and technological exchanges documented in this book.

The international situation offers frightening but easily imagined scenarios to bring to an end the Belle Époque of the trans-Pacific technologists. Regional territorial disputes in East Asia have been growing shriller over the last year or two and China is at the heart of many of these disputes. In addition or conjunction, a contest for hegemony in the western Pacific between China and the US could well occur even if both countries wish to avoid it.

Socio-economic factors, although often more subtle and slower in effecting change, should not be ignored either. China's labor force is going to shrink rather than grow and this change has already impacted the manufacturing sector, including Taiwan's production networks in China. For the first time in decades, labor's share of GDP went up over the last two years so the end of the rural labor surplus is a boon for China's workers, but exporting firms are clearly concerned. Taiwanese firms, such as Hon Hai, have moved inland in search of table workforces, but it is unclear whether such workers are available at a price where Hon Hai remains competitive. Will the Taiwanese networks of firms in electronics be able to move to non-Chinese locations and remain competitive, or was being able to operate in China's institutional environment while taking advantage of China's cheap labor the core advantage of these manufacturing firms in recent years?

Turning to the more skilled side of the labor market, will the transnational technology communities promising bridges to venture capital and equity markets abroad maintain their appeal or will Chinese technologists rely more and more on local institutions for innovation. In 2010, 26 of the 30 Chinese semiconductor firms that held initial public offerings (IPOs) did so in Chinese financial markets and 72 percent of the funding for all the IPOs was raised in these Chinese markets (PWC 2011). These figures appear to suggest that foreigners might want to come to China's equity markets rather than the other way around. However, this author is skeptical that this one year of data signifies the end of the use of foreign institutions of technology entrepreneurship by local technologists. From interviews within the sector over the past year, there seems to be a sorting out of firms, with the more technologically sophisticated firms still planning to list abroad while the firms with a low-cost, relatively low-tech strategy aiming for listing at home. Nevertheless, it is important to keep in mind that these institutional links to the outside world have always been predicated on domestic political arrangements allowing them to operate (Zweig 2002; Fuller 2005).

Taiwan's economic integration with Mainland China is still politically contested in Taiwan despite ECFA, amidst worrisome socio-economic trends at home that some view as the effects of cross-strait integration. While Chapter 7 correctly pointed out that inequality measured in terms of the Gini coefficient has declined since 2001, it has bounced around 0.34 through 2009 with a slight uptick in the final year due to the global financial crisis. Furthermore, in 2010 wages and salaries hit an all-time low as a portion of Taiwan's GDP (Lai 2012). In comparison to the OECD countries, Taiwan's Gini coefficient in 2008 placed it just above the OECD average i.e. slightly higher than average inequality (DGBAS 2011). Nevertheless, it is still hard to blame cross-Strait economic integration's purported hollowing out of Taiwan's industrial economy for the decline in economic equality. The years subsequent to those covered in Chapter 7 actually saw a rise in manufacturing employment to an all-time high of 2.949 million workers in 2011. While a significant number of these workers are foreigners, domestic manufacturing employment reached 2.73 million workers, the highest total since the peak of 2.8 million in 1987. Taiwan is also still running very large trade surpluses with China, with a surplus of US $48.88 billion in 2010. Admittedly, pressures on wages could still occur with high employment and large trade surpluses because the high employment

and large manufacturing exports might be the result of successful wage suppression.

One could be forgiven for thinking ECFA promises much deeper integration, but an examination of the details points to a very shallow trade agreement. ECFA stipulates that Taiwan and China will negotiate four major agreements: merchandise trade, investment protection, service trade and trade-dispute settlement. So far, all that has been agreed upon is an early harvest list of goods in prelude to a merchandise trade agreement and the latter is not expected to be completed until perhaps March or April of 2014. One of the reasons the merchandise trade agreement will take so long is that it will cover the 5000 items not covered in the early harvest list. However, the Taiwanese government has already indicated that certain heavily protected sectors, such as autos and agriculture, will remain so. Thus, even merchandise trade will not be as liberalized as some had previously envisioned.

Similarly, the Taiwanese state is not pursuing deep liberalization of Chinese investment in Taiwan. Chinese firms cannot own controlling shares of Taiwanese firms and they are still barred from investing in strategic manufacturing and service industries. The maximum liberalization envisioned is 97 percent of all manufacturing sectors and 50 percent of all service sectors (CENS 4/2/2012). In the near future, 90 percent of manufacturing sectors are to be opened to Chinese investment up from 42 percent currently (CENS, 2/3/2012). However, the ownership is capped at 10 percent in existing firms and 50 percent in joint ventures with wholly Chinese-owned firms forbidden. Over the three years during which Chinese investment has been allowed into Taiwan, through February of 2012 only US$ 160 million has been invested (CENS, 3/29/2012).

The shallowness of ECFA's economic integration is not surprising for several reasons. First, China is clearly more interested in the political leverage it may gain from ECFA than economic advantages so it is willing to countenance unequal levels of liberalization with China giving more than Taiwan e.g. the early harvest list. Second, Taiwan does not have a strong tradition of liberal economic ideology. Between a history of successful state intervention and its experience of late development, Taiwanese society generally shares a belief in the legitimacy of state intervention and some economic protectionism and a suspicion of across-the-board liberalization. This ideological bent is enshrined in certain state institutions that still have the power to regulate liberalization and intervene in Taiwan's economy, such as Taiwan's Ministry of Economic Affairs. Finally, partisan politics has created a situation where whatever gains creative destruction via deep liberalization might bring, the opposition would highlight the obvious costs while downplaying potential benefits. Such a position resonates with an electorate that is somewhat suspicious of economic liberalism in the first place. ECFA has only managed to garner support because the incumbent KMT has made clear that it will not impose significant adjustment costs on Taiwan through thorough liberalization of Taiwan's economy.

The most ominous threat that might drastically change the deep and increasingly two-way flows of knowledge across the Pacific is the fallout of the Global Financial Crisis. High unemployment in many parts of the EU and the US may prove politically and economically unsustainable over time. Indeed, one could argue that the current era of hyper-globalization was structurally supported by unsustainable American trade deficits. A reversion to sustainable trade patterns may lead to ugly politics of re-adjustment in surplus and deficit countries alike and could very easily undermine the legal and socio-political foundations of international trade and finance. Double movements (radical liberalization and backlashes against it), as Karl Polanyi long ago pointed out, often have ugly political consequences. Political elites on both sides of the Pacific as well as in the EU realize the current patterns of trade and finance are unsustainable, but none has been able to find politically feasible solutions. The ideal solution would be gradual and mutual adjustment that does not lead to a collapse to global trade and investment akin to what happened in the 1930s, but it is far from clear that such a solution can be achieved. The politics are difficult domestically and even more so internationally because for the latter arena a new, different set of agreements, practices and institutions than the current WTO framework would be required (Rodrik 2011).

References

China Economic News Service (CENS), various issues, www.cens.com/.

Directorate General of Budget, Accounting and Statistics (DGBAS), Executive Yuan, Republic Of China (2011). *Social Indicators.*

Fuller, D.B. (2013) "Building Ladders out of Chains: China's Hybrid-led Technological Development in Disaggregated Value Chains," *Journal of Development Studies*, 49 (4) April, 547–563.

Fuller, D.B. (2005) "Creating Ladders out of Chains: China's Technological Upgrading in a World of Global Production." dissertation, MIT, Cambridge, MA.

Lai, Jerry (2012) "Taiwan is model student in Four Little Dragons school, but at back of class," *China Post* January 9. www.chinapost.com.tw/commentary/the-china-post/special-to-the-china-post/2012/01/09/328474/p5/Taiwan-is.htm

Price Waterhouse Coopers (PWC) (2011) *Continued Growth: China's Impact on the Semiconductor Industry 2011 Update.*

Rodrik, D. (2011) *The Globalization Paradox.* New York: W.W. Norton.

Zweig, D. (2002) *Internationalizing China.* Ithaca, NY: Cornell University Press.

Index